First World War
and Army of Occupation
War Diary
France, Belgium and Germany

60 DIVISION
Headquarters, Branches and Services
Commander Royal Artillery
9 April 1915 - 30 November 1916

WO95/3026/6

The Naval & Military Press Ltd
www.nmarchive.com
Published in association with The National Archives

Published by

The Naval & Military Press Ltd

Unit 10 Ridgewood Industrial Park,

Uckfield, East Sussex,

TN22 5QE England

Tel: +44 (0) 1825 749494

www.naval-military-press.com

www.nmarchive.com

This diary has been reprinted in facsimile from the original. Any imperfections are inevitably reproduced and the quality may fall short of modern type and cartographic standards.

© Crown Copyright
Images reproduced by permission of The National Archives, London, England, 2015.

Contents

Document type	Place/Title	Date From	Date To
Heading	WO95/3026/6		
Heading	60th Division C.R.A. 1915 Apl-1916 Nov		
War Diary	Hemel Hempstead	09/04/1915	15/05/1915
War Diary	Bromley	16/05/1915	31/05/1915
War Diary	Bromley Standon, Ware, Herts	01/06/1915	30/06/1915
War Diary	Bromley	01/07/1915	15/09/1915
War Diary	Rollestone Camp	16/09/1915	23/09/1915
War Diary	Bromley	23/09/1915	23/09/1915
War Diary	Rollestone Camp	24/09/1915	26/09/1915
War Diary	Bromley	27/09/1915	05/10/1915
War Diary	S Of Y In Ivory	05/10/1915	05/10/1915
War Diary	Bromley	05/10/1915	05/10/1915
War Diary	Clock House	06/10/1915	06/10/1915
War Diary	Black Narley Lodge	06/10/1915	07/10/1915
War Diary	Drummond	08/10/1915	14/10/1915
War Diary	Bromley	15/10/1915	20/10/1915
War Diary	Drummond	20/10/1915	20/10/1915
War Diary	Terling	21/10/1915	21/10/1915
War Diary	Dummor	22/10/1915	22/10/1915
War Diary	Bromley	22/10/1915	30/10/1915
Heading	War Diary of 60th (London) Divisional Artillery From 1st November 1915 To 30 November 1915		
War Diary	Bromley	02/11/1915	03/11/1915
War Diary	Stansted	04/11/1915	04/11/1915
War Diary	Hadham	05/11/1915	07/11/1915
War Diary	Bishops Stortford	08/11/1915	08/11/1915
War Diary	Bromley	09/11/1915	11/11/1915
War Diary	Stansted	11/11/1915	11/11/1915
War Diary	Hadham	12/11/1915	14/11/1915
War Diary	Bishops Stortford	15/11/1915	15/11/1915
War Diary	Hadham	16/11/1915	19/11/1915
War Diary	Buntingford	20/11/1915	21/11/1915
War Diary	Hadham	22/11/1915	22/11/1915
War Diary	Little Hadham	23/11/1915	23/11/1915
War Diary	Bishops Stortford	23/11/1915	23/11/1915
War Diary	Much Hadham	23/11/1915	23/11/1915
War Diary	Bromley	23/11/1915	23/11/1915
War Diary	Hadham	24/11/1915	24/11/1915
War Diary	Ugley Green	25/11/1915	25/11/1915
War Diary	Bromley	25/11/1915	26/11/1915
War Diary	Widford	27/11/1915	28/11/1915
War Diary	Bromley	29/11/1915	29/11/1915
War Diary	Stansted	30/11/1915	30/11/1915
Heading	War Diary of H.Qs 60th (London) Divisional Artillery From 1st Dec 1915 To 31st Dec 1915 (Volume 12)		
War Diary	Stansted	01/12/1915	01/12/1915
War Diary	Much Hadham	02/12/1915	02/12/1915
War Diary	Stansted	02/12/1915	02/12/1915
War Diary	Bromley	02/12/1915	02/12/1915
War Diary	Standon	03/12/1915	03/12/1915

War Diary	Much Hadham and Bunting Ford	03/12/1915	03/12/1915
War Diary	Bromley	03/12/1915	03/12/1915
War Diary	Much Hadham	04/12/1915	04/12/1915
War Diary	Bishops Stortford	05/12/1915	05/12/1915
War Diary	Stansted	06/12/1915	06/12/1915
War Diary	Manuden	06/12/1915	06/12/1915
War Diary	Bromley	06/12/1915	06/12/1915
War Diary	Much Hadham	07/12/1915	07/12/1915
War Diary	Elsenham	07/12/1915	07/12/1915
War Diary	Bromley	07/12/1915	07/12/1915
War Diary	Elsenham	08/12/1915	08/12/1915
War Diary	Bromley	08/12/1915	08/12/1915
War Diary	Buntingford	09/12/1915	09/12/1915
War Diary	Much Hadham	09/12/1915	09/12/1915
War Diary	Bromley	09/12/1915	09/12/1915
War Diary	Much Hadham	10/12/1915	10/12/1915
War Diary	Buntingford	10/12/1915	10/12/1915
War Diary	Braughing	10/12/1915	10/12/1915
War Diary	Bromley	10/12/1915	10/12/1915
War Diary	Much Hadham	11/12/1915	11/12/1915
War Diary	Bishops Stortford	11/12/1915	11/12/1915
War Diary	Stansted	11/12/1915	11/12/1915
War Diary	Much Hadham	12/12/1915	12/12/1915
War Diary	Buntingford	13/12/1915	13/12/1915
War Diary	Stansted	13/12/1915	13/12/1915
War Diary	Bromley	13/12/1915	13/12/1915
War Diary	Stansted	14/12/1915	15/12/1915
War Diary	Bromley	15/12/1915	15/12/1915
War Diary	Buntingford	16/12/1915	16/12/1915
War Diary	Standon	16/12/1915	16/12/1915
War Diary	Bromley	16/12/1915	16/12/1915
War Diary	Buntingford-Royston Saffron Walden	16/12/1915	16/12/1915
War Diary	Much Hadham	16/12/1915	17/12/1915
War Diary	Dunmow	17/12/1915	17/12/1915
War Diary	Much Hadham	18/12/1915	20/12/1915
War Diary	Bromley	20/12/1915	20/12/1915
War Diary	Stansted	21/12/1915	21/12/1915
War Diary	Bromley	21/12/1915	21/12/1915
War Diary	Stansted	22/12/1915	22/12/1915
War Diary	Much Hadham	22/12/1915	22/12/1915
War Diary	Bromley	22/12/1915	22/12/1915
War Diary	Standon & Bunting Ford	23/12/1915	23/12/1915
War Diary	Stansted	23/12/1915	23/12/1915
War Diary	Bromley	23/12/1915	23/12/1915
War Diary	Much Hadham	24/12/1915	24/12/1915
War Diary	Standon	24/12/1915	24/12/1915
War Diary	Buntingford	24/12/1915	24/12/1915
War Diary	Bromley	25/12/1915	27/12/1915
War Diary	Stansted	28/12/1915	28/12/1915
War Diary	Bishops Stortford	28/12/1915	28/12/1915
War Diary	Stansted	29/12/1915	30/12/1915
War Diary	Much Hadham	31/12/1915	31/12/1915
War Diary	Standon	31/12/1915	31/12/1915
Miscellaneous	60th (London) Divisional Artillery Inspection By Major General Brunker		
War Diary	Much Hadham	01/01/1916	02/01/1916

War Diary	Elsenham	03/01/1916	03/01/1916
War Diary	Bromley	03/01/1916	03/01/1916
War Diary	Much Hadham	04/01/1916	04/01/1916
War Diary	Bromley	04/01/1916	04/01/1916
War Diary	Much Hadham	05/01/1916	05/01/1916
War Diary	Elsenham	05/01/1916	05/01/1916
War Diary	Bromley	05/01/1916	05/01/1916
War Diary	Elsenham	06/01/1916	06/01/1916
War Diary	Stansted	06/01/1916	06/01/1916
War Diary	Elsenham	06/01/1916	06/01/1916
War Diary	Southminster	07/01/1916	07/01/1916
War Diary	Chelmsford	07/01/1916	07/01/1916
War Diary	Elsenham	07/01/1916	07/01/1916
War Diary	Stansted	08/01/1916	08/01/1916
War Diary	Elsenham	08/01/1916	08/01/1916
War Diary	Much Hadham	09/01/1916	09/01/1916
War Diary	Stansted	10/01/1916	10/01/1916
War Diary	Elsenham	10/01/1916	10/01/1916
War Diary	Much Hadham	11/01/1916	12/01/1916
War Diary	Stansted	12/01/1916	14/01/1916
War Diary	Southminster	15/01/1916	19/01/1916
War Diary	Much Hadham	20/01/1916	20/01/1916
War Diary	Southminster	21/01/1916	22/01/1916
War Diary	Much Hadham	22/01/1916	24/01/1916
War Diary	Southminster	25/01/1916	25/01/1916
War Diary	Buntingford	25/01/1916	25/01/1916
War Diary	Southminster	26/01/1916	26/01/1916
War Diary	Boyton	26/01/1916	27/01/1916
War Diary	Sutton Veny	28/01/1916	29/01/1916
War Diary	Boyton	30/01/1916	30/01/1916
War Diary	Sutton Veny	31/01/1916	31/01/1916
War Diary	Corton	31/01/1916	31/01/1916
War Diary	Boyton	31/01/1916	31/01/1916
Miscellaneous	List Of Appendices To War Diary (Vol 1/1916)		
Heading	War Diary of H.Q., 60th (London) Divisional Artillery From 1st February To 29th February 1916 Volume 2		
War Diary	Corton and Boyton	01/02/1916	01/02/1916
War Diary	Corton	02/02/1916	02/02/1916
War Diary	Sutton Veny	03/02/1916	03/02/1916
War Diary	Hindon-Sherrington	03/02/1916	03/02/1916
War Diary	Corton	04/02/1916	06/02/1916
War Diary	Sutton Veny	07/02/1916	07/02/1916
War Diary	Boyton	08/02/1916	08/02/1916
War Diary	Corton	08/02/1916	08/02/1916
War Diary	Boyton	09/02/1916	09/02/1916
War Diary	Corton	10/02/1916	10/02/1916
War Diary	Boyton	10/02/1916	10/02/1916
War Diary	Sutton Veny	10/02/1916	14/02/1916
War Diary	Corton	14/02/1916	15/02/1916
War Diary	Sutton Veny	15/02/1916	15/02/1916
War Diary	Boyton	16/02/1916	16/02/1916
War Diary	Pertwood	17/02/1916	18/02/1916
War Diary	Boyton	19/02/1916	19/02/1916
War Diary	Corton	19/02/1916	19/02/1916
War Diary	Sutton Veny	20/02/1916	20/02/1916
War Diary	Boyton	21/02/1916	22/02/1916

War Diary	Corton	22/02/1916	22/02/1916
War Diary	Sutton Veny	22/02/1916	22/02/1916
War Diary	Boyton	23/02/1916	23/02/1916
War Diary	Corton	23/02/1916	25/02/1916
War Diary	Sutton Veny	25/02/1916	25/02/1916
War Diary	Boyton	26/02/1916	27/02/1916
War Diary	Corton Boyton	28/02/1916	29/02/1916
Miscellaneous	Divisional Exercise 16th February 1916	15/02/1916	15/02/1916
Miscellaneous	Divisional Exercise 16th February 1916 Notes To The Special Instructions Issued Today	15/02/1916	15/02/1916
Heading	War Diary of H.Q. 60th (London) Divisional Artillery From 1st March 1916 To 31st March 1916 Volume 3		
War Diary	Boyton Corton	01/03/1916	04/03/1916
War Diary	Boyton Down	06/03/1916	06/03/1916
War Diary	Corton	07/03/1916	08/03/1916
War Diary	Boyton	09/03/1916	10/03/1916
War Diary	Longbridge Deverill	14/03/1916	14/03/1916
War Diary	Corton	16/03/1916	16/03/1916
War Diary	Boyton	17/03/1916	22/03/1916
War Diary	Longbridge Deverill	23/03/1916	23/03/1916
War Diary	Boyton	24/03/1916	30/03/1916
War Diary	Corton	31/03/1916	31/03/1916
War Diary	Boyton Corton	01/03/1916	04/03/1916
War Diary	Boyton Down	06/03/1916	06/03/1916
War Diary	Corton	07/03/1916	07/03/1916
War Diary	Boyton	09/03/1916	10/03/1916
War Diary	Longbridge Deverill	14/03/1916	14/03/1916
War Diary	Corton	16/03/1916	16/03/1916
War Diary	Boyton	17/03/1916	22/03/1916
War Diary	Longbridge Deverill	23/03/1916	23/03/1916
War Diary	Boyton	24/03/1916	30/03/1916
War Diary	Corton	31/03/1916	31/03/1916
Heading	War Diary of H.Q. 60th (London) Divisional Artillery From 1st April 1916 To 28th April 1916 Volume 4		
War Diary	West Down Salisbury	01/04/1916	06/04/1916
War Diary	Sutton Veny	05/04/1916	05/04/1916
War Diary	West Down Salisbury	07/04/1916	12/04/1916
War Diary	Sutton Veny	12/04/1916	12/04/1916
War Diary	Corton Boyton	15/04/1916	15/04/1916
War Diary	Corton	17/04/1916	18/04/1916
War Diary	Longbridge-Deverill	19/04/1916	19/04/1916
War Diary	Boyton	19/04/1916	19/04/1916
War Diary	Salisbury	22/04/1916	22/04/1916
War Diary	Sutton Veny	24/04/1916	24/04/1916
War Diary	Boyton	26/04/1916	26/04/1916
War Diary	Corton	27/04/1916	27/04/1916
War Diary	Boyton	27/04/1916	28/04/1916
War Diary	West Down Salisbury	01/04/1916	06/04/1916
War Diary	Sutton Veny	05/04/1916	05/04/1916
War Diary	West Down Salisbury	07/04/1916	12/04/1916
War Diary	Sutton Veny	12/04/1916	12/04/1916
War Diary	Corton Boyton	15/04/1916	15/04/1916
War Diary	Corton	17/04/1916	18/04/1916
War Diary	Longbridge-Deverill	19/04/1916	19/04/1916
War Diary	Boyton	19/04/1916	19/04/1916
War Diary	Salisbury	22/04/1916	22/04/1916

War Diary	Sutton Veny	24/04/1916	24/04/1916
War Diary	Boyton	26/04/1916	26/04/1916
War Diary	Corton	27/04/1916	27/04/1916
War Diary	Boyton	27/04/1916	28/04/1916
War Diary	No 23 Canadn Lines Larkhin	01/04/1916	05/04/1916
War Diary	No.3 Boston Camp	06/04/1916	30/04/1916
Heading	War Diary of H.Q. 60th (London) Divisional Artillery From 4th May 1916 To 31st May 1916 Volume 5		
War Diary	Boyton	04/05/1916	04/05/1916
War Diary	Sherrington	05/05/1916	05/05/1916
War Diary	Boyton Corton	06/05/1916	06/05/1916
War Diary	Boyton	08/05/1916	09/05/1916
War Diary	Corton	10/05/1916	11/05/1916
War Diary	Sherrington	12/05/1916	12/05/1916
War Diary	Corton	13/05/1916	16/05/1916
War Diary	Boyton	17/05/1916	18/05/1916
War Diary	Corton	19/05/1916	20/05/1916
War Diary	Boyton	22/05/1916	22/05/1916
War Diary	Sutton Veny	24/05/1916	26/05/1916
War Diary	Corton	27/05/1916	27/05/1916
War Diary	Larkhill	28/05/1916	30/05/1916
War Diary	Boyton	29/05/1916	30/05/1916
War Diary	Heytesbury	31/05/1916	31/05/1916
War Diary	Boyton	04/05/1916	04/05/1916
War Diary	Sherrington	05/05/1916	05/05/1916
War Diary	Boyton Corton	06/05/1916	06/05/1916
War Diary	Boyton	08/05/1916	10/05/1916
War Diary	Corton	10/05/1916	11/05/1916
War Diary	Sherrington	12/05/1916	12/05/1916
War Diary	Corton	15/05/1916	16/05/1916
War Diary	Boyton	17/05/1916	18/05/1916
War Diary	Corton	19/05/1916	20/05/1916
War Diary	Boyton	22/05/1916	22/05/1916
War Diary	Sutton Veny	24/05/1916	26/05/1916
War Diary	Corton	27/05/1916	27/05/1916
War Diary	Larkhill	28/05/1916	30/05/1916
War Diary	Boyton	29/05/1916	30/05/1916
War Diary	Heytesbury	31/05/1916	31/05/1916
Heading	War Diary of H.Q. 60th (London) Divisional Artillery From 1st June 1916 To 22nd June 1916 Volume 6		
War Diary	Corton Boyton	01/06/1916	01/06/1916
War Diary	Sutton Veny	02/06/1916	02/06/1916
War Diary	Warminster	03/06/1916	04/06/1916
War Diary	Corton	06/06/1916	08/06/1916
War Diary	Corton Boyton	12/06/1916	14/06/1916
War Diary	Sherrington	15/06/1916	15/06/1916
War Diary	Corton	15/06/1916	15/06/1916
War Diary	Boyton	16/06/1916	17/06/1916
War Diary	Corton	19/06/1916	19/06/1916
War Diary	Boyton	20/06/1916	20/06/1916
War Diary	Codford	21/06/1916	22/06/1916
Miscellaneous	Nominal Roll of Officers Warrant Officers N.C.O's And Men Proceeding Overseas With Headquarters 60th (London) Divisional Artillery	21/06/1916	21/06/1916
War Diary	Corton Boyton	01/06/1916	01/06/1916
War Diary	Sutton Veny	02/06/1916	02/06/1916

Type	Location / Title	From	To
War Diary	Warminster	03/06/1916	04/06/1916
War Diary	Corton	06/06/1916	08/06/1916
War Diary	Corton Boyton	12/06/1916	14/06/1916
War Diary	Sherrington	15/06/1916	15/06/1916
War Diary	Corton	15/06/1916	15/06/1916
War Diary	Boyton	16/06/1916	17/06/1916
War Diary	Corton	19/06/1916	19/06/1916
War Diary	Boyton	20/06/1916	20/06/1916
War Diary	Codford	21/06/1916	22/06/1916
War Diary	Southampton	22/06/1916	22/06/1916
War Diary	Le Havre	23/06/1916	24/06/1916
War Diary	Petit Houvin	25/06/1916	25/06/1916
War Diary	St Pol	25/06/1916	25/06/1916
War Diary	Hermaville	26/06/1916	26/06/1916
War Diary	La Targette	27/06/1916	27/06/1916
War Diary	Ecurie	27/06/1916	27/06/1916
War Diary	Flers	28/06/1916	28/06/1916
War Diary	Ecurie	29/06/1916	29/06/1916
War Diary	Warlus	29/06/1916	29/06/1916
War Diary	St Pol	29/06/1916	29/06/1916
War Diary	Ligny St. Flochel	30/06/1916	30/06/1916
War Diary	St Michel-Sur-Ternoise	30/06/1916	30/06/1916
War Diary	La Targette De	30/06/1916	30/06/1916
Operation(al) Order(s)	51st Divisional Artillery Operation Order No.26	25/06/1916	25/06/1916
Miscellaneous	No.2772/A, Highland Division	26/06/1916	26/06/1916
Miscellaneous	Reference Para.2 Of XVII Corps Order No.13 Of 20th June	24/06/1916	24/06/1916
Miscellaneous	Headquarters 60th Division (For Information)	26/06/1916	26/06/1916
Miscellaneous	Instructions Regarding the Attachment of the 60th Division to 51st (Highland) Division	27/06/1916	27/06/1916
Miscellaneous	Instructions for Training Battalions of 60th Division in Back Area		
Miscellaneous	Points To Which Attention Should Be Directed During Tours Of Instruction In Trenches	23/06/1916	23/06/1916
Heading	War Diary of Headquarters 60th Divisional Artillery From 1st July 1916 To 31st July 1916 (Volume 7) 1916		
Heading	War Diary of Headquarters 60th London Divl Artillery From 1st August 1916 To 31st August 1916 (Volume 8)		
War Diary	Berthonval	02/08/1916	02/08/1916
War Diary	Etrun-Aux-Rietz	03/08/1916	03/08/1916
War Diary	Fund De Vase	04/08/1916	04/08/1916
War Diary	Roclincourt	05/08/1916	05/08/1916
War Diary	Neuville-St-Vaast	06/08/1916	06/08/1916
War Diary	Roclincourt	07/08/1916	08/08/1916
War Diary	Mt St-Eloy	09/08/1916	09/08/1916
War Diary	Aux Rietz	10/08/1916	10/08/1916
War Diary	Neuville	11/08/1916	11/08/1916
War Diary	Ecoivres	11/08/1916	11/08/1916
War Diary	Aux Rietz	12/08/1916	12/08/1916
War Diary	La Folie	13/08/1916	13/08/1916
War Diary	Ecurie	13/08/1916	13/08/1916
War Diary	Roclincourt	14/08/1916	15/08/1916
War Diary	S.W. Of Thelus	15/08/1916	15/08/1916
War Diary	Camblain L'Abbe	16/08/1916	16/08/1916
War Diary	Neuville-St-Vaast	17/08/1916	17/08/1916
War Diary	Ecoivres	18/08/1916	18/08/1916

Type	Location	Date From	Date To
War Diary	Etrun, Aux Rietz	19/08/1916	19/08/1916
War Diary	Fermont Capelle	20/08/1916	20/08/1916
War Diary	Berthonval	21/08/1916	21/08/1916
War Diary	Notredame De Lorette	21/08/1916	21/08/1916
War Diary	Roclincourt	22/08/1916	23/08/1916
War Diary	Berthonval	24/08/1916	24/08/1916
War Diary	Aux Rietz	25/08/1916	25/08/1916
War Diary	Neuville	26/08/1916	26/08/1916
War Diary	Camblain	27/08/1916	27/08/1916
War Diary	Fond De Vase	27/08/1916	27/08/1916
War Diary	Somme	28/08/1916	28/08/1916
War Diary	Roclincourt	29/08/1916	29/08/1916
War Diary	Aux Rietz	30/08/1916	31/08/1916
Operation(al) Order(s)	Operation Scheme No.1	05/08/1916	05/08/1916
Miscellaneous	Artillery Scheme-Raid No.1		
Map	Map		
Miscellaneous	Operation Scheme No.2	05/08/1916	05/08/1916
Miscellaneous	Artillery Scheme-Raid No.2		
Map	Map		
Miscellaneous	Preliminary Warning	01/08/1916	01/08/1916
Miscellaneous	Operation Scheme No.3		
Miscellaneous	Artillery Scheme Raid No.3		
Map	Map		
Miscellaneous	Artillery Scheme No.4		
Map	Map		
Miscellaneous	Artillery Scheme No.5	18/08/1916	18/08/1916
Miscellaneous	Artillery Scheme "Christabel"	22/08/1916	22/08/1916
Miscellaneous	Artillery Scheme "Delilah"		
Heading	War Diary of Headquarters 60th Divl Artillery From 1st To 30th Sept 1916 (Volume 9)		
War Diary	Mt St Eloi	01/09/1916	01/09/1916
War Diary	Fond De Vase	02/09/1916	02/09/1916
War Diary	Etrun	03/09/1916	03/09/1916
War Diary	Mt St Eloi	04/09/1916	04/09/1916
War Diary	Hermaville	04/09/1916	04/09/1916
War Diary	Neuville St Vaast	05/09/1916	05/09/1916
War Diary	Fond De Vase	06/09/1916	06/09/1916
War Diary	Neuville	07/09/1916	07/09/1916
War Diary	Capelle Fermont Frevin Capelle	08/09/1916	08/09/1916
War Diary	Etrun Neuville	09/09/1916	09/09/1916
War Diary	Fort George	09/09/1916	09/09/1916
War Diary	Maroeuil	10/09/1916	10/09/1916
War Diary	Neuville	11/09/1916	11/09/1916
War Diary	Hermaville	12/09/1916	12/09/1916
War Diary	Ligny St Flochel	12/09/1916	12/09/1916
War Diary	Berthonval	13/09/1916	13/09/1916
War Diary	Fond De Vase	14/09/1916	14/09/1916
War Diary	Roclincourt	15/09/1916	15/09/1916
War Diary	Neuville	16/09/1916	17/09/1916
War Diary	Agnez-Les-Duisans	18/09/1916	18/09/1916
War Diary	Roclincourt	19/09/1916	19/09/1916
War Diary	Neuville	20/09/1916	20/09/1916
War Diary	Acq Laresset Etc	21/09/1916	21/09/1916
War Diary	Aux Rietz	22/09/1916	22/09/1916
War Diary	Etrun	23/09/1916	24/09/1916
War Diary	Neuville	24/09/1916	25/09/1916

War Diary	Capelle Fermont	26/09/1916	26/09/1916
War Diary	Mt St Eloi	26/09/1916	26/09/1916
War Diary	Anzin	27/09/1916	27/09/1916
War Diary	Neuville	28/09/1916	28/09/1916
War Diary	Anzin	29/09/1916	30/09/1916
Miscellaneous	Artillery Scheme Ermywtrude (Ref. Attached Diagram)		
Map	Map		
Miscellaneous	Artillery Scheme "Flossie"		
Miscellaneous	Artillery Scheme "Gertle"	06/09/1916	06/09/1916
Heading	War Diary of Headquarters 60th. Divisional Artillery From 1st October 1916 To 31st October 1916 Volume 10		
War Diary	Neuville St Vaast	01/10/1916	02/10/1916
War Diary	Fond De Vase	02/10/1916	02/10/1916
War Diary	Etrun Etc	03/10/1916	03/10/1916
War Diary	Roclincourt	04/10/1916	04/10/1916
War Diary	Laresset	05/10/1916	05/10/1916
War Diary	Ecoivres	06/10/1916	06/10/1916
War Diary	Aux Rietz Etc	07/10/1916	07/10/1916
War Diary	Ligny St Flochel	08/10/1916	08/10/1916
War Diary	Roclincourt	08/10/1916	08/10/1916
War Diary	Aubigny	09/10/1916	09/10/1916
War Diary	La Targette	10/10/1916	10/10/1916
War Diary	Neuville St Vaast	11/10/1916	11/10/1916
War Diary	Hermaville	12/10/1916	12/10/1916
War Diary	Ecoivres Etc	13/10/1916	13/10/1916
War Diary	Fond De Vase	14/10/1916	14/10/1916
War Diary	Roclincourt	15/10/1916	16/10/1916
War Diary	Vimy	16/10/1916	16/10/1916
War Diary	Hermaville	17/10/1916	17/10/1916
War Diary	Aubigny	17/10/1916	17/10/1916
War Diary	Ecoivres	18/10/1916	18/10/1916
War Diary	Savy	19/10/1916	20/10/1916
War Diary	Fond De Vase	20/10/1916	20/10/1916
War Diary	Etrun Aux Rietz	21/10/1916	21/10/1916
War Diary	La Targette	22/10/1916	23/10/1916
War Diary	Acq Laresset	24/10/1916	25/10/1916
War Diary	Hermaville	26/10/1916	26/10/1916
War Diary	Ecoivres Etc	27/10/1916	27/10/1916
War Diary	Roclincourt Acq	28/10/1916	28/10/1916
War Diary	Maroeuil	29/10/1916	29/10/1916
War Diary	Capelle Fermont	30/10/1916	30/10/1916
War Diary	Hermaville	31/10/1916	31/10/1916
War Diary	Mont St Eloy	01/07/1916	01/07/1916
War Diary	Fond De Vase	02/07/1916	02/07/1916
War Diary	Anzin	04/07/1916	04/07/1916
War Diary	Ecurie	05/07/1916	05/07/1916
War Diary	Neuville St Vaast	06/07/1916	06/07/1916
War Diary	Hermaville	07/07/1916	07/07/1916
War Diary	Haute Cloque	08/07/1916	08/07/1916
War Diary	Ligny St Flochel	09/07/1916	09/07/1916
War Diary	Ecoivres	09/07/1916	09/07/1916
War Diary	La Targette	10/07/1916	10/07/1916
War Diary	Fond De Vase	11/07/1916	11/07/1916
War Diary	Aubigny	13/07/1916	13/07/1916
War Diary	Hermaville	14/07/1916	15/07/1916

Type	Description	Start	End
War Diary	Warlus	16/07/1916	16/07/1916
War Diary	Mt St Eloy	16/07/1916	17/07/1916
War Diary	Neuville	18/07/1916	18/07/1916
War Diary	Etrun	19/07/1916	19/07/1916
War Diary	Neuville St.V	20/07/1916	20/07/1916
War Diary	Anzin	20/07/1916	20/07/1916
War Diary	Acq Laresset	21/07/1916	21/07/1916
War Diary	Fond De Vase	22/07/1916	22/07/1916
War Diary	Ecurie	23/07/1916	23/07/1916
War Diary	Berthonval	24/07/1916	24/07/1916
War Diary	Ecurie	25/07/1916	26/07/1916
War Diary	Camblain	27/07/1916	27/07/1916
War Diary	Ecurie	28/07/1916	29/07/1916
War Diary	Vimy Ridge	30/07/1916	31/07/1916
War Diary	Fond De Vase	31/07/1916	31/07/1916
Operation(al) Order(s)	60th Division Order No.1	10/07/1916	10/07/1916
Operation(al) Order(s)	51st (Highland) Division Operation Order No.61	08/07/1916	08/07/1916
Operation(al) Order(s)	60th (London) Divisional Artillery Operation Order No.1	11/07/1916	11/07/1916
Operation(al) Order(s)	51st Divisional Artillery Operation Order No.27	12/07/1916	12/07/1916
Operation(al) Order(s)	51st (Highland) Divisional Artillery Operation Order No.28	14/07/1916	14/07/1916
Miscellaneous	Combined Bombardment (Ref. Trench Map Roclincourt 1:10,000)	22/07/1916	22/07/1916
Miscellaneous	Artillery Scheme	23/07/1916	23/07/1916
Heading	War Diary of Headquarters 60th Divl Artillery From 1st To 30th Nov 1916 (Volume 11)		
War Diary	Aubigny	01/11/1916	02/11/1916
War Diary	Maroeuil	03/11/1916	03/11/1916
War Diary	Frevin Capelle	03/11/1916	03/11/1916
War Diary	Neuville St. Vaast	03/11/1916	03/11/1916
War Diary	Aubigny	04/11/1916	06/11/1916
War Diary	Boubers Etc	07/11/1916	07/11/1916
War Diary	Neuville Etc	07/11/1916	07/11/1916
War Diary	Aubigny	07/11/1916	08/11/1916
War Diary	Etree-Wamin	09/11/1916	09/11/1916
War Diary	Occoches	10/11/1916	10/11/1916
War Diary	Ailly-Le-Haut-Clocher	11/11/1916	11/11/1916
War Diary	Ailly Etc	12/11/1916	13/11/1916
War Diary	Longpre	14/11/1916	14/11/1916
War Diary	Ailly	15/11/1916	15/11/1916
War Diary	Longpre	16/11/1916	20/11/1916
War Diary	Marseilles	22/11/1916	22/11/1916
War Diary	Ailly	23/11/1916	23/11/1916
War Diary	Longpre	24/11/1916	24/11/1916
War Diary	Marseilles	25/11/1916	30/11/1916
Miscellaneous	First Army No.G.S.468	01/11/1918	01/11/1918
Operation(al) Order(s)	(Third) Army Order No.87 Ref Map Lens 1/100000	01/11/1916	01/11/1916
Miscellaneous	March Table 60th Divisional Ammunition Column & Personnel Heavy T.M. Battery Issued With Third Army No.97	01/11/1916	01/11/1916
Operation(al) Order(s)	60th Divisional Artillery Operation Order No.2	04/11/1916	04/11/1916
Operation(al) Order(s)	Operation Order No.37 By Brigadier General R.J.G. Elkington C.M.G. Commanding 56th Divnl. Artillery	04/11/1916	04/11/1916
Miscellaneous	First Army No.G.S. 468	05/11/1916	05/11/1916
Miscellaneous	To C.R.A. 60th Divl Artillery A.&.Q. A.P.M	05/11/1916	05/11/1916

Type	Description	Date	Date
Miscellaneous	A Form Messages And Signals		
Operation(al) Order(s)	60th Divisional Artillery Operation Order No.3	04/11/1916	04/11/1916
Operation(al) Order(s)	60th Divisional Artillery Operation Order No.4		
Operation(al) Order(s)	60th Divisional Artillery Operation Order No.5		
Operation(al) Order(s)	60th Divisional Artillery Operation Order No.6	06/11/1916	06/11/1916
Operation(al) Order(s)	60th Divisional Artillery Operation Order No.7	08/11/1916	08/11/1916
Operation(al) Order(s)	60th Divisional Artillery Operation Order No.8	09/11/1916	09/11/1916
Operation(al) Order(s)	Third Army Order No.89	05/11/1916	05/11/1916
Miscellaneous	March Table 60th Divisional Artillery Issued With Third Army Order No.89	05/11/1916	05/11/1916
Operation(al) Order(s)	Third Army Order No.90	06/11/1916	06/11/1916
Miscellaneous	60th Divisional Artillery March Table Issued With Third Army Order No.90	06/11/1916	06/11/1916
Miscellaneous	A Form Messages And Signals		
Miscellaneous	First Army No.G.S. 468	05/11/1916	05/11/1916
Miscellaneous	60th Division With Reference to Q/5885	11/11/1916	11/11/1916
Miscellaneous	60th Division Q/5885	12/11/1916	12/11/1916
Miscellaneous	60th Divn Q.D.519	11/11/1916	11/11/1916
Miscellaneous	C.R.A. H.Q. 179th Infantry Brigade	13/11/1916	13/11/1916
Miscellaneous	60th Division-Entrainments Longpre to Marseilles	13/11/1916	13/11/1916
Operation(al) Order(s)	60th Divisional Artillery Operation Order No.9	15/11/1916	15/11/1916
Miscellaneous	To 302nd F.A. Bde D.A.G	12/11/1916	12/11/1916
Operation(al) Order(s)	60th Division Order No.11	15/11/1916	15/11/1916
Miscellaneous	Table Of Personnel Animals & Vehicles Proceeding		
Miscellaneous	Programme of Entrainment	16/11/1916	16/11/1916
Miscellaneous	Programme of Entrainment	17/11/1916	17/11/1916
Miscellaneous	Following Amendments to Schedule "A" And Programme of Entrainment	16/11/1916	16/11/1916
Operation(al) Order(s)	60th Divisional Artillery Operation Order No.10	15/11/1916	15/11/1916
Miscellaneous	Schedule "A"		
Miscellaneous	G/S.427	16/11/1916	16/11/1916
Miscellaneous	Table Of Personnel Animals And Vehicles Proceeding On The 18th And 19th November 1916	19/11/1916	19/11/1916
Miscellaneous	Programme Of Entrainment	18/11/1916	18/11/1916
Miscellaneous	G/S.427/2	17/11/1916	17/11/1916
Miscellaneous	Programme Of Entrainment	18/11/1916	18/11/1916
Operation(al) Order(s)	60th Divisional Artillery Operation Order No.11	17/11/1916	17/11/1916
Miscellaneous	Schedule "A"	17/11/1916	17/11/1916
Miscellaneous	G/S.428	18/11/1916	18/11/1916
Miscellaneous	Table Of Personnel Animals & Vehicles Proceeding On The 20th/21st November 1916	21/11/1916	21/11/1916
Miscellaneous	Programme Of Entrainment	20/11/1916	20/11/1916
Operation(al) Order(s)	60th Divisional Artillery Operation Order No.12	18/11/1916	18/11/1916
Miscellaneous	Schedule "A"	18/11/1916	18/11/1916
Miscellaneous	G/S. 429	20/11/1916	20/11/1916
Miscellaneous	Programme Of Entrainment	22/11/1916	22/11/1916
Miscellaneous	Programme Of Entrainment	23/11/1916	23/11/1916
Miscellaneous	Table Of Personnel Animals And Vehicles Proceeding On The 22nd And 23rd November 1916	22/11/1916	22/11/1916
Operation(al) Order(s)	60th Divisional Artillery Operation Order No.12	21/11/1916	21/11/1916
Miscellaneous	Schedule "A"		
Miscellaneous	G/S. 431	21/11/1916	21/11/1916
Miscellaneous	Table Of Personnel Animals And Vehicles Proceeding	24/11/1916	24/11/1916
Miscellaneous	Programme Of Entrainment	24/11/1916	24/11/1916
Operation(al) Order(s)	60th Divisional Artillery Operation Order No.12.b	21/11/1916	21/11/1916
Miscellaneous	Schedule "A"		

Heading   60th Division Asst Dir Med Services 1915 Aug-1915 Dec 1916 Jun-1916 Nov

WO 95/3026/6

60TH DIVISION

C. R. A.

~~JUN - NOV 1916~~

1915 APL — 1916 NOV

60TH DIVISION

Army Form C. 2118.

Headquarters R.A. 2/2 London Division.

Sheet 1

WAR DIARY
or
INTELLIGENCE SUMMARY.
(Erase heading not required.)

Place	Date	Hour	Summary of Events and Information	Remarks and references to Appendices
Hemel Hempstead	9.4.15		The Artillery of the 2/2 London Division, less the 2/5* & 2/6*' 2.A Brigades moved to its War Station on this date arriving at Boxmoor Station at the following times.	
			2/7* Bde. 7.15 AM	
			" 11.45 AM	
			2/8* 8.45 AM.	
			2/2 Heavy Battery. 10.15 AM.	
			All horses were examined by the Veterinary Officer before leaving the Station.	
			The "Marching in State" was as follows.	
			Officers. O.R. Chargers. Riding. Draught. Guns. Rifles.	
			H.Q.R.A 2 9 4 NIL NIL NIL NIL	
			7* Bde. 14 553 35 NIL 103 9.15 PR. B.L.C. 68	
			8* Bde. 7 343 14 11 41 NIL 36	
			2/2 Heavy 5 139 NIL 8 2 NIL 22	
			The Brigade then moved into their Billets as follows	

Army Form C. 2118.

Headquarters R.A. 2/2 London Division.

WAR DIARY
or
INTELLIGENCE SUMMARY.

(Erase heading not required.)

Instructions regarding War Diaries and Intelligence Summaries are contained in F. S. Regs., Part II. and the Staff Manual respectively. Title pages will be prepared in manuscript.

Title pages 2

Place	Date	Hour	Summary of Events and Information	Remarks and references to Appendices
Hemel Hempstead	9.4.15	6.30 pm	2/7th Bde. HEMEL HEMPSTEAD Headquarters THE MANSE ALEXANDRA ROAD. 2/8th Bde. HEMEL HEMPSTEAD, BOXMOOR. do. BOXMOOR HALL. 2/2 Heavy Battery. BOXMOOR · GREENEND. do 9 HORSECROFT ROAD, BOXMOOR. An isolation hospital for suspected cases, other than mange, has been established at the Rose & Crown, HEMEL HEMPSTEAD. The 1st Hant's Heavy Battery which arrived from PORTSMOUTH and WEYMOUTH on 7th April has gone into billets at SHENDISH with Headquarters at SHENDISH HOUSE. The Divisional Artillery Headquarters will be shared at THE MANSE, ALEXANDRA ROAD at 11 am.	
	10.4.15	6.30 am	The C.R.A arrived at HEMEL HEMPSTEAD.	
"	11.4.15	6.30 pm	Nil	
"	12.4.15	6.30 pm	4 15 P.R. B.L.C guns Mark I arrived from IRELAND and were allotted to 2/7th Bde. The C.R.A. visited the gun park of the 2/7th Bde & then visited the 1st Hant's Heavy Battery at SHENDISH when he learnt that 3 horses had been sent	15ft. 15ft. 65/7

Army Form C. 2118.

WAR DIARY
INTELLIGENCE SUMMARY.

Headquarters R.A. 2/2 London Division

Instructions regarding War Diaries and Intelligence Summaries are contained in F.S. Regs., Part II. and the Staff Manual respectively. Title pages will be prepared in manuscript.

(Erase heading not required.)

3

Place	Date	Hour	Summary of Events and Information	Remarks and references to Appendices
Hemel Hempstead	12.4.15	6.30 am	to the Veterinary Hospital at St ALBANS with mange & that 3 horses was suspected of mange.	1577.
do	13.4.15	6.30 PM	The CRA went to St ALBANS in the afternoon to see the G.O.C. 2/2 London Division.	1577.
do	14.4.15	6.30 PM	ibid.	1577.
do	15.4.15	6-30 PM	Major G.T. Daniells 2/7th Brigade + Major F.B. Osborne proceeded to Salisbury Plain to attend Artillery Practice of Wessex + East Anglian Divisions. 4 15 Pr B.L.C Guns Mark IV arrived this day from IRELAND.	1577.
do		7. P.M.	A telephone message was received from H.Q. St ALBANS stating that no officers were to travel in Motor Cars or bicycles between 7 PM + 6 AM on nights 15th 16th 17th April except on duty + with Pass Word	1577.
do	16.4.15	10. am	An Aeroplane was reported by the guard at the 2/7th Brigade Gun Park at MARCHMONT FARM flying from WEST to EAST at 2.45 a.m.	1577.
do	17.4.15	6.30 PM	R.J.	1577.

Army Form C. 2118.

Sheet 4

WAR DIARY
or
INTELLIGENCE SUMMARY.
(Erase heading not required.)

HEADQUARTERS R.A. 2/2 LONDON DIVISION.

Instructions regarding War Diaries and Intelligence Summaries are contained in F. S. Regs., Part II. and the Staff Manual respectively. Title pages will be prepared in manuscript.

Place	Date	Hour	Summary of Events and Information	Remarks and references to Appendices
HEMEL HEMPSTEAD	18.4.15	6.30 PM	nil.	15f.t
do	19.4.15	6.30 PM	nil.	15f.t
do	20.4.15	6.30 PM	nil.	15f.t
do	21.4.15	6.30 PM	nil.	15f.t
do	22.4.15	6.20 PM	nil.	15f.t
do	23.4.15	6.30 PM	Col. LANE A.D.V.S. came this morning to see the C.R.A. He reported that there were no fresh cases of mange, & that a number of cured horses would shortly be distributed to the Division	15f.t
do	24.4.15	6.30 PM	nil.	15f.t
do	25.4.15	6.20 PM	nil.	15f.t
do	26.4.15	6.30 PM	Capt. Monagh of the Royal Automobile Club reported for duty with motor car. General Altby G.O.C 2/2 London Division being on sick leave the C.R.A took command of the Division	15f.t
do	27.4.15	6.30 PM	The C.R.A this day went to H.Q 2/2 London Division St ALBANS.	15f.t
do	28.4.15	4 P.M	29 Remounts were received from the Remount Officer 2/2 London Division. They were allotted as follows	15f.t

Army Form C. 2118.

Sheet 5.

HEADQUARTERS R.A. 2/2 LONDON DIVISION.

WAR DIARY or INTELLIGENCE SUMMARY
(Erase heading not required.)

Instructions regarding War Diaries and Intelligence Summaries are contained in F.S. Regs., Part II. and the Staff Manual respectively. Title pages will be prepared in manuscript.

Place	Date	Hour	Summary of Events and Information	Remarks and references to Appendices
HEMEL HEMPSTEAD	28.4.15	4 P.M.		
			Chargers. Riding. Artillery. Light Draught. Heavy Draught	
			HEADQUARTERS R.A. 1 3 - - -	
			2/7 F.A. Bgde - - 5 - -	
			2/8 How. Bgde. 1 3 - 6 2	
			2/2 HEAVY BATTERY. - 2 - - 2	
			2/1 HANTS HEAVY BY. - - - 4 -	
			Three horses under instructions from the Veterinary Officer Mr Prudames were temporarily isolated in the stables of GADEBRIDGE HUTMENTS, with the exception of Ross allotted to 2/1 HANTS HEAVY By. which were isolated in the sick lines of the Battery at SHENDISM PARK	15/f
do	29.4.15	7. P.M	Major G. P. Daniells 2/7 Brigade gave a lecture at ST MARY'S HALL, HEMEL HEMPSTEAD on the Artillery tactics of the various East Anglian Divisions which he had witnessed on Salisbury Plain. Major Malcolm A.A. & Q.M.G. 2nd .... G.S.O.2 Col. Dunlop G.S.O.1 of the 2/2 LONDON DIVISION were present, Col Dunlop afterwards criticising the lecture. The G.O.C. 2/2 LONDON DIVISION having returned from sick leave, the CRA	15/f

Army Form C. 2118.

Sheet 6

WAR DIARY
or
INTELLIGENCE SUMMARY.

(Erase heading not required.)

HEADQUARTERS R.A. 2/2 LONDON DIVISION

Instructions regarding War Diaries and Intelligence Summaries are contained in F. S. Regs., Part II. and the Staff Manual respectively. Title pages will be prepared in manuscript.

Place	Date	Hour	Summary of Events and Information	Remarks and references to Appendices
HEMEL HEMPSTEAD	29.4.15	7 P.M	Relinquished command of the Division.	57.
do	30.4.15	6.30 P.M	Major Pinky, Divisional Musketry Instructor, gave a lecture at the Headquarters of the 2/2 Heavy Battery, on how to teach recruits the elements of musketry, trigger pressing & aiming.	57.

for b.f.Arson Capt
Staff Captain, R.A.
2/2nd London Division, T.F.

1577 Wt. W10791/1773 500,000 1/15 D. D. & L. A.D.S.S./Forms/C. 2118.

Army Form C. 2118.

WAR DIARY
or
INTELLIGENCE SUMMARY.
(Erase heading not required.)

Headquarters R.A 2/2 London Division.   Sheet 1

Place	Date	Hour	Summary of Events and Information	Remarks and references to Appendices
HEMEL HEMPSTEAD	1-5-15	3 P.M.	Telegram received from H.Q. London District that 2 officers are wanted for reinforcements overseas. No units stated.	
		11.15 PM	Telegram received that 1/2 London FA Bde are dispatching 600 rounds 15 pr B.L.C Ammunition.	A.H.
	2-5-15	9 P.M.	600 rounds 15 pr Ammunition received from 1/2 London FA Bde. Taken on charge by 2/7 F.A. Bde	
		12.30 PM	600 rounds 15 pr Ammunition taken on charge by 2/4 FA Bde at Rickmansworth	
		2.30 PM	Gun drill & turnouts inspected by DRA.O.C in company with Majors	
HANWORTH.	3-5-15	11.30 AM	C.R.A inspected stables of Hants Heavy Battery at Shendish	A.H.
		2.45 PM	G.O.C 2/2 London Division inspected gundrill of 2/7 F.A. Bde at Marchmont Farm.	A.H.
	4-5-15	4 P.M.	War office telephoned to say that officers required for reinforcements overseas were to be Field Gunners. Names of 2/Lt Vick (2/5 FA BDE) & Lt Brasset (2/8 FABDE) forwarded	A.H.

Army Form C. 2118.

Headquarters R.A. 2/2 London Division

Sheet 2

WAR DIARY
or
INTELLIGENCE SUMMARY.
(Erase heading not required.)

Instructions regarding War Diaries and Intelligence Summaries are contained in F. S. Regs., Part II and the Staff Manual respectively. Title pages will be prepared in manuscript.

Place	Date	Hour	Summary of Events and Information	Remarks and references to Appendices
HEMEL HEMPSTEAD	5.5.15		Nil.	
	6.5.15	11 AM.	C.R.A. & Staff Capt. R.A. met Lt Col. DUNLOP G.S.O.1 at cross roads 2 mile west of KINGS LANGLEY. The scheme set for the 2/8th Howitzer BRIGADE was to support the infantry crossing the River GADE at ABBOTS MILL BRIDGE & KINGS LANGLEY BRIDGE. The 2/8 HOWITZER BRIGADE formed part of an advanced guard. The Batteries went in position behind a wood west of BARNES LODGE. Observers went to a flank at 250 and 400 yds distance. Col Dunlop pointed out that this was a bad position as this was not the slightest cover from aircraft, & both batteries were in a straight line at regular intervals instead of being placed irregularly, also he pointed out that the O.C. 2/8 Howitzer Bde. was wrong in placing his batteries personally, & not leaving this to his B.C.s	6/7.
"	7.5.15	4.30 PM	C.R.A. went to Headquarters 2/London Division & learnt that the Division was to move at short notice to the neighbourhood of BISHOPS STORTFORD	6/7.

Army Form C. 2118.

Headquarters R.A. 2/2 London Division.

Sheet 3.

WAR DIARY
or
INTELLIGENCE SUMMARY.

(Erase heading not required.)

Instructions regarding War Diaries and Intelligence Summaries are contained in F. S. Regs., Part II. and the Staff Manual respectively. Title pages will be prepared in manuscript.

Place	Date	Hour	Summary of Events and Information	Remarks and references to Appendices
HEMEL HEMPSTED	8.5.15	11.20 a.m	C.R.A. went over to Headquarters to confer about move. Telegram sent to III ARMY to say that Artillery could not move by road.	Apt.
"	9.5.15		Nil.	Apt.
"	10.5.15	1 P.M.	Brigadier General BIDDULPH C.R.A. 1/EAST ANGLIAN DIVISION came over to confer about positions for his Brigade.	Apt.
"	11.5.15		Nil.	Apt.
"	12.5.15		Nil.	Apt.
"	13.5.15	2.30 P.M.	One Brigade of EAST ANGLIAN DIVISION arrived BOXMOOR.	Apt.
"	14.5.15	1 P.M.	Train schedule received.	Apt.
"	15.5.15	10 A.M.	10.8 to motor lorries arrived to take stores & baggage to BOXMOOR STATION.	Apt.
H. BROMLEY	16.5.15	5 P.M.	The DIVISIONAL ARTILLERY moved to BISHOPS STORTFORD area arriving BISHOPS STORTFORD STATION at the following times.	Apt.
			1st HANTS HEAVY BATTERY 8.35 A.M.	
			2/1 LONDON HEAVY BATTERY & H.Q. R.A. 10.5 A.M.	
			2/8 HOWITZER BRIGADE 11.35 A.M.	

Army Form C. 2118.

Sheet 4

Headquarters. R.A. 2/2 London Division.

WAR DIARY
or
INTELLIGENCE SUMMARY.

(Erase heading not required.)

Instructions regarding War Diaries and Intelligence Summaries are contained in F.S. Regs., Part II and the Staff Manual respectively. Title pages will be prepared in manuscript.

Place	Date	Hour	Summary of Events and Information	Remarks and references to Appendices
BROMLEY	16.5.15	5. P.M.	2/7 F.A. BRIGADE 1.5 P.M.	
			do 2.45 P.M.	
			Baggage Train 4.0 P.M.	
			2/5 + 2/6 BGDE DETAILS 8.45 P.M.	
			The units then marched from BISHOPS STORTFORD to their billeting areas which	
			were as follows.	
			2/5 F.A. BGDE DETAILS STANDON.	
			2/6 " " " WIDFORD.	
			2/7 FA BGDE MUCH HADHAM.	
			2/8 HOWITZER BGDE STANDON. PUCKERIDGE and BRAUGHING.	
			2/2 HEAVY BATTERY. BRAUGHING.	
			1st HANTS HEAVY BATTERY BRAUGHING	
			The Baggage & Ammunition of the units were transported from BISHOPS STORTFORD	
			by 10 2ton W.O. Motor Lorries.	
			The Headquarters Divisional Artillery was established at BROMLEY	
			and the Offices opened at 12 noon.	

Army Form C. 2118.

Sheet 5.

Headquarters R.A. 2/1 London Division.

WAR DIARY
or
INTELLIGENCE SUMMARY.
(Erase heading not required.)

Instructions regarding War Diaries and Intelligence Summaries are contained in F. S. Regs., Part II. and the Staff Manual respectively. Title pages will be prepared in manuscript.

Place	Date	Hour	Summary of Events and Information	Remarks and references to Appendices
BROMLEY.	16.5.15	7 p.m.	The Strength in Nets was as follows.	
			Officers. O.R. Horses. Guns. Wagons	
			2/1 F.A. Bde Details 4 90 Nil Nil Nil	
			2/5 F.A. Bgde Details 2 71 Nil Nil Nil	
			2/6 " " 19 615 134 17 12	
			2/7 F.A Bgde 12 433 56 Nil 6	
			2/8 How. Bgde 3 199 14 Nil 5	
			2/2 London Heavy Battery 9 213 81 4 6	
			Hants Heavy Battery 1 9 8 Nil Nil	
			H.Q. R.A.	Appx.
	17.5.15		Nil.	Appx.
	18.5.15	10.30am	C.R.A. arrived at BROMLEY.	Appx.
"	19.5.15		Nil.	Appx.
"	20.5.15	6 p.m.	48 Remounts received from St ALBANS taken on charge by 2/7 F.A. Bgde.	Appx.
"	21.5.15		Nil	Appx.
"	22.5.15		Nil	Appx.
"	23.5.15		Nil	Appx.

Army Form C. 2118.

Sheet 6

WAR DIARY
or
INTELLIGENCE SUMMARY.

Headquarters R.A. 2/2 London Division

(Erase heading not required.)

Place	Date	Hour	Summary of Events and Information	Remarks and references to Appendices
BROMLEY	24.5.15	5.P.M	C.R.A reported to His G.O.C. at BISHOPS STORTFORD.	15/7.
	25.5.15		Nil	15/7.
	26.5.15	11.A.M.	G.O.C. 2/2 LONDON DIVISION. visited &inspected the units of Divisional Artillery	15/7.
"	27.5.15	3.P.M.	C.R.A conferred with G.O.C re arrangements for moving 2/5 & 2/6 Bgdes from London.	15/7.
	28.5.15	11.30am	8 Remounts received from BISHOPS STORTFORD taken on charge by H.Q. R.A.	15/7.
	29.5.15	2.30pm	*Inspection of Horses of Divisional Artillery by Col. LONG.	15/7.
"	30.5.15		Nil	15/7.
"	31.5.15		Nil	15/7.

* The following Officers were submitted to HEADQUARTERS Staff Captain, R.A.
2/2nd London Division, T.F. 15/7/150.
2/2 London Division for a fortnights attachment to a battery at the front
to proceed about June 12th

Major S.P.DANIELS 2/7 F.A. BGDE.

Major F.B. OSBORNE 2/8 HOW BGDE and Major F.H. CHAPLIN HANTS HEAVY BATTERY. 15/7.

WAR DIARY
or
INTELLIGENCE SUMMARY.
(Erase heading not required.)

Army Form C. 2118.

Place	Date	Hour	Summary of Events and Information	Remarks and references to Appendices
Bromley Standon, Ware, Herts.	June 1	10.30	C.R.A. and staff were present at a tactical scheme arranged for the 2/7th. London F.A.Brigade by Col. Dunlop, G.S.O.(1)	
		4 p.m	Inspection by C.R.A. and Staff of the area Furneux Pelham, Brent Pelham, Stocking Pelham, Little Hormead, Great Hormead, Hare Street, and Buntingford, with special regard to its desirability and accommodation as a billeting area. Inspection showed area to be generally satisfactory, and its sanitary condition not inferior to that of other similar villages.	
	2	2.30	C.R.A. visited G.O.C. at Headquarters, and discussed the question of the location of the 2/6th London F.A.Brigade.	
	4	10.30	C.R.A. visited Hutment Stables (Much Hadham).	
		-	Billeting parties for the 2/5th. London F.A.Bde., which is to be quartered in and about Hadham Hall, and Little Hadham arrived today.	
	6	-	Definite orders received from Headquarters that 2/5th. Bde., is to move from London on the 9th inst. and the 2/6th. on the 15th. instant.	
	7	11a.m	C.R.A. saw the G.O.C. at Headquarters, and discussed the question of the accommodation for the 2/6th. Brigade. The G.O.C. finally decided that 100 tents are to be allotted for this unit, which will be encamped at Much Hadham.	

Army Form C. 2118.

WAR DIARY
or
INTELLIGENCE SUMMARY.
(Erase heading not required.)

Instructions regarding War Diaries and Intelligence Summaries are contained in F. S. Regs., Part II and the Staff Manual respectively. Title pages will be prepared in manuscript.

Place	Date	Hour	Summary of Events and Information	Remarks and references to Appendices
Bromley, Standon, Ware, Herts.	June 8	10.30a.m	C.R.A. inspected site for the encampment of 2/6th. Brigade.	
		3.30	G.O.C. arrived to inspect the site for encampment of 2/6th. Bde., and was met by C.R.A.	
	9	2 p.m } 4.25p.m }	Arrival of trains conveying the 2/5th. London F.A.Bde. from London to Bishops Stortford.	
		2.15	C.R.A. and staff visit billeting area allotted to the 2/5th. Bde.	
	10	12.0	C.R.A. present at lecture on work with the Director, by Col. Dunlop, G.S.O.(1)	
		2.30p.m	Lt. Col. Sir Charles Allen, Comndg. 2/5th. Bde. at Hadham Hall reported himself to C.R.A.	
		9.30 p.m	6 Officers' Chargers for Headquarters, Divisional Artillery, received from Bishops Stortford (by train from Remount Depot, St. Albans).	
	11	11am.	C.R.A. visited units at Puckeridge and Braughing.	
	12	2.45	C.R.A. met O.C. 2/6th. London F.A.Bde. and explained arrangements for the encamping of this Brigade at Much Hadham (Moor Place)	
	14	10a.m	G.O.C. inspected 2/5th. Bde. at Hadham Hall etc. C.R.A. present.	
	15	2.25pm } 4.25pm }	Arrival of the 2/6th. London F.A.Bde. from London at the Bishops Stortford Station. Units proceeded by march route to the Camp, Much Hadham, Moor Place. Second train met by C.RA., first by Staff Captain.	
			Strength of 2/6th. Bde. on arrival:-	

Army Form C. 2118.

WAR DIARY
or
INTELLIGENCE SUMMARY.
(Erase heading not required.)

Instructions regarding War Diaries and Intelligence Summaries are contained in F. S. Regs., Part II and the Staff Manual respectively. Title pages will be prepared in manuscript.

Place	Date	Hour	Summary of Events and Information	Remarks and references to Appendices
Bromley, Standon, Ware, Herts.	June 16		17 Officers, 618 other ranks, 112 horses.	
		10 am	Route march arranged for the 1/1st. Hants Heavy Battery; Battery inspected on the march by the C.R.A.	
	17	11am	C.R.A. inspected 2/2nd. London Heavy Battery R.G.A.	
		11am	C.R.A. inspected the 2/8th. London Ammunition Column at Standon, and the Divisional Artillery Headquarters stables at Westfield Farm.	
	18	10.30am	C.R.A. inspected 2/6th. Bde. at the Camp, Much Hadham, (Moor Place), and the Ammunition Column which is billeted at Widford.	
	21	10am	C.R.A. inspected the section of the 2/8th. (Howitzer) Bde., which is to take part in a proposed Concentration of the Division on Friday next, 25th. inst.	
		4p.m	C.R.A. and staff attended the first of a series of six Veterinary First-aid Lectures which are to be given at Hadham Hall and Much Hadham, (Moor Place), camp to the officers of the Artillery by Mr. Healy, M.R.C.V.S.	
	22	10.15am	C.R.A. inspected the Driving Drill of the batteries of the 2/7th. Bde.	
		4 pm	C.R.A. attended second lecture at Hadham Hall by Mr. Healy, M.R.C.V.S.	
	23	10.15am	C.R.A. inspected a section of the 2/6th. Bde, which is to take part in the Concentration tomorrow.	

Army Form C. 2118.

WAR DIARY
or
INTELLIGENCE SUMMARY.
(Erase heading not required.)

Instructions regarding War Diaries and Intelligence Summaries are contained in F. S. Regs., Part II. and the Staff Manual respectively. Title pages will be prepared in manuscript.

Place	Date	Hour	Summary of Events and Information	Remarks and references to Appendices
Bromley, Standon, Ware, Herts.	June 23	10 am	C.R.A. received G.O.C. at Moor Place - inspection by G.O.C. of the 2/6th. Bde, and the 2/6th. Ammunition Column at WIDFORD.	
	24	11 am	C.R.A. inspected 2/18th. Battery, 2/7th. Bde.	
		4 pm	C.R.A. and staff attended fourth lecture by Mr.Healy, M.R.C.V.S., at the Camp, Moor Place.	
	25	10.15am	C.R.A. and Staff proceeded to FURNEUX PELHAM. and witnessed concentration scheme of the 2/4th and 2/6th. London Infantry Brigades in co-operation with the Artillery. C.R.A. watched the Left Column file past.	
		12.45	C.R.A. met the G.O.C. who witnessed the concentration.	
	26	9.15am	Brigade Major R.A., in company with Col. Dunlop, G.S.O. (1), visited LEXHAM, near BRAINTREE by arrangement and viewed miniature Artillery Range used by one of the Brigades of the 2/1st South Midland Division.	
		10.30am	C.R.A. attended final lecture of 1st. series by Mr. Healy, M.R.C.V.S., at Much Hadham, (MOOR PLACE).	
	28	10.15 am	C.R.A. inspected 2/6th. Bde. at work at MUCH HADHAM.	
		11.30am	C.R.A. inspected Gun epaulments at STANDON, constructed by the 2/8th. London (Howitzer)Bde., after the model of these used by the 1/8th. London (Howitzer) Bde. with the B.E.F.	

1577 Wt.W10791/1773 500,000 1/15 D. D. & L. A.D.S.S./Forms/C. 2118.

Army Form C. 2118.

WAR DIARY
or
INTELLIGENCE SUMMARY.
(Erase heading not required.)

Instructions regarding War Diaries and Intelligence Summaries are contained in F. S. Regs., Part II. and the Staff Manual respectively. Title pages will be prepared in manuscript.

Place	Date	Hour	Summary of Events and Information	Remarks and references to Appendices
Bromley, Standon, Ware, Herts.	June 28	2.30pm	C.R.A. and Staff visit ground selected as a site for a Divisional Artillery School for the establishment of which the C.R.A. is applying for sanction.	
	29	11 am	C.R.A. and staff attend lecture in Director work given to 2/6th. Bde. at EXNELLS by Col. Dunlop, G.S.O. (1)	
		2.30pm	C.R.A. and staff visit Polo Ground, HADHAM ROAD, to arrange for the accommodation of the Divisional Artillery tomorrow at an inspection of the Division by Sir Leslie Rundle, G.O.C. in C., Central Force.	
		6.pm to 11 pm	C.R.A.'s staff arrange for reception of 102 horses (remounts) at BISHOPS STORTFORD and distribute them to the units.	
	30	10.30	Inspection of the 2/2nd. London Divisional Artillery at the Polo Ground, HADHAM ROAD, by the G.O.C. in C. Central Force, the 2/6th. London Infantry Brigade being drawn up in adjacent Field to the North of the Polo ground. The following, in addition to the rest of the personnel of the Units who paraded (dismounted, were the mounted troops of the Divisional Artillery present:-	
			2/5th. London F.A.Brigade. 1 Section (Mounted).	
			2/6th. Do. 2 Sections (Do?)	

Army Form C. 2118.

WAR DIARY
or
INTELLIGENCE SUMMARY.
(Erase heading not required.)

Instructions regarding War Diaries and Intelligence Summaries are contained in F. S. Regs., Part II. and the Staff Manual respectively. Title pages will be prepared in manuscript.

Place	Date	Hour	Summary of Events and Information	Remarks and references to Appendices
Bromley, Standon, Ware, Herts.	June. 30		2/7th. London F.A. Brigade. 3 Sections (Mounted), six wagons of the Ammunition Column.	
			2/8th. London F.A.(How) Bde. 1 Section (no wagons) mounted.	
			2/2nd. London Heavy Battery R.G.A. Nil (mounted).	
			1/1st. Hants Heavy Battery R.G.A. 2 sections and 2 A & S wagons.	
		3 pm to 6 pm	First day's inspection by Brig. Gen. Drake, Inspector of Horse and Field Artillery. Brigadier General Drake inspected the 2/5th., 2/6th and 2/7th. Brigades by batteries at their work in the field and camp.	

[signature]

Colonel, C.R.A.

2/2nd. London Division.

Army Form C. 2118.

WAR DIARY
or
INTELLIGENCE SUMMARY.
(Erase heading not required.)

HEADQUARTERS R.A. 2/2 LONDON DIVISION.

Sheet 1.

Place	Date	Hour	Summary of Events and Information	Remarks and references to Appendices
BROMLEY	JULY 1	10 AM	Brig General DRAKE inspected RH + RFA, inspected 2/2 LONDON HEAVY BATTERY and 1/HANTS HEAVY BATTERY at BRAUGHING.	65°F
	2	11:30	Inspected 2/2 Howitzer Battery at PUCKERIDGE and saw driving drill.	65°F
		12.0	" " " 2/21 " " at STANDON. visited AMMUNITION COLUMN	65°F
	3		Found a dug out constructed by the AMMUNITION COLUMN.	65°F
	4		nil	65°F
	5		nil	65°F
	6		nil	65°F
	7		nil	65°F
	8	9 AM	Home Service Officers & men proceed to COLCHESTER.	65°F
			nil	
		9 PM	Night Concentration march on the road WESTMILL - PUCKERIDGE - STANDON GREEN END - HIGH CROSS.	65°F
	9		nil	65°F
	10		nil	65°F
	11		nil	65°F

HEADQUARTERS R.A. 2/2 LONDON DIVISION. WAR DIARY Army Form C. 2118.

Instructions regarding War Diaries and Intelligence
Summaries are contained in F. S. Regs., Part II.
and the Staff Manual respectively. Title pages
will be prepared in manuscript.

INTELLIGENCE SUMMARY.

Sheet 2

(Erase heading not required.)

Place	Date	Hour	Summary of Events and Information	Remarks and references to Appendices
BROMLEY.	July 12		Q.J.	S/T
	13		R.J.	S/T
	14	9.30 am	Concentration March in the Neighbourhood of DANE END	S/T
	15		Mil. Lef/Keeton HANTS HEAVY BATTERY PROCEEDED to a artillery training school WENDOVER	S/T
	16		R.J.	S/T
	17		R.J.	S/T
	18		Q.J.	S/T
	19		Information received from Divisional Headquarters that HQ 2/5 FA BRIGADE will move into CAMP at STANSTED CRA inspects his camping ground at STANSTED.	S/T S/T S/T
	20		Q.J.	
	21		R.J.	
	22		Field Day in continuation of concentration march of 14 July. Columns Rendezvous at ST EDMUNDS COLLEGE. Position taken up at POTTERS GREEN + LEVENS GREEN.	Rif 2 O.S 29
		9.30 am		
		10.45		
		11.30	Retirement over RIVER RIB to positions by BARTRAMS FARM	S/T

Army Form C. 2118.

Sheet 3

WAR DIARY
INTELLIGENCE SUMMARY.

HEADQUARTERS R.A. 2/2 LONDON DIVISION

(Erase heading not required.)

Place	Date	Hour	Summary of Events and Information	Remarks and references to Appendices
	July			
BROMLEY	22	11.30am	nil STANDON LODGE.	577
	23		nil	1577
	24		nil	1577
	25		nil	1577
	26		nil	1577
	27		nil	1577
	28		Information received that G.O.C. III Army will inspect Ashkey Camps.	1572
	29	10.15am	C.R.A. meets G.O.C. III Army outside KING EDWARDS HORSE STABLES LITTLE HADHAM ROAD. The G.O.C. inspected 2/12 BATTERY at HADHAM HALL the horse lines of the 2/5th AMMUNITION COLUMN, the 2/18 BATTERY. and the 2/19th BATTERY. The G.O.C. also inspected the 2/6th BRIGADE in camp at MUCH HADHAM MOOR PLACE.	
	30	11.30am	A.A. & Q.M.G. 2/London Division visited the proposed site for a/a/s/s camp for the 2/6th F.A. BRIGADE in MOOR PLACE PARK.	577

Army Form C. 2118.

Sheet 4.

WAR DIARY
or
INTELLIGENCE SUMMARY

(Erase heading not required.)

HEADQUARTERS R.A. 2/2 LONDON DIVISION

Instructions regarding War Diaries and Intelligence Summaries are contained in F. S. Regs., Part II. and the Staff Manual respectively. Title pages will be prepared in manuscript.

Place	Date	Hour	Summary of Events and Information	Remarks and references to Appendices
	JULY			
BROMLEY	31	10.0 am	C.R.A. Judges in driving competitions between the different artillery Brigades.	Lyt.

Lytton.
Staff Captain, R.A.
2/2nd London Division, T.F.

1577 Wt.W10791/1773 500,000 1/15 D. D. & L. A.D.S.S./Forms/C. 2118.

Army Form C. 2118.

WAR DIARY
or
INTELLIGENCE SUMMARY.
(Erase heading not required.)

HEADQUARTERS R.A. 2/6 LONDON DIVISION

Instructions regarding War Diaries and Intelligence Summaries are contained in F. S. Regs., Part II. and the Staff Manual respectively. Title pages will be prepared in manuscript.

Sheet 1

Place	Date	Hour	Summary of Events and Information	Remarks and references to Appendices
BROMLEY.	AUGUST 1		NIL	
	2	11.0 AM	Divisional Sports at BISHOPS STORTFORD. 2/1st LONDON BRIGADE.R.F.A & 1/1. HANTS HEAVY BATTERY gave driving display under M.T. Rules.	WPJ
	3		Nil.	WPJ WPJ
	4	11.0 AM	Divisional Sanitary Officer inspected new Camping ground for 2/6 BRIGADE, & advised as to placing of latrines, horse troughs etc	WPJ
		12.30 AM	1/1. BARNES inspected certain fields taken as drill grounds, horse lines etc with a view to stiffening rates.	WPJ
	5	10. AM	2/5th BRIGADE received 82 remounts from ST.ALBANS. These brought by road to LITTLE HADHAM.	SPJ
	6	9.30 AM	2/5th BRIGADE moved by road from billets at HADHAM HALL, LITTLE HADHAM, ALBURY and PATMORE HEATH into camp at BURTON END. STANSTED. ESSEX. Marching in strength. 21 Officers. 528 other ranks 430 horses 12 guns & limbers 9 vehicles. Transport was supplied by the A.S.C & by the 2/1st BRIGADE.	WPJ

WAR DIARY or INTELLIGENCE SUMMARY.

Army Form C. 2118.
Sheet 2.

HEADQUARTERS. R.A. 2/2 LONDON DIVISION.

Place	Date	Hour	Summary of Events and Information	Remarks and references to Appendices
BROMLEY	AUGUST 7	9.30am	C.R.A visits D.A.D.O.S. 2/2 LONDON DIVISION with reference to his supply of grooming requisites.	Apt.
	8	3.30pm	Telegram received from central forces requiring the name of a captain as reinforcement for 47th DIVISIONAL AMMUNITION COLUMN. The name of Captain FOURGER 2/5th BRIGADE submitted	
		4.0 PM	Telegram received from HEADQUARTERS that 2/Lt ANDERSON 2/5 BGDE Lt ULLMAN 2/1 " Lt WEBSTER 2/8 (HOW) " 2/Lt C.J. BROWNE 2/2 HEAVY BATTY. will report personally to Embarkation Commandant at SOUTHAMPTON as reinforcements for 1st LINE UNITS.	Apt.
	9	11. PM	C.R.A inspected Camp of 2/5 BRIGADE at STANSTED & went also to see H.Q.O.C with regard to the move of the HEAVY BATTERIES from BRAUGHING.	G.S.7
	10	3. PM	Telegram received from A.D.V.S. that 90 remounts are to be fetched from REMOUNT FIELD, BISHOPS STORTFORD. Telegraphic mistake 19 remounts	

HEADQUARTERS R.A. 2/2 LONDON DIVISION.

Army Form C. 2118.

Sheet 3

WAR DIARY
or
INTELLIGENCE SUMMARY.
(Erase heading not required.)

Instructions regarding War Diaries and Intelligence Summaries are contained in F. S. Regs., Part II. and the Staff Manual respectively. Title pages will be prepared in manuscript.

Place	Date	Hour	Summary of Events and Information	Remarks and references to Appendices
BROMLEY	August 10	6 P.M.	Orders issued by 2/7th BRIGADE	SPA
	11	10.30 A.M.	Telegraph received that 80 REMOUNTS to be issued at 6 P.M. from BISHOPS STORTFORD, 20 to 2/8th BRIGADE, 40 to 2/6th AMMUNITION COLUMN.	SPA
	12.		Nil.	SPA
	13	12.0	G.O.C. 2/2 LONDON DIVISION inspects Divisional Artillery Miniature Ranges. Orders issued that the designation of the Division is changed to the 60th (LONDON) DIVISION.	SPA
	14	8. P.M.	Captain WOOTON. A.S.C. rejoins for duty on his return from FRANCE.	SPA
	15	8.40 A.M.	2/5th + 2/6th Brigades R.F.A concentration march. 2/5th Rear Camp at BURTON END, STANSTED at 9.15 A.M. 2/6 Rear Camp at MOOR PLACE, MUCHHADHAM at 8.40 A.M. The former march by TAKELEY and 2/6 by GREEN TYE – TRIMS GREEN – at BUSH END returns, the latter march by road for 1½ mils N of WALLBURY CAMP.	SPA
	16.	12.0 noon	The 2/8th LONDON HOWITZER BRIGADE moved from billets at STANDON and PUCKERIDGE into Camp at SILVERLEYS. BISHOPS STORTFORD by road, the horses being in the Hut Stables. They were inspected on the route by the G.O.C. 60th (LONDON) DIVISION.	Left

1577 Wt.W10791/1773 500,000 1/15 D. D. & L. A.D.S.S./Forms/C. 2118.

Army Form C. 2118.

HEADQUARTERS R.A. 60th (LONDON) DIVISION.

Sheet 4.

WAR DIARY
or
INTELLIGENCE SUMMARY.
(Erase heading not required.)

Instructions regarding War Diaries and Intelligence Summaries are contained in F. S. Regs., Part II. and the Staff Manual respectively. Title pages will be prepared in manuscript.

Place	Date	Hour	Summary of Events and Information	Remarks and references to Appendices
BROMLEY	16	2:30 PM	9/s marching in strength had 16 officers. 342 other ranks 227 horses 2 guns limbers 12 vehicles.	lsft
	17	9.0. AM	The 2/7 London Brigade. R.F.A. moved from billets at MUCH HADHAM into camp at STANSTED by road. They were inspected en route by the G.O.C. Marching in strength 18 officers 468 other ranks 508 horses 12 guns & limbers, 28 vehicles.	lsft.
	18	7.0 AM 11.15 AM	2/5th & 2/6th Brigades march from camps at STANSTED & MOOR PLACE to concentrate at HATFIELD HEATH. Inspected en route at half interval on the hrak by the G.O.C. III Army. Horses watered & fed on the hrak before marching home.	lsft
	19	9.0 AM	1/Hants Heavy Battery moved by march route from billets at BRAUGHING into camp at SILVERLEYS, BISHOPS STORTFORD, marching in strength 4 officers 118 other ranks, 44 horses, 2 guns + limbers 6 vehicles.	
		10:30	2/2 London Heavy Battery moved by march route from billets at BRAUGHING into camp at SILVERLEYS, BISHOPS STORTFORD, BISHOPS STORTFORD, their tents had not	lsft

Army Form C. 2118.

Sheet 5

WAR DIARY
or
INTELLIGENCE SUMMARY.
(Erase heading not required.)

HEADQUARTERS, R.A. 60th (LONDON) DIVISION

Instructions regarding War Diaries and Intelligence Summaries are contained in F.S. Regs., Part II and the Staff Manual respectively. Title pages will be prepared in manuscript.

Place	Date	Hour	Summary of Events and Information	Remarks and references to Appendices
BROMLEY.	AUGUST 19	10.30 AM	arrived when Hy got into Camp. Marching in Strength 3 Officers 171 other ranks 44 horses 8 vehicles.	left.
		12.30 PM	C.R.A granted 3 days leave. Colonel S. Wishart V.D. O.C. 2/6 London Brigade R.F.A assumes temporary command.	
	20		Nil	
	21		Information received re: Headquarters R.A. 60th London Division will move into Camp.	left.
	22	12.30	C.R.A returns from leave.	left.
	23.		Nil.	left.
	24	10.0 AM	Concentration march of all units. Rendezvous in Hallingbury Park.	left.
	25		Nil	left.
	26.	10.30 AM	Inspection of 2/8" How Bgde 2/1 London Heavy Batty + 1/Hants Heavy Batty by G.O.C III Army in field behind Silverleys Camp.	left.
		12.30	C.R.A inspects reinforcing draught of 2/7th Brigade.	
		3.0 PM	draught of the 2/6th Brigade and later a	left.
	27	3.0 PM	Col Long inspects 2/6 Brigade Horses.	left.
	28		Nil.	left.

Army Form C. 2118.

Sheet- 6

WAR DIARY
or
INTELLIGENCE SUMMARY.
(Erase heading not required.)

HEADQUARTERS R.A. 60th LONDON DIVISION

Instructions regarding War Diaries and Intelligence Summaries are contained in F. S. Regs., Part II. and the Staff Manual respectively. Title pages will be prepared in manuscript.

Place	Date	Hour	Summary of Events and Information	Remarks and references to Appendices
	AUGUST			
BROMLEY	29	10.0 AM	C.R.A inspects reinforcing draught of 4 artificers of 2/8th LONDON BRIGADE.	15/1
	30		Nil.	15/2
	31		Nil.	15/3
				15/4

W.S. ?son
Staff Captain, R.A.
60th London Division, T.F.

1577 Wt.W10791/1773 500,000 1/15 D. D. & L. A.D.S.S./Forms/C. 2118.

HEADQUARTERS R.A. 60th LONDON DIVISION. WAR DIARY or INTELLIGENCE SUMMARY.

Army Form C2118.

Instructions regarding War Diaries and Intelligence Summaries are contained in F. S. Regs., Part II and the Staff Manual respectively. Title pages will be prepared in manuscript.

(Erase heading not required.)

Place	Date	Hour	Summary of Events and Information	Remarks and references to Appendices
BROMLEY.	SEPTEMBER			
	1	12.0	Divisional Artillery Concentrate at WOODSIDE GREEN for practice in Ceremonial Drill + marching past.	15ft.
	2	10.30 a.m.	G.O.C. inspects Divisional Artillery Range at BROMLEY whilst officers of 2/6th Brigade are being instructed.	15ft.
	3		Nil	15ft.
	4		Nil	15ft.
	5		Nil	15ft.
	6	5 p.m.	C.R.A. confers with G.O.C. + Infantry Brigadiers about the formation of a composite force to act as a reinforcement to any of the three Systems of defence (East Coast) under III Army. The 2/7 Brigade chosen.	15ft.
	7	2 p.m.	Hozrso of the 2/8th Howitzer Brigade transferred as follows 39 to 2/6 Brigade 4 to 2/5 Brigade 11 to 2/7 Brigade and 1 to Divisional Artillery Headquarters.	15ft.
		3.0	Lecture by Lt Col Burrowes G.S. on "Notes from the front" attended by C.R.A, Staff + officers of R.A.	15ft.
	8	5.30 p.m.	Lecture by Lt Col Dunlop G.S. on Cooperation between Artillery + Infantry.	15ft.

Army Form C. 2118.

Sheet 2

HEADQUARTERS R.A. 60TH LONDON DIVISION

WAR DIARY
or
INTELLIGENCE SUMMARY.
(Erase heading not required.)

Instructions regarding War Diaries and Intelligence Summaries are contained in F. S. Regs., Part II. and the Staff Manual respectively. Title pages will be prepared in manuscript.

Place	Date	Hour	Summary of Events and Information	Remarks and references to Appendices
BROMLEY.	9	7.32am	Lt R.C. NASH and drafts from 2/6, 2/7 & 2/8 Brigades proceeded from BISHOPS STORTFORD to reinforce units overseas	15ft.
		10AM	C.R.A inspects the 25th Brigade in full marching order ready to march away as for an emergency.	
		12.AM	Inspection of 2/6th Brigade in full marching order ready to march away as for an emergency. O.T.I P.W O.W O.J.	15ft 15ft 15ft
	10			
	11			
	12			
	13	10.30	Information received that the Divisional Artillery will proceed to WEST DOWN SALISBURY PLAIN for GUN PRACTISE from 16th to 28th. 100 rounds per Battery to be taken.	15ft
	14	6.AM	Information received cancelling previous days arrangements. Only one Battery to proceed to practise with guns horses ammunition for the rest of the Brigades. Brigades to proceed singly. 2/19th Battery 2/4 Brigade chosen as depot Battery	65ft

1577 Wt.W10791/1773 500,000 1/15 D.D.&L. A.D.S.S./Forms/C. 2118.

WAR DIARY
INTELLIGENCE SUMMARY

Army Form C. 2118.
Sheet 3

HEADQUARTERS R.A. 60th LONDON DIVISION

Place	Date	Hour	Summary of Events and Information	Remarks and references to Appendices
BROMLEY	14	6	Waggons to carry ammunition sent by 2/5th Brigade and 2/2 London Heavy Battery.	Sgt.
	15	6.30	2/1" Brigade entrain at ELSENHAM first train left 6.42 am 2nd train 4.49 am detrained at PATNEY (G.W. Railway) marched to 7. AUSTRALIAN LINES, ROLLESTONE CAMP. When the Brigade went into Huts.	Sgt.
ROLLESTONE CAMP	16		Nil.	
"	17		2/19th Battery fired on WEST DOWN RANGE. 100 rounds allowed + fired	Sgt.
"	18		2/20" Battery fired " " " " "	Sgt.
"	19		2/18" Battery " " " " "	Sgt.
"	20		Nil	Sgt.
"	21		2/17 Battery fired on WEST DOWN RANGE. The G.O.C. & Col DUNLOP watched practice.	Sgt.
"	22		2/16 " " " " " Capt NAPIER G.S.O. (2) watched practice.	Sgt.
"	23		2/15 " " " " "	Sgt.
			2/12 Battery fired on WEST DOWN RANGE. The Inspector General R.H. & R.A. watched practice & instructed officers. The G.O.C. III Army was also present.	Sgt.

Army Form C. 2118.

Sheet 4

WAR DIARY
or
INTELLIGENCE SUMMARY.
(Erase heading not required.)

HEADQUARTERS R.A. 60TH LONDON DIVISION.

Instructions regarding War Diaries and Intelligence Summaries are contained in F.S. Regs., Part II. and the Staff Manual respectively. Title pages will be prepared in manuscript.

Place	Date	Hour	Summary of Events and Information	Remarks and references to Appendices
BROMLEY	23.		Inspection by G.O.C. of the Composite forces in QUENDON PARK. 2/1st Brigade turned out as for an emergency having horses & water carts sent by 2/5 & 2/6 Brigades	1/1
	24.		2/13 Battery fired on WEST DOWN RANGE	1/1
	25.		2/14 " " " " "	1/1
ROLLESTONE CAMP	26.		2/5th Brigade & 2/9 Battery (Depot Battery) left AMESBURY STATION 8.40 P.M. G.O.C III Army was present.	1/1
	27.	4.10 P.M.	2/5 Brigade & 2/9 Battery arrived ELSENHAM STATION 2.40 A.M. & 3.45 A.M.	1/1
	28.		Nil	1/1
BROMLEY	29.		Entraining practice at ELSENHAM by 2/8th Brigade 1/1 Kent Heavy Battery & 2/2 London Heavy Battery.	1/1
	30.		Entraining Practice at ELSENHAM STATION by 2/7 Brigade.	1/1

K. Arison.
Staff Capt.
60th (London) Divisional Artillery.

HEADQUARTERS
58th (London) DIVISIONAL ARTILLERY.

Instructions regarding War Diaries and Intelligence
Summaries are contained in F.S. Regs., Part II.
and the Staff Manual respectively. Title pages
will be prepared in manuscript.

Army Form C. 2118.

Sheet I

WAR DIARY
or
INTELLIGENCE SUMMARY.
(Erase heading not required.)

Hour, Date, Place	Summary of Events and Information	Remarks and references to Appendices
BROMLEY. October 1.	Divisional Tactical Exercise in the Neighbourhood of EASTON LODGE DUNMOW.	
10.30 a.m	2/5 & 2/4 BRIGADES RFA rendezvous at road junction 300 x S of A in TAKELEY. Orders handed to O.C. 2/5 & 2/4 Brigades at 10.45 A.M. 2/4 TAKELEY Cross Roads + 2/5 they are to place themselves under the orders of A/5 O.C. 180th Infy Bde & 181st Infy Bdes respectively.	S.O.S. 29
11.30 a.m	2/5th Bde in action 200 yards N of Y in WARISH HALL objective enemy infantry lining wood from BROOK END to range of wood N of First B in LITTLE CANFIELD HALL. 2/4th Bde in action 150 S of the HOLE objective from the limit of the objective of the 2/5th Bde to the Junction of HIGH WOOD and the main Road 200 x E of the First E in STAKE STREET. The cooperation of the 8/4 Brigade with its right	
2.0 [illegible]		

HEADQUARTERS
60th (LONDON) DIVISIONAL ARTILLERY.

Army Form C. 2118.

Sheet 2

Instructions regarding War Diaries and Intelligence Summaries are contained in F.S. Regs., Part II. and the Staff Manual respectively. Title pages will be prepared in manuscript.

WAR DIARY
or
INTELLIGENCE SUMMARY.
(Erase heading not required.)

Hour, Date, Place	Summary of Events and Information	Remarks and references to Appendices
BROMLEY. October. 1.	Infantry Brigade was hindered owing to the HORSE being unavailable to wheeled traffic. Telephonic communication between the 2g/. Bat. Hqrs & the Arty Bat. Hqrs was not established. At the end of hostilities the 2/1st Brigade had to march to EASTON LODGE PARK to water & feed horses. This necessitated a detour of about 2 miles & greatly delayed the return of the Brigade to Camp.	
2.	Entraining practice at ELSENHAM STATION was carried out the day by the 2/6th Brigade R.F.A.	K/T S/T
3.	Entraining practice at ELSENHAM STATION by 2/5" Bde.	W.S.T.
	Nil.	

WAR DIARY
or
INTELLIGENCE SUMMARY.
(Erase heading not required.)

Army Form C. 2118.

Sheet 3

Instructions regarding War Diaries and Intelligence Summaries are contained in F.S. Regs., Part II. and the Staff Manual respectively. Title pages will be prepared in manuscript.

Hour, Date, Place	Summary of Events and Information	Remarks and references to Appendices
Bromley, 3rd October 5.30 P.m.	Orders received from Divisional Headquarters that the Division will move from its present Camping area into Bivouac formation in the area Dunmow – Stebbing – Braintree – How. Street – Leaden. –	60th London Div. Orders No. I. off
Bromley, 4th October 9.30 a.m.	Orders issued to Artillery Brigades and Heavy Batteries for the move into their Bivouac areas.	Read. 60th London Div. Arty. Orders No. 7. Read.
5th October 9. a.m.	The 2/5 L. Brigade R.F.A. the head of the Artillery Column arrived at the rendezvous at starting point (Cross junction S. of Y. in Priory) at 9 a.m. but the column was unable 6 move. forward owing to the 181 L Infantry Brigade and the 2/6 London Field Ambulance not being clear. –	
Road Junction 9.10 a.m. S. of Y. in Priory.	The head of the column passed the starting point at 9.10 a.m. in the following order. 2/5 Bty. 2/6 Bty. 2/7, 2/8 Bty. 1 Section of H.Q. & 1 Section South Heavy Battery	

WAR DIARY
or
INTELLIGENCE SUMMARY.

(Erase heading not required.)

Army Form C. 2118.

Sheet 4

Hour, Date, Place	Summary of Events and Information	Remarks and references to Appendices
Oundle 5/10/15 11-45 am	Pri. arrived at Oundle. Received Billeting Telegraph with the O-Clerk there —	
12. 0 noon	Artillery Column reached Oundle. 2/5th Bde — proceeding to Stibbing, where Brenner was the O.C. 179th Infantry Brigade — The "B" Bty proceeding to New Street where it came under the orders of the O.C. 180th Infantry Brigade. — 2/7th Brigade proceeding to Hewitt where it came under the orders the O.C. 181st — Infantry Brigade. The O.C. 181st Infantry Bde was not having room for the 2/7 Brigade at Hewitt this latter Brigade bivouacked at Little Common. RW	

WAR DIARY
or
INTELLIGENCE SUMMARY.
(Erase heading not required.)

Army Form C. 2118.

Sheet 5

Hour, Date, Place	Summary of Events and Information	Remarks and references to Appendices
Clyd Kens. 6/10/15 Luncar - 9.30am	Orders Received from Divisional Headquarters	
10.0am	Orders issued to 2/9th Batt. on Mt Stunde Heavy Battery, to march via Pension Inn to Black Notley, Lies Brigade under the orders of O.C. Infantry Brigade. -	R.A. 7. R.A. 8.
12.30pm	CRA. & COff report to GOC at 12.20 pm at Black Notley Lodge. -	
12.40pm	Orders issued to 2/3", 2/6", 2/7 "Batts" to concentrate with their respective Infantry Brigades, reporting progress to Black Notley Lodge. -	R.A. 10. to R.A. 14
Black. Notley Lodge - 6.10-15 2.20pm	Information received that Kent Heavy Battery was in position S.W. of Hyde Wood Farm -	
3.10pm	Message from 2/5 Batt. that Battery was re adjusted arrived Black Notley.	

Army Form C. 2118.

Sheet 6

WAR DIARY
or
INTELLIGENCE SUMMARY.
(Erase heading not required.)

Instructions regarding War Diaries and Intelligence Summaries are contained in F.S. Regs., Part II and the Staff Manual respectively. Title pages will be prepared in manuscript.

Hour, Date, Place	Summary of Events and Information	Remarks and references to Appendices
4.0 P.m.	Information Received that 2/6th Battn were in Sheldon to the left of Gore Farm —	
4.20 P.m.	Information Received that a strong force of the enemy were massed B. of Blackwater and as advancing on Brasenose —	
Black Notley Lodge — 5/10/15 — 4.30 P.m	Orders issued to 2/6th Bn and their Scouts Heavy Battery to Laurel Oak between three Cross Roads —	R. A. 15. R. A. 16.

Army Form C. 2118.

Sheet 7

WAR DIARY
or
INTELLIGENCE SUMMARY.
(Erase heading not required.)

Hour, Date, Place		Summary of Events and Information	Remarks and references to Appendices
6/10/15	6.15 pm	Hants Heavy Battery & 2/8 How Bde were ordered to return to bivouac	RW
	6.30 pm	Div Artillery Headquarters for night 6-7 were at Black Notley Hall	
7/10/15	4.0 am	Bde Major & Staff Capt report for orders to O.C. 181st Inf Bde. Retirement commenced at 6.30 am covered by the Brie & 2/7 Hampshire at Black Notley.	
		The 2/6 Bde retired from White Notley by Bolts Green & Fayers Farm; at 10 am 2/7 Bde retired by sections, their retreat being covered by the 2/23rd Battalion.	
		The Hants Hvy Battery were in position near Wilkins Green	
	2.20 pm	Operations ceased artillery returned to bivouac areas as follows. 2/8 Bde — Great Dunmow 2/6 Bde 1/1 Hants 2/7 Bde — Little Dunmow 2/5 Bde — Stebbing	
		Div Art Headquarters at Clock House Dunmow Orders received that Divisional Artillery Hvbahm & Company Area independently.	RW

WAR DIARY
or
INTELLIGENCE SUMMARY.
(Erase heading not required.)

Army Form C. 2118.

Sheet 6

Hour, Date, Place	Summary of Events and Information	Remarks and references to Appendices
Oct 8 M Sorrow 8 AM	Divisional Artillery leave billets at Sorrow, march via Tixeley. Units proceed to respective Camps at Stanshed, Bishops Stortford & Much Hadham arriving in Camp at 12 noon.	
11 2 pm	C.R.A 2nd Bde. Major gen Stanshed to attend practice of same Model held by 2/5 Bde. + 2/7 Bde. Preliminary Staff Ride to select positions ordnance maps.	Nil
12	G.R.A. Staff present at Lunch. Brens letter G.O.C. + Staff of Divn. accompany him on Staff Ride with reference to Tactical Exercise to be carried out by the Division with Troops on the 14th inst.	Nil
13 2.30 pm	Conference on the subject of Manoeuvres Oct 5-8 at Drill Hall Market Square, Bishops Stortford. All mounted Officers of Division attending.	Nil
14 9 am	Tactical Exercise by Troops of Division.	
10.30	PELHAM FORD to GLAPGATE. Divisional Artillery in position, allotted by 10.30 - 2/5 London Bde attached to 179 Inf Bde, 2/6 Bde to 180 Inf Bde + 2/7 Bde. 181st Inf Bde. Headquarters R.A. at White Farm Wheat + Oats HQrs of Manoeuvre.	
12.15	Whole Front commences rapid Artillery concentrating fire attack on the 9 Brigades on front portion of enemy of front for ten minutes. Switching to other portions of the said line. 2 Phase of fire for 5 minutes on front opposite new Field Artillery Bde.	
1.15	Several attacks commence to attack enemy positions. 2/8 London Heavy Battery + 111 Howitzer Battery engage	
1.45	Howitzer Bde + 2/2 Heavy Battery + 111 Howr enemy's Batteries + Reserves. Transportation to Camp at about 7 pm.	Nil

WAR DIARY
or
INTELLIGENCE SUMMARY.
(Erase heading not required.)

Army Form C. 2118.

Sheet 9

Instructions regarding War Diaries and Intelligence Summaries are contained in F.S. Regs., Part II. and the Staff Manual respectively. Title pages will be prepared in manuscript.

Hour, Date, Place		Summary of Events and Information	Remarks and references to Appendices
Oct 15th Sunday	2.0 pm	Lt Col A.S. Dunlop inspects Practice Range reports of Gunner Practice at Salisbury Plain	
18.	10.30	CRA The Major attended at Headquarters in superintend matters	Mem
	2 pm	Major Carl Bell from France called with reference the appointment of a new	Mem
19.		of Subalterns in the Division	
		Divisional Artillery take part in a III Army Exercise move from	
		old present Company area towards the Coast. The 2/2 London Hy.	
		Battery were attached to take on Div Am Col. The Artillery starts	
		2/5 Lon Bde 2/6, 2/7 at 6 -11 Hours move towards Bishops Stortford - Dunmow	
	12.10	Road. Head of Column moves East of crossroads at Priory at 12.00 pm	
		at the respective billeting areas at Sq. Little Dunmow at 2.30 pm.	
	3.30	CRA & Staff without the Brigades proceed by car.	
	4.0	CRA visits Artillery Bivouacs & Billets	
	7.0	G.O.C. confers with CRA at Sw H.Q.	Mem
Oct 20th	9 am	Divisional Operation Orders received 2/7 Bde allotted to 179 Inf Bde	
	7.30	2/5 Bde RFA to 181 Inf Bde	
	10.30	The Divisional Artillery east with three composite Home 9/1 Bdes	
		2/6 + 2/8 Bde + 111 How By proceed by Range to Manor Green to Chatley	

Army Form C. 2118.

Sheet 10

WAR DIARY
or
INTELLIGENCE SUMMARY.
(Erase heading not required.)

Instructions regarding War Diaries and Intelligence Summaries are contained in F.S. Regs., Part II. and the Staff Manual respectively. Title pages will be prepared in manuscript.

Hour, Date, Place	Summary of Events and Information	Remarks and references to Appendices
Oct 20 Dunmurry 12.15	C.R.A. Staff arrived at Terling	
12.45	2/6 2/8 R.E. with Horses occupy position in neighbourhood of Home Farm near White Notley	
12.50	CRA reports to GOC at Bin HQ. RQC r&R & inspect gun position	
6.0	CRA returns to Terling to the Vicarage where he makes his Headquarters	PW
6.30	Units return to horses billets in the neighbourhood	
Oct 21 Terling	Orders to relieve on tomorrow. Bdes receive orders from the 2nd/Bde.	
9.30	CRA meets GOC at Chatley & renders other visits/matters of various lines	
12.50	CRA at Bn HQ at Little Braxon. Proceeds to Filest with GOC	
3.45	Operation ceases. Return arrive in their billets areas soon after 4 pm with exception of 2/5 Bde who arrive at 6.30 pm	PW
6.30		
Oct 22 Dunmow Bin Air lumn Dunmow proceeds to respective Corps.	
8.40	arriving about 12.20.	

WAR DIARY
or
INTELLIGENCE SUMMARY.
(Erase heading not required.)

Army Form C. 2118.

Sheet 11

Hour, Date, Place	Summary of Events and Information	Remarks and references to Appendices
Bromley	Dormant	
Oct 22. 12.30	G.O.C's call with reference to arrangements for Artillery Area at Shorncliffe. Purchasing Brampley Brindleyford for Artillery units	
" 23.	Col Nisbet, Col Bolling, Capt Jones proceed to Shorncliffe to attend the Refresher Course for Senior Officers.	Nil
" 25. 10.a.m	Col Army Inspector of Remounts inspects horses at Schorncliffe Camp belonging to the 2/5 How Battery 2/2 Bde & Battery 11 Hants Heavy Battery	Nil
2 – 4 p.m	15 Battery under Major Enser attend Divisional Artillery Range at Bromley. Very useful series fires.	Ammunition
" 26.	School Master Goodwin commenced a 15 days Course of lectures on Map Reading to the Div Artillery	
9.30	G.R.A & Bde Major proceed to H.Q's to meet G.O.C on inspection matters	
10 a.m	Inspector of Remounts inspects 2/5 & 2/7 Bde Horses	
3 p.m	at Standen	
2 – 4 p.m	18th Battery & 2/7 Bde under Capt Fordyke attend Divisional Artillery Miniature Range at Bromley	
3.30	G.R.A & goes to H.Q. to meet G.O.C & Sir Charles Allen O.C & 2/5 Bde	Nil

Army Form C. 2118.

Sheet 12

WAR DIARY
or
INTELLIGENCE SUMMARY.
(Erase heading not required.)

Instructions regarding War Diaries and Intelligence Summaries are contained in F.S. Regs., Part II and the Staff Manual respectively. Title pages will be prepared in manuscript.

Hour, Date, Place		Summary of Events and Information	Remarks and references to Appendices
Bromley			
Oct 27 -	10. am	Inspection of horses of 2/6 Sou Bde at Much Hadham by Col Roney.	
		2/8 "Sou How Batty, 2/2 Sou & 1/1 Hants Heavy Batteries move to their billeting areas at Puckeridge & Bishops Stortford.	
		C.R.A. attends at H.Q's Bishops Stortford.	
	2 - 4pm	14 * Battery 2/5 Bde attends Div Artillery Miniature Range	Pass
Oct 28 *	10. am	CRA proceeds to Standon Puckeridge, Braughing & Bishops Stortford to inspect the Billets of the 2/8 How, 2/2 Sou & 1/1 Hants Hvy Battery	Pass
Oct 29 -		Two 5" howitzer guns limbers + 4 ammunition wagons, 2 S.S. Wagons + 3/5 complete rounds of ammunition received by the 2/8" Countermortbatt. Bde.	Pass
	3.0	C.R.A. & Bde major proceed to Conference at 1/4 pro Statford.	
Oct 30 -	10 am	Board held at Bromley H.Q's with reference to W. Enders by Mrs 2/7 "Bde.	Pass

A.G. Northey Capt.
for Staff Captain, R.A.
60 London Division, T.F.

(73989) W4141—463. 400,000. 9/14. H.&J.Ltd. Forms/C. 2118/10.

Confidential

War Diary

of

60th (London) Divisional Artillery.

From 1st November 1915 ... to 30 November 1915.

Army Form C. 2118.

HEAD QUARTERS 60TH (LONDON) DIVISIONAL ARTILLERY **WAR DIARY** or **INTELLIGENCE SUMMARY.**

Sheet 1.

(Erase heading not required.)

Instructions regarding War Diaries and Intelligence Summaries are contained in F.S. Regs., Part II. and the Staff Manual respectively. Title pages will be prepared in manuscript.

Hour, Date, Place		Summary of Events and Information	Remarks and references to Appendices
	November		
BROMLEY	2	DIVISIONAL ARTILLERY HEADQUARTERS moved from Camp at Bromley into billets at BROMLEY.	left
"	3	64 (L.D.) Remounts taken on charge by 2/6 Bde. Instruction on Miniature Range BROMLEY 2/3 Batty 2/5th Bde.	left
STANSTED	4	Tactical exercise 2/5th and 2/7th Bdes cooperating with 180th and 179th Inf Bdes respectively.	left
HORSHAM	5	Remounts inspected by C.R.A.	left
	6	n.d.	left
	7	n.d.	left

HEADQUARTERS 60th (LOND) DIVISIONAL ARTILLERY. **WAR DIARY** or **INTELLIGENCE SUMMARY**.

Army Form C. 2118.

Sheet 2.

(Erase heading not required.)

Instructions regarding War Diaries and Intelligence Summaries are contained in F.S. Regs., Part II. and the Staff Manual respectively. Title pages will be prepared in manuscript.

Hour, Date, Place		Summary of Events and Information	Remarks and references to Appendices
BISHOPS STORTFORD	8th	Lectures in Drill Hall on Ammunition Supply in the Field.	6/T
BROMLEY	9th	Instruction on Miniature Range. 2/6 Batty.	6/T
		2/6 Bde. attend.	
	10.	Following Officers proceeded overseas as reinforcements from 2/6 Bde. 2nd/Lt BARROW	
		" WHITTEN	
		2/1 Bde. " WILKINSON	
		" FOLINGSBY.	
	11	Instruction on Miniature Range 2/13 Batty. 2/5th Bde.	6/T
		Lt. K. HARDING	
		2/8th Bde. attached 2/5Bde. proceeded overseas as reinforcement	6/T
STANSTED		for 1st Line Unit.	6/T

Army Form C. 2118.

HEADQUARTERS 60th (LOND) DIVISIONAL ARTILLERY. WAR DIARY or INTELLIGENCE SUMMARY.

Sheet No III

(Erase heading not required.)

Instructions regarding War Diaries and Intelligence Summaries are contained in F.S. Regs., Part II. and the Staff Manual respectively. Title pages will be prepared in manuscript.

Hour, Date, Place	Summary of Events and Information	Remarks and references to Appendices
HADHAM 12th	DIVISIONAL ARTILLERY HEADQUARTERS moved from BROMLEY to OLD OFFICES, MUCH HADHAM.	
13th	Nil.	bfr
14th	Nil.	
BISHOPS STORTFORD 15.	Farriery course for officers commences at BISHOPS STORTFORD.	bfr
HADHAM 16.	Draft of 27 drivers from 2/6th Bde in gisted by CRA	bfr
17.	Nil.	bfr
		bfr

(73989) W4141—463. 400,000. 9/14. H.&J.Ltd. Forms/C. 2118/10.

Army Form C. 2118.

WAR DIARY
or
INTELLIGENCE SUMMARY.
(Erase heading not required.)

HEAD QUARTERS 60th (LONDON) DIVISIONAL ARTILLERY   Sheet 4.

Instructions regarding War Diaries and Intelligence Summaries are contained in F.S. Regs., Part II. and the Staff Manual respectively. Title pages will be prepared in manuscript.

Hour, Date, Place	Summary of Events and Information	Remarks and references to Appendices
18th	Nil.	S/L
19th	Nil.	S/L
BUNTINGFORD 20th	1 Section 1/1 HANTS HEAVY BATTERY arrived from Training School LUTON, strength 1 officer, 60 other ranks, 38 Horses.	S/L
21st	Nil	
HADHAM 22nd	Colonel H. WEIR having resigned his appointment Colonel H.A. BUTLER takes over command # 20 C.R.A. Divisional Artillery.	S/L
LITTLE HADHAM 23rd	Tactical exercise for 2/6th and 2/8th Bdes.	S/L
BISHOPS STORTFORD 23	Staff of 58 Squadron from A/F. Rode passed going to B.E.F. FRANCE	S/L

(73989) W4141—463. 400,000. 9/14. H.&J.Ltd. Forms/C. 2118/10.

HEADQUARTERS 60th LONDON DIVISIONAL ARTILLERY.

Army Form C. 2118.

WAR DIARY
or
INTELLIGENCE SUMMARY.
(Erase heading not required.)

Sheet 6.

Hour, Date, Place	Summary of Events and Information	Remarks and references to Appendices
MUCH HADHAM. 23	Inspection of billets & Central Feeding by Officers of CENTRAL FORCE.	SA.
BROMLEY.	Instruction on Miniature Range. 2/19th BATTY. CRA present.	SA.
	Tactical exercise 2/5th Bde.	SA.
HADHAM. 24th	CRA watches 2/6th Bde. at Gun Drill and Battery manoeuvres, & inspects the horses.	SA.
UGLEY GREEN. 25th	Tactical exercise for 2/7th Bde. Report centre UGLEY GREEN (W. of EASENHAM STATION) at 11. A.M. CRA and Bde Major present.	SA.
BROMLEY.	Instruction on Miniature Range 2/17th Battery 2/6th Bde.	SA.
26th	Tactical exercise for 2/6th Bde.	SA.

Army Form C. 2118.

Sheet 6.

HEADQUARTERS 60th (LONS) DIVISIONAL ARTILLERY.

WAR DIARY
or
INTELLIGENCE SUMMARY.
(Erase heading not required.)

Instructions regarding War Diaries and Intelligence Summaries are contained in F.S. Regs., Part II. and the Staff Manual respectively. Title pages will be prepared in manuscript.

Hour, Date, Place		Summary of Events and Information	Remarks and references to Appendices
BROMLEY.	26.	Instruction on Miniature Range. 2/20th Batty 2/7th Bde.	KP.
WIDFORD	27.	C.R.A inspects Horses and Harness of 2/6 Bde. Amm. Column at WIDFORD.	KP.
"	28.	36 (18 pr Ammunition Waggons arrived.	KP.
BROMLEY	29.	Instruction on Miniature Range. 2/18th Batty 2/7th Bde. Guns 18 pr Q.F. [arrived for 2/5th, 2/6th & 2/7 Bdes. Limbers Ammunition Wagons]	KP.
STANSTED	30	CRA inspects 2/5th Bde at Gun Drill, also horses, stables, billets.	KP.

Johnson. Capt.
Staff Captain, R.A.
60th London Division, T.F.

(73969) W4141—463. 400,000. 9/14. H.&J.Ltd. Forms/C. 2118/10.

Confidential

War Diary

of

H.Qs. 60th (London) Divisional Artillery.

From 1st Dec 1915 to 31st Dec 1915.

(Volume 12)

Headquarters R.A.
60 (Lon) Divisional Artillery.

WAR DIARY
INTELLIGENCE SUMMARY

(Erase heading not required.)

Army Form C. 2118.

Instructions regarding War Diaries and Intelligence Summaries are contained in F.S. Regs., Part II. and the Staff Manual respectively. Title pages will be prepared in manuscript.

Hour, Date, Place	Summary of Events and Information	Remarks and references to Appendices
10 a.m. 1/12/15. STANSTED	C.R.A, accompanied by Bde Major, inspected 2/18th Battery, 2/7th Bde. a/t. Drill order. Very very wet. The inspection harness and clothes of the Bde	
11 - 1 hr	and noted that drivers and gunnery are very badly needed for the stables. 50 horses (L.D.1) arrive for 2/5th Bde	absent
10.30 a.m. 2/12/15 MUCH HADHAM	A.A. + Q.M.G. 60th (Lon) Div. (in absence of G.O.C) accompanied by C.R.A inspects men of the billets, cook houses, messes etc of 2/6th Bde. R.F.A	
10.0 a.m. STANSTED	A.D.C. to C.R.A. meets Lt. W.A.C. CLERY, R.E. at STANSTED. Lt. CLERY on behalf of 3rd Army arranges speeding examination of the 2/5th Bde at 10 a.m and 2/7th Bde at 2/pm	
3.0 pm BROMLEY	C.R.A visits miniature Range (In Armoury) at BROMLEY, but practice of 2/18th Battery has to be cancelled owing to rain	absent
10.0 a.m 2/12/15. STANDON	C.R.A, accompanied by Bde. Major, inspects 2/8th Bde, 2/2nd Battery and 2/1st (HANTS) Battery at their watering order.	

(73929) W4141—463. 400,000. 9/14. H.&J.Ltd. Forms/C. 2118/10.

Headquarters
2nd (Co. of Lon) Divisional Artillery

WAR DIARY or INTELLIGENCE SUMMARY.
(Erase heading not required.)

Army Form C. 2118.

Instructions regarding War Diaries and Intelligence Summaries are contained in F.S. Regs., Part II and the Staff Manual respectively. Title pages will be prepared in manuscript.

Hour, Date, Place	Summary of Events and Information	Remarks and references to Appendices
10.30 am 3/12/15 (morning) to 2 pm MUCH HADHAM and BUNTINGFORD	Divl Arty examined 2/1st Bde RFA, 2/2 and 2/1st Batteries in artillery	
3 pm BROMLEY	CRA inspected 2/1st C Battery, 2/1st Bde re-Manual Regulations	
4/12/15 9.30 am MUCH HADHAM	CRA visits 2/1st Bde, accompanied by Asst Major	
12.30 pm "	GOC also appeared from the 2/1st Bde, and recommended him for a commission	
	1200 rounds 18PR Q.F. ammunition arrived at MUCH HADHAM STATION for 2/1st Bde.	
5/12/15 BISHOPS STORTFORD	CRA inspected GOC and took 2/1st Ammn Col at STANSTED	
10.30 am STANSTED	CRA accompanied by Bde Major, inspects Rising stores, petrol in major contracts by Sgt NOAKES detailed from Reserve Cavalry Regt. Also inspected QR 50 remounts received by 2/1st Bde from Remount Depot, ORMSKIRK.	
6/12/15 10 am MANUDEN		

Headquarters
60 (?) Divisional Artillery

Army Form C. 2118.

WAR DIARY
or
INTELLIGENCE SUMMARY.
(Erase heading not required.)

Instructions regarding War Diaries and Intelligence Summaries are contained in F.S. Regs., Part II. and the Staff Manual respectively. Title pages will be prepared in manuscript.

Hour, Date, Place	Summary of Events and Information	Remarks and references to Appendices
6/12/15 (continued)		
2.30 pm BROMLEY	CRA inspected 1/1st (?) Battery 2/1st Bde at parade in the Artillery Manoeuvre Range	none
7/12/15		
9.30 am MUCH HADHAM	CRA, accompanied by Bde. Major, inspected Riding Class under the instruction of Serjt FOX assisted by an Reserve Cavalry Regt.	
10.30 am ELSENHAM	Watched ordinary practice under supervision of Capt. SAUNDERS, 2/1st C/L Battery, LONDON Regt, of A 2/5st Bde.	
11.0 am "	Capt. HOUTEN, R.D.C. & CRA, watched practice Board at ELSENHAM	
2.30 pm BROMLEY.	CRA inspected 2/1st A Battery, 2/1st Bde at Artillery Manoeuvre Range	none
8/12/15		
10 am ELSENHAM	CRA, accompanied by STAFF CAPTAIN, watched entraining practice under Capt. SAUNDERS, of 2/1st C Bde, RFA.	
2.30 pm BROMLEY	inspected 2/1st A Battery, 2/1st Bde at practice at the Artillery Manoeuvre Range	none

Headquarters
60 (North) Divisional Artillery

Army Form C. 2118.

WAR DIARY
or
INTELLIGENCE SUMMARY.
(Erase heading not required.)

Instructions regarding War Diaries and Intelligence Summaries are contained in F.S. Regs., Part II and the Staff Manual respectively. Title pages will be prepared in manuscript.

Hour, Date, Place	Summary of Events and Information	Remarks and references to Appendices
9/12/15		
10 am BUNTINGFORD.	CRA accompanied by ADC, attended ENTRAINING parties, inspected Capt. SPINNERS 1st 2/185th Bde. The 2nd pts (RA) Staff attended the 2/g	
9.30 am MUCH HADHAM.	CRA accompanied Bde. Major, inspected Sergt FOX'S riding class at HADHAM	
2.30 pm BROMLEY.	inspect 2/1st Battery, 2/7th Bde. RFA at parade in the Innovative Range. APDA	
10/12/15		
9.30 am MUCH HADHAM	CRA accompanied by Bde. Major, inspected Sergt FOX'S riding class	
12.30 pm BUNTINGFORD	attend ENTRAINING parties of 1/2nd Heavy Battery, afterwards inspecting	
12.0 noon BRAUGHING.	2/pt Amm Col at morning sheds	
2.30 pm BROMLEY.	inspects 2/3rd Battery, 2/17th Bde. at the Innovative Range.	APDA
11/12/15		
9.30 am MUCH HADHAM	CRA accompanied by Bde. Major inspected Sergt. FOX'S riding class.	
10.30 am BISHOPS STORTFORD.	saw GSC as regards proposed BOARD on equipment of 2/1st Bde.; also saw our GSO(1) as Training and DAA+QMG; also saw DADOS with regard to the authorisation of a model "ADAPTER" intended to allow the Hale DIAL SIGHT to be fitted to the 18 PR. Q.F. Gun.	

Headquarters
60 Div Divisional Artillery

Army Form C. 2118.

WAR DIARY
or
INTELLIGENCE SUMMARY.
(Erase heading not required.)

Instructions regarding War Diaries and Intelligence Summaries are contained in F.S. Regs., Part II. and the Staff Manual respectively. Title pages will be prepared in manuscript.

Hour, Date, Place	Summary of Events and Information	Remarks and references to Appendices
11/12/15 (continued) STANSTED. 12.30 pm	CRA accompanied by Bde Major, inspected 2/1st Bde Stables and Gun Park, and 2/1V_PS & 2/1V_PS Battery Offices, mens' equipment, billets, cooking utensils, tools, Army Book 408, ammunition, Cook-house, Mess Rooms &c.	Appx
12/12/15 (SUNDAY) MUCH HADHAM 11 am	Received message from H/F (HANTS) Heavy Battery Tex-B419, GSM BREEKS from WAR OFFICE was to inspect the Battery tomorrow — Battery at 222 by HQR OFFICE who the 1st IX (HANTS) Heavy Battery — CRA has received no reference from HANTS, 60th (LOND) DIV. Battery telegraphed Bdqrs. 60th DIV, THIRD ARMY, and CENTRAL FORCE accordingly. Asked O.C. 1/1st HANTS Battery to take opportunity of informing GEN BREEKS that Battery has no guns or other equipment will not all been handed over to other units; only horses and harness left.	none

Headquarters
60th (Lon) Divisional Artillery

WAR DIARY
INTELLIGENCE SUMMARY
(Erase heading not required.)

Army Form C. 2118.

Hour, Date, Place	Summary of Events and Information	Remarks and references to Appendices
10 am 13/12/15 BUNTINGFORD	Inspection of 1st C. DIVN'S HVY BATY by BRIG GEN. BREEKS — CRA + Brig Major present	
11.30 STANSTED	CRA accompanied by Bde Major inspected Riding Class under Sergt NOAKES, and then 2/1C AM Batty, 2/5th Bde, on Battery Gun Drill	good
2.30pm BROMLEY	inspected 2/2nd Batty, 2/5th Bde at Riding from Range	
14/12/15 10.30 am STANSTED	accompanied by Bde Major inspected Riding Class	
" "	do — do — inspected 2/7th Bde in Dismounted Range Practice	
" "	— do — do — visited the stable Rooms of 4/5th Bde and the Offices Letters, Books,"	
1 pm "	lunch at 2/5th R.F.A. 2/5th Bde	
10.30 to 1 pm "	Staff Captain inspected interior economy of 2/10 a + 2/1a batteries, 2/7th a bde. Appx	
15/12/15 5.30 am STANSTED	BSM and ASC Drivers are given to trying on equipment of 2/1st ADB Bde (Lond) extr J—169).	
2 pm BROMLEY	— accompanied by Col. WISHART Comg 2/5 Bde. inspected 2/1st Batty 2/5th Bde and from Ranchmanship	good

Headquarters
60th Div: Divisional Artillery

WAR DIARY
or
INTELLIGENCE SUMMARY.
(Erase heading not required.)

Army Form C. 2118.

Instructions regarding War Diaries and Intelligence Summaries are contained in F.S. Regs., Part II and the Staff Manual respectively. Title pages will be prepared in manuscript.

Hour, Date, Place	Summary of Events and Information	Remarks and references to Appendices
13/11/15 Lyndhurst Bustinford	BRA (and RSO) Examined Error of training in respect of 2/2nd N.Y. Arty	
15 Noon STANDON	" inspected training station on 2/2/2nd Batty, 2 9pr Bde.	
3pm BROMLEY	2/Lt Tan R. Lithe Min Range practice of 2/11/8 Bn.F.S, 2/9 Bde	
2.30pm BUNTINGFORD-ROYSTON- STAPLE WALDEN	CRA. accompanied by Bde Major inspected area noted as dragon and run of far winter camp of artillery portion of Div.	
MUCH HADHAM	Result of the examination of Officer and N.C.O. by Lt. CLEARY, RA received results very satisfactory	9000
17/11/15 10 AM MUCH HADHAM	Staff Capt inspected magazine arrangements drill of M. H. Hospl. and heat [?]	
11 AM DUNMOW	CRA accompanied by G.S.O.(I) reports at 9 ARMY HQRS. the Inferior unit Group Army. New guns practice to be carried out. Details been at SOUTHMINSTER. Some upon as outside – Sig It (M.M) was to make fair [?] in the own	apps
18/12/15	" accompanied by Bde Major inspected – Billing Arrgts of Guns and Amm waggons of 2/6th Bde, Amm: requisite stores of 2/6th Bde.	apps
9.30AM MUCH HADHAM	"	apps
19/12/15	NIL	
29/12/15 9.30AM MUCH HADHAM	CRA, accompanied by Bde Major, inspected Billing Residence of 2/4th Bde	
2.30pm BROMLEY	" inspected Min Range practice of 2/14 K Battr, 2/7 K Bde.	

Army Form C. 2118.

HEADQUARTERS.
60th (LON) DIVISIONAL ARTILLERY

WAR DIARY
or
INTELLIGENCE SUMMARY.
(Erase heading not required.)

Instructions regarding War Diaries and Intelligence Summaries are contained in F. S. Regs., Part II. and the Staff Manual respectively. Title pages will be prepared in manuscript.

Hour, Date, Place		Summary of Events and Information	Remarks and references to Appendices
2.0 PM	21/12/15 (cont?)	Assumes command of 60th (LON) DIV	
	STANSTED	MAJOR-GEN E.S. BULFIN relieving B.G.C. GEN. CALLEY	
22/12/15			
10 AM	STANSTED	GRA visit 2/5th and 2/7 L.B. to arrange for musketry by A.O.C. Columns	over
2.15 PM	BROMLEY	inspects 2/18th Battery, 2/5th Bde, at new Range Practice	over
	—	Return of Stephen Smith forwarded to DADOS — (serial nos 307, 10/12/15)	
23/12/15			
9.30 AM	STANSTED	Inspection by G.O.C. 60th LON. DIV of 2/5th Bde (9.30 AM) and 2/7 L.F.Bde (10.30 AM) — G.R.A. + the larger portion; RSM Tompkins, 2/15th Bde, and the N.Co. 17-Lt 2/17th Bde presented to G.O.C. for his approval of the application for Commission — Improvement of 2/6th Bde armament	
—	MUCH HADHAM	Course of Lectures on Improvement of 2/6th Bde armament	over
2.15 PM	BROMLEY	GRA, inspects 2/18th Battery, 2/7 L.F.Bde at new Range	
23/12/15			
10.50 AM	STANDON + BUNTING FORD STANSTEAD	GRA, accompanied by Bde Major, inspects 2/5th Bde, and 2/2nd LON. M. Battery.	
3 PM		" " " inspects 2/5th Bde at practice at the new Range	
		(month) Gun Range	
2 PM	BROMLEY	2/Lt. JANE (late 2/15 R.S.Br) 1/6th Bde, at practice at new Range	over

HEADQUARTERS
60th (LONDIVISIONAL ARTILLERY   WAR DIARY
                                     or
                         INTELLIGENCE SUMMARY.
                           (Erase heading not required.)

Army Form C. 2118.   9

Instructions regarding War Diaries and Intelligence
Summaries are contained in F.S. Regs., Part II.
and the Staff Manual respectively. Title pages
will be prepared in manuscript.

Hour, Date, Place	Summary of Events and Information	Remarks and references to Appendices
24/12/15		
10.30 am MUCH HADHAM	Inspection of 3/4th Bde by GOC, 60th LON DIV, and of 2/6 FORS (11.30 AM -	
to STANDON	STANDON) and 3/5th LON HOW BDES, (2.15 PM - BUNTINGFORD) -	
1.30 PM BUNTINGFORD	CRA known Brigades, One Horse contract. GOC to see inspect ac. Mann Hospital	
4 PM BENTLEY	CRA moved 2/10th Battery 2/5th Bde to MUCH HAD.	good
25/12/15	nil	???
26/12/15	nil	????
27/12/15	nil	????
28/12/15 STANSTED	CRA known that 2/5th and 2/6th Bdes to arrange inspection by MAJOR GEN TMS	
2 PM	BRUNKER. Inspected 3/RH FA xxx mot Gen. BRUNKER arrived at gate	} See APP NO IX I
4 WORN (BISHOPS STORTFORD)		
29/12/15		
9.30 am STANSTED	Inspection of 2/5th Bde (4 batteries) by GEN BRUNKER - see programme APP I	good
2. PM	" " " CRA accompanied by BDE	for inspection of
30/12/15 "	" 2/17th Bde (4 batteries) and 2/5th Bde (Ndrs) by GEN BRUNKER -	batteries.
9.30 am STANSTED	see APP I - CRA, accompanied by BDE MAJOR, present	
" "		
4.30 pm		good

HEADQUARTERS
60 (LON) DIVISIONAL ARTILLERY. **WAR DIARY**
or
INTELLIGENCE SUMMARY.

Army Form C. 2118.

(Erase heading not required.)

Instructions regarding War Diaries and Intelligence Summaries are contained in F. S. Regs., Part II. and the Staff Manual respectively. Title pages will be prepared in manuscript.

Hour, Date, Place	Summary of Events and Information	Remarks and references to Appendices
31/1/15		
9.30 AM MUCH HADHAM	Inspection by Gen BRUNKER of 2/4th Bn (by battalion) - see APP I	APPENDIX I
3 0 M STAN BOW	" " " " " 2/5th Bde (order) — " — . CRA	
	Same Inspected inspection; this Also continued CRAP inspection of 2/6th Bde.	XXX

H. H. Boulter
Colonel
CRA 60th (London) Div.

Appendix I

60th (LONDON) DIVISIONAL ARTILLERY.

INSPECTION
by
Major-General BRUNKER.

PROGRAMME.

Wednesday 29th Dec.	9.30 a.m.	2/12th Batty)	
	10.30 "	2/13th do)	2/5th London
	11.30 "	2/14th do)	Brigade at
	12.30 "	Amn Column)	STANSTED.
	2.0 p.m.	Officers Ride)	
	2.15 "	N.C.Os Ride)	2/7th London
		(1 ride per batty)	Brigade at
	2.30 "	Drivers Ride)	STANSTED.
		(2 rides per batty))	
Thursday 30th Dec.	9.30 a.m.	2/18th Batty)	
	10.30 a.m.	2/19th do)	2/7th London
	11.30 a.m.	2/20th do)	Brigade at
	12.30 a.m.	Amn. Column)	STANSTED.
	2.0 p.m.	Officers ride)	
	2.15 "	N.C.O.s ride)	2/5th London
		(as above))	Brigade at
	2.30 "	Drivers ride)	STANSTED.
		(as above))	
Friday 31st Dec.	9.30 a.m.	2/15th Batty)	
	10.30 "	2/16th do)	2/6th London
	11.30 "	2/17th do)	Brigade at
	12.30 "	Amn Column)	MUCH HADHAM.
	2.30 p.m.	Officers ride)	
	2.45 "	N.C.O.s ride)	2/8th London
		(as above))	Brigade at
	3.0 "	Drivers ride)	STANDON.
		(as above))	
Saturday 1st Jan 16.	9.30 a.m.	Officers ride)	
	9.45 "	N.C.Os Ride)	2/6th London
		(as above))	Brigade at
	10.0 "	Drivers ride)	MUCH HADHAM.
		(as above))	
	11.0 "	2/21st Batty)	2/8th London
	11.30 "	2/22nd do)	Brigade at
	12.0 p.m.	Amn Col.)	STANDON.
	2.30 "	2/2nd Lon Hvy)	
		Batty.)	2/2nd London
	3.30 "	Officers ride)	Heavy Battery
	3.45 "	N.C.Os ride)	R.G.A. at
		(as above))	HUNTINGFORD.
		Drivers ride)	
		(as above))	

H.H. HANWORTH.
Major.
Brigade Major.
60th London Divl. Artillery.

Army Form C. 2118.

WAR DIARY
or
INTELLIGENCE SUMMARY.
(Erase heading not required.)

Instructions regarding War Diaries and Intelligence Summaries are contained in F.S. Regs., Part II. and the Staff Manual respectively. Title pages will be prepared in manuscript.

Hour, Date, Place		Summary of Events and Information	Remarks and references to Appendices
1/1/16	MUCH HADHAM	Inspection of 2/1st α Bde and 2/1st Bde by Brig.-Gen. J.M.S. BRUNKER.	See Appx I
1.30 A.M.			
8 P.M.	—do—	Inspects of R.H. & R.F.A. Wagon nurses from Hagm. and in inspection of 2/8th (How.) Bde is now held.	
11 up.m	—do—	Through to lead-communication of Divl. ARTY reviews and communicated.	
2/1/16	—do—	Nil	
31/1/16			
10 A.M.	ELSENHAM	CRA, accompanied by Bde Major, inspects the buildings & area about to be proposed to occupies — do — Hq 2/7 LND AMM COL on arr of completion of Divl. am.	
2.30 A.M.	BROMLEY	2/17 JAMS organises training parties (2/19 α Bn.Bty) in connection with Bromley Range.	
4/1/16	MUCH HADHAM		
9 A.M.		Arrival at west of RAC ammn.-drivers (Mr BLACK) attached to the Hqrs.	
3 P.M.	—do—	A.A. section, 60th Div. calls will refuse to the rear of Hqrs 2/7 α AMM COL to ELSENHAM.	

WAR DIARY
or
INTELLIGENCE SUMMARY.

(Erase heading not required.)

Army Form C. 2118. 2

Instructions regarding War Diaries and Intelligence Summaries are contained in F. S. Regs., Part II. and the Staff Manual respectively. Title pages will be prepared in manuscript.

Hour, Date, Place	Summary of Events and Information	Remarks and references to Appendices
4/1/16 (cont^d) BROMLEY		
2 P.M.	Practice of 2/1st R.Bty. on miniature Range — 2/Lt JANE present	
5/1/16		
1 P.M. MUCH HADHAM	CRA inspects 2/16 R.BDE at Battery Headquarters	
10.30 A.M. —do—	Lt BARCLAY from Divl Hdqrs calls to arrange for observations of shooting of Divl ARTY	
" ELSENHAM	STAFF CAPT. arrives at ELSENHAM to arrange matter reconnaissance for 2/2nd LON Hvy. Batty which is to be practise three models of the 2/1st LOND ARM WL.	
2 P.M. BROMLEY.	Artillery practice of 2/1st R.Battery — 2/Lt JANE present	
6/1/16		
9.0 A.M. ELSENHAM	2/2nd LON Hvy Batty marches from BUNTINGFORD to ELSENHAM	
—do— —do—	STAFF CAPTAIN visits Hdqrs with reference to arrangements for shooting Ammunition of 2/2nd Hvy Batty. and for billeting and catering the personnel of the Batty.	
2. 2 P.M. STANSTED	CRA inspects offrs of 2/1st & 2/2nd LF & 2/DES at practise on a miniature Range and Sand model Range	

Army Form C. 2118.

WAR DIARY
or
INTELLIGENCE SUMMARY.
(Erase heading not required.)

Instructions regarding War Diaries and Intelligence Summaries are contained in F.S. Regs., Part II and the Staff Manual respectively. Title pages will be prepared in manuscript.

Hour, Date, Place		Summary of Events and Information	Remarks and references to Appendices
2 PM	6/1/16 ELSENHAM	2/LT JANE inspects STABLES at 2/7M.DDICKS House & thought it suitable. Rep. Off. 2/2nd HVY BATTY.	—
9 AM	7/1/16 SOUTHMINSTER and CHELMSFORD	CRA with BDE MAJOR, B/M (JM) DIV., to CHELMSFORD, and proceeded SOUTHMINSTER to inspect site of proposed training Range; met MAJOR R.A. AUSTIN, who will have opposite training facilities.	—
3 PM	ELSENHAM	STAFF CAPTAIN proceed to ELSENHAM to inspect work of DOR in connexion with the accommodation of the 2/2nd HVY BATTY and the arrangements for anti inshore enemy.	—
9.30 AM	8/1/16 STANSTED	LT. G. LR WISELY and M/CAPT. R. MULVEY, LA RES BDE, RFA, WOOLWICH, report to Off. 2/15th BDE. to gun-instruction on 18 PR equipment.	—
10 AM	9/1/16 ELSENHAM	CRA inspects 2/2 ND LON. HVY BATTY.	—
10 AM	MUCH HADHAM	CRA inspects PUBLIC HOUSE (HQ 2/1 RESVE BATTY. being JACK)	
10.30 AM	— do —	MAJOR OLIVER (1/17th BDE.) acted with reference to the Board of Examiner the equipment of the 2/15th BDE.	—

Army Form C. 2118.

WAR DIARY
or
INTELLIGENCE SUMMARY.
(Erase heading not required.)

Instructions regarding War Diaries and Intelligence Summaries are contained in F.S. Regs., Part II. and the Staff Manual respectively. Title pages will be prepared in manuscript.

Hour, Date, Place	Summary of Events and Information	Remarks and references to Appendices
10.30 AM 10/1/16 STANSTED	Inspection of horses of 2/5TH and 2/7TH BDES and 2/2ND LON HVY BATTY by Col DAD Remounts	appd
4 PM 11/1/16 FELSTEAD	CRA Present	nil
10.30 AM MUCH HADHAM	Inspection of horses of 2/6TH & 2/4 BDES RFA by DAD Remounts	nil
1.2 PM AND EDSANDON	CRA Present	
12/1/16		
11.0 AM MUCH HADHAM	Inspection of 1/4 BDE RFA recog. room etc by G.O.C. 2/1st LON DIV	appd
2.30 PM STANSTED	CRA Present	nil
13/1/16	CRA inspects 2/19TH BATTY RFA re artillery manoeuvre range	nil
14/1/16	NIL	nil
15/1/16 SOUTHMINSTER	CRA and BDE. MAJOR proceed to 3rd ARMY Artillery Camps	nil
10.30 AM 16/1/16	CRA inspects Artillery Range and tests R. Detonation of R 2/1 B.2 BDE RFA nr SOUTH MINSTER STATIONS	appd
11.30 AM 17/1/16	do	
10 AM to 3.30 PM	Practice 15/2/16TH & 12/1 ISR BATTYS RFA nr the Artillery Range	nil

(73989) W4141-463. 400,000. 9/14. H.&J.Ltd. Forms/C. 2118/10.

Army Form C. 2118.

WAR DIARY
or
INTELLIGENCE SUMMARY.
(Erase heading not required.)

Instructions regarding War Diaries and Intelligence Summaries are contained in F.S. Regs., Part II. and the Staff Manual respectively. Title pages will be prepared in manuscript.

Hour, Date, Place	Summary of Events and Information	Remarks and references to Appendices
18/1/16 SOUTHMINSTER 9 AM to 3.30 PM	Practice by 2/17th & 2/15th Batty's RFA — GOC THIRD ARMY present with Staff during part of the practice	
19/1/16 — Do —		
9 AM to 3 PM	Practice by 2/16th Batty, RFA — Staff Officer from THIRD ARMY attended various practice	
20/1/16 MUCH HADHAM 9 AM to 5 PM	CRA accompanied by BDE Major return to MUCH HADHAM in connection with future arrangements for the move of the Division to SALISBURY PLAIN Later return to SOUTHMINSTER.	
21/1/16	Departure of 2/1st BDE to SOUTHMINSTER.	
9.0 AM to 4 PM SOUTHMINSTER	Practice of 2/12th, 2/13th, & 2/14th Batty's, 2/5th BDE, RFA at Artillery Range.	
22/1/16 9 AM to 1.30 PM — DO —	Practice of 2/17th & 2/14th Batty's RFA. GOC BURTON DIV. and Staff officer present with the practice	
3 PM MUCH HADHAM	CRA accompanied by BDE Major return to Div Arty Hqrs, MUCH HADHAM.	
23/1/16	Nil	
24/1/16	CRA accompanied by BDE Major return to SOUTHMINSTER. BDE RFA delivery	

Army Form C. 2118.

WAR DIARY
or
INTELLIGENCE SUMMARY.
(Erase heading not required.)

Instructions regarding War Diaries and Intelligence Summaries are contained in F.S. Regs., Part II and the Staff Manual respectively. Title pages will be prepared in manuscript.

6

Hour, Date, Place	Summary of Events and Information	Remarks and references to Appendices
25/1/16 SOUTHMINSTER	Practice by 2/18th & 2/19th BATTY/S RFA in Gatling Range — BRIG. GEN. BREEKS Inspected of RH + RFA attached the practice.	nom
9.0AM to 4PM	ADVANCE PARTY of 2/8th BDE. Leave for CODFORD STN, SALISBURY	See APP. A post.
BUNTINGFORD		nom
	We await events no hope required change by fire	nom
	All 2/1, 1st and 2nd Division men returned to WAR OFFICE	
26/1/16		
9.0AM to 1.30PM SOUTHMINSTER	Practice by 2/20th BATTY. 4/7th BDE, RFA Practice of 6.6/7 LOW DIV. ARTY not watched.	See APP B
	BRIG. GEN. BREEKS attended. BN ARTY Exercises — BISHOPS STRATFORD for SUTTON VENY	
BOYTON	2/1/B 2/R & 2/1 BDE. ARTY nifonn BISHOPS STRATFORD & BUNTINGFORD respectively	Appx D, I Field PO
	for NOON + 1 Camp, BOYTON	Appx E app. FO
27/1/16		
— DO —	2/1/A RDE, RFA, Transport STARTED for No 3 CAMP, BOYTON	nom
28/1/16 SUTTON VENY	NIL	
10AM to 1.30PM	CRA Accompanied by ADE MASTER took 2/1/A, 2/16A, 2/17A & 2/18 BDE BOYTON	nom

(73989) W4141-463. 400,000. 9/14. H.&J.Ltd. Forms/C. 2118/10.

Army Form C. 2118.

2

WAR DIARY
or
INTELLIGENCE SUMMARY.
(Erase heading not required.)

Instructions regarding War Diaries and Intelligence Summaries are contained in F.S. Regs., Part II. and the Staff Manual respectively. Title pages will be prepared in manuscript.

Hour, Date, Place		Summary of Events and Information	Remarks and references to Appendices
30/1/16	BOYTON.	2/1 E. BDE, RFA, from XII NOV CAMP, BOYTON	See APP Figure.
31/1/16	SUTTON VENY	Inspection of 2" LONDON DIV by F.M. LORD FRENCH, C—in—C, Home Forces	See APP G.
1030 am			
3 P.M.	CORTON.	Inspection of SCDs of 60th LON DIV ARTY by G.OC., 60th LON DIV — CRA 2 BDE MAJOR Anson	See APP H
4 P.M.	BOYTON	Arrival of 2/16th BATTY, 2/1 4th BDE, RFA from MUCH HADHAM	govt.

[signature]

List of Appendices to War Diary (Vol 1/1916)

1st Jan 1916 - 31st Jan 1916.
_____

(1) Programme of Inspection by Major Gen Bruce.

(2) State of adv. Party of 2/8th Bde. 25/1/16.

(3) Marching-in State - H.Q. R.A. Welsh Div. 26/1/16.

(4) " " " "   2/8th Bde.   26/1/16.

(5) " " " "   2/8th Bde.   26/1/16.

(6) " " " one "   H.Q. R.A. Welsh Div. 26/1/16.

(7) " " " "   2/7th Bde.   30/1/16.

(8) Inspection of Div. by F.M. Viscount French. (Orders &c. &c.) 30/1/16

(9) Marching in State of 2/16th Battery R.F.A. 31/1/16.

CONFIDENTIAL.

WAR DIARY

of

H.Q., 60th. (LONDON) DIVISIONAL ARTILLERY.

From 1st. February to 29th. February 1916.

VOLUME 2.

Army Form C. 2118

WAR DIARY
or
INTELLIGENCE SUMMARY.
(Erase heading not required.)

Instructions regarding War Diaries and Intelligence Summaries are contained in F.S. Regs., Part II. and the Staff Manual respectively. Title pages will be prepared in manuscript.

Hour, Date, Place		Summary of Events and Information	Remarks and references to Appendices
10 AM	1 FEB CORTON and BOYTON	CRA accompanied by STAFF CAPT, inspects camps of 2/5th, 2/6th, 2/7th + 2/8th BDES, RFA	
2.30 PM	2 FEB CORTON	BDE MAJOR visits area selected to the 60th (LON) DIV ARTY for training	
10.0 AM	3 FEB SUTTON VENY - HINDON - SHERRINGTON	BDE MAJOR took reconnce of training area	
9.30 PM	4 FEB CORTON	CRA, accompanied by STAFF CAPT, inspects camps of 2/5th, 2/6th, 2/7th + 2/8th BDES, RFA, and arrange with O.C. HORSE Coy. DIVL. TRAIN as to supply arrangements for BDES.	
3.0 PM	5 FEB CORTON	CRA visits 2/5th BDE. Camp.	
	6 FEB	NIL	
11.0 PM	7 FEB SUTTON VENY	Lt.COL. R.J. MACHUGH reports to CRA on assuming command of 2/5th BDE. RFA	
9.30 AM	8 FEB BOYTON	CRA, accompanied by BDE MAJOR) inspects 2/8th BATTY RFA, at manoeuvre.	
2.30 PM	CORTON	CRA and DOR.E. inspects site selected as RFA. ranges for gun-parks.	
9.30 AM	9 FEB BOYTON	CRA accompanied by BDE. MAJOR inspects 2/8th BATTY RFA at manoeuvres	

(73989) W4141—463. 400,000. 9/14. H.&J.Ltd. Forms/C. 2118/10.

Army Form C. 2118.

(2)

WAR DIARY
or
INTELLIGENCE SUMMARY.

(Erase heading not required.)

Instructions regarding War Diaries and Intelligence Summaries are contained in F.S. Regs., Part II and the Staff Manual respectively. Title pages will be prepared in manuscript.

Hour, Date, Place		Summary of Events and Information	Remarks and references to Appendices
9.30 AM	10 FEB 1916 CORTON	(LT. COL. for (LONO) DIV. inspects Corps of 2/3/5, 2/4/5, and 2/6th BDES, RFA	
11.0 AM	BOYTON	and BDE. MAJOR present. G.O.C. visits artillery training area.	
3.0 PM	BOYTON	CRA, accompanied by BDE. MAJOR, visits 2/6th BDE RFA while at manoeuvre.	
	SUTTON VENY	LT COL W DARLEY, RFA, reports to CRA on assuming command of 2/6th BDE. RFA.	
6.30 PM	11 FEB	CAPT. P. E. WOOTTON, A.D.C. to CRA, reports to HODGES, DIV. ARTY., on going on leave.	
	— DO —	from MAJOR HARDHAM, whom he relieved as STAFF OFFICER with DIV. ARTY.	
		ARTY. rear party left Cohorton with rear of DIVISION to SUTTON VENY.	
9.30 AM	12 FEB	CRA, accompanied by BDE MAJOR inspect area allotted to DIV. ARTY on	
		18th inst.	
6.0 PM	13 FEB.	CAPT W. G. PISON, STAFF CAPT, proceeds to SOUTHAMPTON for embarcation	
		to B.E.F. in FRANCE.	
10.30 AM	14 FEB SUTTON VENY	G.O.C. holds conference with DIV. HODQRS. on DIV. exercise to be held on 18 Feb.	
2.0 PM	— DO —	COL RAINSFORD, R.F.A., reports to CRA and assumes command of the 2/17th LOND. BDE, R.F.A.	
3. 15 PM	CORTON	CRA lectures to Offrs 9th DIV. ARTY on the "organisation of artillery into Groups" DUTY	
9.30 AM	15 FEB CORTON	G.O.C. accompanied by CRA visits O. C. BDES, RFA ser. 2/5th BDES, R.F.A., Group	
11 AM	— DO —	COL FERRAR, Inspector of Remounts, inspects horses of 2/5th BDES, RFA. —	

CRA Amm—

Army Form C. 2118.

WAR DIARY
or
INTELLIGENCE SUMMARY.
(Erase heading not required.)

Instructions regarding War Diaries and Intelligence Summaries are contained in F.S. Regs., Part II. and the Staff Manual respectively. Title pages will be prepared in manuscript.

Hour, Date, Place		Summary of Events and Information	Remarks and references to Appendices
4.0 PM	15 FEB 19/6 SUTTON VENY	ORDERS for DIVL movement 16th issued to all units.	—
1.0 PM	16 FEB	DIVL moves without incident to relevant stations	—
1.0 AM	BOYTON	COL FERRAR inspects horses of 2/1st BDE RFA. – CRA Inspects orders issued that DIVL recruits not to be held beyond 17 Febry.	—
9.0 AM	17 FEB PERTWOOD	DIVL service at the Municipal General – PERTWOOD – GREAT RIDGE even. Twenty nine firms add. 2/1st & 1/8th BDES observing. 1st BC Inspection of Horses branded Col FERRAR at 11.0 AM	See Appendices I and Appendix II
	18 FEB	NIL	None
10.0 AM	19 FEB BOYTON & CORTON	CRA, accompanied by ASC, inspects Camps of 2/1st, 2/1st, 2/1st, & 2/1st BDES RFA.	—
10 FEB	20 FEB SUTTON VENY	CAPT W.G. FISON STAFF CAPT, returns from attachment GHQ B.E.F., FRANCE.	—
		CAPT WOOTTEN ASC & CRA, proceeds to LONDON on duty leave	—
10.0 AM	21 FEB BOYTON	CRA, accompanied by BDE MAJOR, inspects 2/1 15 BDE RFA at — maneuvers	—
9.30 AM	22 FEB BOYTON	" " " inspects 2/1st BDE at — manoeuvres	—
2.30 PM	CORTON to	Inspects of GHQ2 Genl insp Company 8th DIV. RARTY.	—
4.15 PM	BOYTON	Staff from Nth T.F. ARTY TRAINING SCHOOL at BOYTON.	—
6.15 PM		DIV Ambulance attacked to CRA notes. 12 officers, 257 OR. (Deferred)	—

Army Form C. 2118. (4)

WAR DIARY
or
INTELLIGENCE SUMMARY.
(Erase heading not required.)

Instructions regarding War Diaries and Intelligence Summaries are contained in F.S. Regs., Part II and the Staff Manual respectively. Title pages will be prepared in manuscript.

Hour, Date, Place		Summary of Events and Information	Remarks and references to Appendices
	1916		
9.30 pm	22 FEB (cont'd) SUTTON VENY	2/Lieuts HAINES and WESTON, Reserve Officers from Southern Command Reserve report to CRA by order of the War Office and are posted to 2/1st & 2/2nd BDES, RFA, respectively.	
2 pm	23 FEB BOYTON	CRA, accompanied by BDE MAJOR, inspects 2/18th & 2/19th BATTYS RFA at manœuvre.	
2.30 pm	BOYTON	Inspection of all officers of the 59th DIVL ARTY. by CAPT FLADGATE in No 2 Camp, CORTON	
2.30 pm	CORTON	AA & QMG, SOUTHERN COMMAND, inspects Centre of 59th DIVL ARTY — CRA and STAFF & CAPT. present.	
	24 FEB	Private carried. — heavy snowstorm	
2.30 pm	CORTON	CRA lectures to Officers of 59th DIVL ARTY on "Some points in Artillery Training".	
10 am	25 FEB CORTON	BDE, accompanied by BDE MAJOR 59th DIVL ARTY. inspects 2/4th & 2/5th & 2/6th BDES, RFA.	
5.15 pm	SUTTON VENY MAJOR R.N. PRINGLE R.F.A. reports to CRA by order of War Office as Life of dublin of BDE MAJOR to fill vacancy heavy ammunition.		

(73989) W4141—463. 400,000. 9/14. H.&J.Ltd. Forms/C. 2118/10.

Army Form C. 2118.

WAR DIARY
or
INTELLIGENCE SUMMARY.
(Erase heading not required.)

Instructions regarding War Diaries and Intelligence Summaries are contained in F.S. Regs., Part II. and the Staff Manual respectively. Title pages will be prepared in manuscript.

Hour, Date, Place		Summary of Events and Information	Remarks and references to Appendices
	26th FEB BOYTON	Major H H HANWORTH assumed command of DIVN. AMMUNITION COLUMN. Heavy Snow. Parades cancelled.	R.P.
	27th FEB	Snow.	R.P.
10. A.M.	28th FEB CORTON BOYTON	C.R.A. accompanied by BDE MAJOR, visits all Camps. Snow.	R.P.
2. P.M.	29th FEB CORTON BOYTON	C.R.A. accompanied by BDE MAJOR visits Camps and inspects drafts for DIVL AMN. COLUMN and BTYS.	R.P.

(73989) W4141—463. 400,000. 9/14. H.&J.Ltd. Forms/C. 2118/10.

DIVISIONAL EXERCISE, 16th FEBRUARY, 1916.

SPECIAL INSTRUCTIONS to the 60th (London) Divisional Artillery, in continuation of Orders and Instructions already issued.

Reference 1" O.S. Map - Sheet 282.

Hour of starting. The 2/5th Brigade (less 2/12th Battery), 2/7th Brigade and 2/8th Brigade, (less 2/22nd Battery) - all less Ammunition Columns - will move from their camps as follows :-

2/5th Bde.	7.15 a.m.
2/7th Bde.	6.45 a.m.
2/8th Bde.	Follows in rear of 2/5th Bde.

Route - All units : By SHERRINGTON, thence by road leading S. by W. from road junction S. of I in SHERRINGTON, by points 355, 680, and 500, to road fork N. of the E of CHICKLADE BOTTOM Fm, thence W. to road fork at point 388.

2/5th and 2/8th Brigades : By CHICKLADE, road junction S. of second N in KNOYLE DOWN Fm., thence N.W. to ~~the second intersection of the contour line 600 with the road leading N.W. to point 689. This point is about ½ mile S. of the T of UPPER PERTWOOD BUSHES. The areas in which positions will be occupied will be communicated later in the day.~~

[margin note: Road fork N. of the E of KNOYLE DOWN FM.]

~~The 2/12th Battery will march by the road leading S. by W. from the Y of TYTHERINGTON and follow in rear of the party of the enemy from the 179th Infantry Brigade from the cross tracks ½ mile E. by N. of point 745 onwards.~~

2/7th Brigade. From point 388 by road leading S.W to road fork 300 yards S. of O of HINDON, thence W. by N. by cross roads at point 530 to road fork at point 717, thence by road leading E. by N. to a point to be selected about 300 yards distant from the road fork at point 717. The wire of the fence on the N. side of the road will be cut here and a position occupied by the Brigade in the adjoining field.

(Note. A guard will be placed at the opening so made to prevent the straying of cattle and sheep from the field and the wire will be repaired as soon as the Brigade leaves).

-2- (continued)

Allotment of Brigades and Batteries.
The 2/5th Brigade, R.F.A. will co-operate with the 181st Infantry Brigade, and the 2/7th Brigade with the 180th Infantry Brigade.
The 2/21st Battery will support both attacks.

Special Batteries. One Battery of the 2/5th and one Battery of the 2/7th Brigade will be detailed to act directly under the orders of the O.C., 181st Infantry Brigade and the O.C., 180th Infantry Brigade respectively. O's C. 2/5th and 2/7th Brigades will send the O's C. these batteries to report to the Infantry Brigadiers on arrival at the theatre of operations.
An officer will be detailed by each of the above Brigades to go forward with the Infantry advance to act as observation officers. He should take telephones and wire, if available, and signallers.

Ammunition. 5 rounds of blank ammunition per gun will be taken.

Transport. First Line transport will accompany units.

Rations & Feeds. Haversack rations and feeds will be taken.

Ground sheets. Ground sheets will be taken by the 2/12th Battery only.

Gallopers, etc. Lieutenant H.E.Brown, 2/16th Battery will act as galloper to G.O.C., 60th Division, and report to him at the cross roads at point 654, just N. of T in TWO MILE DOWN, at 10 a.m.
O.C., 2/6th London Brigade will also detail 2 trumpeters to report with Lieutenant Brown, at the same time and place.

Orders. O.C. Brigades and 2/21st Battery will meet the C.R.A. at the above cross roads at 9.30 a.m.

Orderlies. Two mounted orderlies will be detailed by O.C. Brigades and 2/21st Battery, to report to Brigade Major at 9.30 a.m., at above cross roads.

          H.H.HANWORTH.
            Major
          Brigade Major,
      60th (Ldn) Divl. Artillery.

Elm Lodge,
 Sutton Veny,
  Wilts.
February 15th. 1916.

DIVISIONAL EXERCISE - 16th FEBRUARY, 1916.

NOTES TO THE SPECIAL INSTRUCTIONS ISSUED TODAY.

Report Centre.   At 10 a.m. the C.R.A. will establish his report centre at Divisional Headquarters.

Brigade Report Centres. These will be notified to the C.R.A. as soon as decided upon.   Notice of a change of report centre should be given as soon as possible, and the old report centre must be kept open until the new one is established.

Reports. Half hourly progress reports will be made to the Divisional Artillery Report Centre.

Routes.   With reference to the routes laid down in the special Instructions referred to, the following amendments will be made :-

2/7th Brigade.   There will be no need to cut the wire of the fence referred to as westwards from a point about 300 yards to the W. of point 654 the wire will be found to have been removed.

2/8th Brigade.   The head of the column will halt at the cross roads 500 yards W. of the first C of CHICKLADE.

Orders.   The C.R.A. will meet the O.C., 2/8th Brigade at the cross roads 500 yards W. of the first C in CHICKLADE at 9.30 a.m. ;   the O.C., 2/5th Brigade at 9.40 a.m. at the cross roads S. of the second N of KNOYLE DOWN Fm. ;   the O.C., 2/7th Brigade at cross roads at point 654 at 9.45 a.m.

Batteries, composition of.   Only firing batteries are required -first line wagons need not be on parade.

Horses and Horseholders for Colonel Saunders, etc. to be at cross roads at point 654 at 9. 45 a.m.

-2- (Continued)

Designation of targets. The following table will be used in designating targets tomorrow :-

	1" Map.	Artillery Training Map.
A.	Point 748.	B 23 c 1 2
B.	Wood 400 yards S. of R in REDDING HANGING	LOWER SUTTON WOOD H 5 b
C.	Wood 800 yards S. of HAM in HAMMERSMITH	PERTWOOD WOOD. H 5 a c
D.	Road over ROOK HILL	Road over ROOK HILL H 4 a
E.	Tree on ridge 300 yds. W. of road on ROOK HILL	B 28 c 1 1
F.	Point 776, Clump of trees FURZE HEDGE BARN	FURZE HEDGE BARN B 27 c

H.H.HANWORTH.
Major,
Brigade Major,
60th (Ldn) Divl. Artillery

Elm Lodge,
Sutton Veny
15/2/16.

CONFIDENTIAL.

WAR DIARY.

of

H.Q., 60th. (London) Divisional Artillery.

From 1st. March 1916 to 31st. March 1916.

VOLUME 3.

WAR DIARY of INTELLIGENCE SUMMARY.

H.Q. 60th (London) Divisional Artillery

Army Form C. 2118.

Instructions regarding War Diaries and Intelligence Summaries are contained in F.S. Regs., Part II and the Staff Manual respectively. Title pages will be prepared in manuscript.

(Erase heading not required.)

Hour, Date, Place	Summary of Events and Information	Remarks and references to Appendices
9.30 A.M. MARCH 1st to 5th BOYTON & CORTON	C.R.A. inspected Artillery Lines and Camps.	(RD)
10. A.M. MARCH 6th BOYTON DOWN	C.R.A. inspects 2/2nd LT. Battery at manoeuvre.	(RD)
11. A.M. MARCH 7th CORTON	G.O.C. 60th Div. visits lines of 2/5th and 2/7th BDES	(RD)
MARCH 8th —	Training stopped by Snow.	(RD)
10. A.M. MARCH 9th & 10th BOYTON	C.R.A. inspects 2/21st LT and 2/15th BTYS at manoeuvre.	(RD)
9. P.M. MARCH 14th LONGBRIDGE-DEVERILL	2/1st LT and 2/15th BTYS engaged in Tactical Exercises with 179th INF. BDE. Div. Arty. Head on Part VII. W.E. New Armies for lines remaining on Form VIII for men	(RD)
11. A.M. MARCH 16th CORTON	C.R.A. inspects new draft for D.A.C.	(RD)
10. A.M. MARCH 17th BOYTON	C.R.H. inspects 2/20th BTY at manoeuvre	(RD)
10. A.M. MARCH 21st & 22nd BOYTON	C.R.A. inspects 2/16th and 2/13th BTYS at manoeuvre.	(RD)
8.30 A.M. MARCH 23rd LONGBRIDGE-DEVERILL	2/18th and 2/9th BTYS engaged in Tactical exercise with 181st INF. BDE.	(RD)
10 A.M. MARCH 24th BOYTON	C.R.A. inspects 2/20th BTY at manoeuvre.	(RD)
10. A.M. MARCH 27th BOYTON	C.R.A. inspects 2/5th BDE at Gun Drill	(RD)
MARCH 28th —	Training stopped by Snow.	(RD)
10. A.M. MARCH 29th BOYTON	C.R.A. inspects 2/7th BDE at Gun Drill. Advance and Range Parties marched to LARKHILL.	(RD)
10. A.M. MARCH 30th BOYTON	C.R.A. inspects 2/8th BDE at Gun Drill	(RD)
2.30 P.M. MARCH 31st CORTON	H.Q. Div. Arty. 2/5th and 2/7th BDES moved by march route to LARKHILL, SALISBURY PLAIN, to carry out practice on WEST DOWN ARTY. Range. Fair progress made with BDE and BTY Training during the month, but training much interfered with by bad weather.	(RD)

SUTTON VENY
31.3.16

W.N. Mutter Colonel
C.R.A. 60th (London) Divl. Artillery

Army Form C. 2118.

WAR DIARY
of
INTELLIGENCE SUMMARY.

H.Q. 60th (London) Divisional Artillery

(Erase heading not required.)

Instructions regarding War Diaries and Intelligence Summaries are contained in F.S. Regs., Part II and the Staff Manual respectively. Title pages will be prepared in manuscript.

Hour, Date, Place	Summary of Events and Information	Remarks and references to Appendices
9.30 A.M. MARCH 1st 04th BOYTON CORTON	C.R.A. inspected Artillery lines and camps.	
10. A.M. MARCH. 6th BOYTON Bury	C.R.A. inspects 2/1st A Battery at manoeuvre	RR
11. A.M. MARCH 7th CORTON	G.O.C. 60th Div. visits lines of 2/5th and 2/7th BDEs	RR
— MARCH 8th —	Training stopped by Snow.	RR
10. A.M. MARCH 9th 10th BOYTON	C.R.A. inspects 2/21st and 2/15th BTYs at manoeuvre.	RR
9. A.M. MARCH. 14th Longbridge Deverill	2/12th and 2/15th BTYs engaged in tactical exercise with 179th Inf. Bde. Div. Arty placed at Part VII with new names for tactical exercise on Jan VIII for men	RR
11 A.M. MARCH. 16th CORTON	C.R.A. inspects new drags for D.A.C.	RR
10. A.M. MARCH. 17th BOYTON	C.R.A. inspects 2/20th BTY at manoeuvre.	RR
10. A.M. MARCH 21st 22nd BOYTON	C.R.A. inspects 2/16th and 2/13th BTYs at manoeuvre	RR
8.30 A.M. MARCH. 23rd Longbridge Deverill	2/18th and 2/14th BTYs engaged in tactical exercise with 181/2 Inf. Bde.	RR
10 A.M. MARCH. 24th BOYTON	C.R.A. inspects 2/20th BTY at manoeuvre	RR
10. A.M. MARCH 27th BOYTON	C.R.A. inspects 2/5th A BDE at Gun Drill	RR
— MARCH 28th —	Training stopped by Snow.	RR
10. A.M. MARCH 29th BOYTON	C.R.A. inspects 2/7th BDE at Gun Drill. Advance and Rear guards marched to Larkhill.	RR
10. A.M. MARCH 30th BOYTON	C.R.A. inspects 2/8th BDE at Gun Drill	RR
8.30 A.M. MARCH 31st CORTON	H.Q. Div. Arty 2/5th and 2/7th BDEs formed to march route to Larkhill. Salisbury Plain to carry out practice on West Down Arty range. Few parades made with BDE and BTY training during the month but training much interfered with by bad weather.	RR

H.A. Britten Colonel
Comdg 60th (London) Divl Artillery

SUTTON VENY
31.3.16

CONFIDENTIAL.

WAR DIARY.

of

H.Q., 60th. (London) Divisional Artillery.

From 1st. April, 1916 to 28th. April, 1916.

VOLUME No 4.

April

WAR DIARY
of
INTELLIGENCE SUMMARY.
(Erase heading not required.)

H.Q. 60th DIVN ARTILLERY.

Army Form C. 2118.

Instructions regarding War Diaries and Intelligence Summaries are contained in F.S. Regs., Part II and the Staff Manual respectively. Title pages will be prepared in manuscript.

Hour, Date, Place		Summary of Events and Information	Remarks and references to Appendices
9.30 a.m	1st & 6th WEST DOWN } SALISBURY }	2/5th and 2/7th BDES carry out artillery practice on alternate days.	Rec.
—	5th SUTTON VENY	Divisional Notification med that Divn Artly is on Part VII. W.E.	Rec.
9.30 a.m	7th & 12th WEST DOWN } SALISBURY }	2/6th and 2/8th BDES carry out Artillery Practice on alternate days.	Rec.
6 p.m	12th SUTTON VENY	H.Q. R.A. returned to SUTTON VENY. BRIG. GENERAL H. SIMPSON - BAIKIE took over duties of C.R.A. from Colonel H.M. BUTLER.	Rec.
9.05 a.m	15th CORTON, BOYTON.	C.R.A. visits all camps and inspects 2/5th BDE in Stables.	Rec.
9.30 a.m	17th CORTON.	C.R.A. inspects 2/6th BDE in Stables	Rec.
10. a.m	18th CORTON.	C.R.A. inspects turn out of vehicles by D.A.C.	Rec.
8.30 a.m	19th LONGBRIDGE - DEVERILL	2/6th BDE took part in tactical exercise with 180th INF BDE.	Rec.
6.1 pm	19th BOYTON	C.R.A. lectured 2/6th BDE on lessons to be learnt from the mornings exercise	Rec.
9.30 a.m	22nd SALISBURY	BDE. MAJOR proceeded to SALISBURY to interview DADR re horse supply	Rec.
9.0 am	24th SUTTON-VENY	DIVN ARTY commenced musketry practice.	Rec.
9.45 am	26th BOYTON.	C.R.A. visited 2/12th, 2/13th, 2/17th 2/22nd BTYS and D.A.C. at drill	Rec.
—	27th CORTON } BOYTON }	All ranks confined to camps and prepared to move in connection with IRISH riots	Rec.
—	28th "	A found 18-pr BTY per BDE joined from ROLLESTONE camps, and a 5inch HOWITZER BTY from T.F. School WINCHESTER.	Rec.

SUTTON VENY
1st May. 1916.

J. Mm. Baikie
BRIG - GENERAL
CMDG 60th DIVN ARTILLERY

WAR DIARY
INTELLIGENCE SUMMARY

Army Form C. 2118.

HQ 64th DIVN ARTILLERY

Instructions regarding War Diaries and Intelligence Summaries are contained in F.S. Regs., Part II. and the Staff Manual respectively. Title pages will be prepared in manuscript.

(Erase heading not required.)

Hour, Date, Place			Summary of Events and Information	Remarks and references to Appendices
9.30 am	1st & 6th	WEST DOWN SALISBURY	2/5th and 2/7th BDES carrying out artillery practice in alternate days	CC
"	5th	SUTTON VENY	Divn'l Artillery ordered that Divn Arty in on Par VII W.E.	CC
9.30 am	7th & 12th	WEST DOWN SALISBURY	2/6th and 2/8th BDES carrying out artillery practice in alternate days	CC
6 pm	12th	SUTTON VENY	H.R. RH attached to SUTTON VENY. Bris G/ General H Simpson - Baikie Coys for duties of CRA from Colonel H M BUTLER.	CC
9.45 am	15th	CORTON, BOYTON	CRA visits all camps and inspects 2/5th BDE in stables	CC
11.30 am	17th	CORTON	CRA inspects 1/4th BDE in stables	CC
10 am	18th	CORTON	CRA inspects Harness & vehicles of DAC	CC
" am	19th	LONGBRIDGE DEVERILL	2/6th BDE took part in trekking exercise with 186th Inf BDE	CC
6 pm	19th	BOYTON		CC
4.30 am	22nd	SALISBURY	CRA lectured 2/6 BDE on lessons to be learnt from the morning's exercise	CC
9.0 am	24th	SUTTON VENY	BDE MAJOR proceeded to SALISBURY to witness DADR & horse supply	CC
9.15 am	26th	BOYTON	C.R.A. visits 2/12th, 2/13th, 2/17th & 2/23rd BTYS and DAC at drill	CC
"	27th	CORTON BOYTON	Attempts confined to camp and prepared to move in trenches not Irish uni-	CC
"	28th	"	A fourth 18-pr Bty per BDE joined from RolESTONE CAMP and a Field Howitzer BTY from T.F. School WINCHESTER	CC

SUTTON VENY
1st May 1916

[signature] Stampfordwalker
BRIG-GENERAL
CMDG 64th DIVN ARTILLERY

WAR DIARY or INTELLIGENCE SUMMARY

Army Form C. 2118

Place	Date	Hour	Summary of Events and Information	Remarks and references to Appendices
No 2B Canadu Huts Larkhill	1916 April 1			
	2			
	3			
	4			
	5			
No 3. Boyton Camp	6		2/12, 2/13 & 2/14th Batteries returned from Larkhill.	
	7		Fire Alarm practised.	
	8		Church Parade. Inspection by C.O. of all horses proceeded to Division placed under War Establishment Part VII. 5 men proceeded to Weymouth on Cookery Course. 5 men transferred to 'No 6. I.T.B Artillery Training School Luton.	
	9		Church Parade. Col. Lane A.D.V.S. called. Lt. N.H. King returned from Course of Gunnery, Shoeburyness. 2/Lt B.S. Hickens returned from Course of Telephony, Woolwich. Brigade on Sly.	
	10		Brigade Emergency alarm practised. Lt. S.G. Price proceeded on 7 days leave. 2/Lt A.E. Whitehead on H. Major H. Bayley took over command of 2/13th Battery.	
	11		B.Q.M.S. Rain re-engaged for duration of War. Cabl. N.S. Hockett proceeded on 7 days leave. Lt. A.H. Scott + 2/Lt N.G. Harrison att. Att. 2/Lt P.L. Haycock proceeded on 4 days leave.	
	12		2/Lt N.G.P. Dawson admitted to Hospital Tidworth. 810 Pkts. Ammn. booked to Brigade, 2/Bat. Joy attached to Artillery clerk. 2/Lt H. Thompson posted to 2/13th Bdr. 2/Lt A.E. Whitehead posted to B.A.C. C.R.A. lectured all B.C.s in Corporals Room of 2/8th Bde. Capt. A.S. Scott + 2/Lt N.F. Couchman proceeded on 4 days leave.	
	13		Lts. A.E. Prager + N.J. Runch proceeded on 4 days leave. 2416 Dvr Newt taken on strength of Brigade 2 men transferred to B.A.C. 158,000 rounds 303 MkVII S.A.A. returned to O.C. Tidworth.	
	14		Major J.A. Williams proceeded on 7 days leave. 2 sergts attached from 47th Reserve Bty. Newdon for Instructional purposes.	

WAR DIARY or INTELLIGENCE SUMMARY

Army Form C. 2118

Place	Date	Hour	Summary of Events and Information	Remarks and references to Appendices
No 3 Bordon Camp	April 1916 16		Brigadier General H.A.D. Simpson Baikie C.B. having assumed command of the 60th Div. Arty. is taken on the strength of the division. Col. H.H. Butler is struck off the strength.	
	17		3 chargers fetched from Netheravon. Lecture to Officers on shoeing by Capt. Sheffield. Capt A.A. Edwards proceeded to Lark Hill on course of gunnery. 1 man sent on Cookery Course, Bethnal Green. 195 wagon collected from 2/2 Bn. Lon. Regt. 5 men transferred to No 6 Artillery Training School, Hilsea. Capt. I.A.W. McGowan proceeded on 4 days leave. Lt. A.J. Price sent on 7 days leave.	
	18		No. 4 Gun Bty. out of bounds owing to sickness. R.S.M. Hager reported for duty. 70 mules transferred to 60th Lon. D.A.C. Visit of C.R.A. & Ds C. Bden of 60th Lon. Div. Arty. 4 18 Pr Wagons with Limbers fetched from Ordnance Depot Warminster.	
	19		Board on unserviceable clothing. D.A.D.O.S. representative present. 30 remounts received from Remounts Bulford; 9 K.D. from Vet. Hosp. Salisbury.	
	20		4 men to Sutton Veney for Dental Treatment. New Establishment of Officers. Lt. A.H.A. Stair & 2/Lt. J. Maier proceeded on 4 days leave.	
	22		Visit of 9.O.C. 60th Lon. Div. 4 18 Pr gun & wagons fetched for New Battery from Warminster. 2/Lt. D.H. Waddington proceeded on 4 days leave.	
	24		3 men proceeded to Borden for Cold-shoeing Course. Courses on 1 man Range-Finder, & Burger under R.P.O. Instructors began. 1 horse destroyed (gran leg 13741 12th Bty). Lt. N.H. King sent on 4 days leave.	
	25		Visit of C.R.A. Lt. C.R. de Traine proceeded on 4 days leave	
	26		Instruction in Cable laying by Capt. Fludgate. 1 horse destroyed (14033 1/4 Bty). Inspection of Barrack Furniture by D./C. Barracks. Lt. W.H. Lunch sent on Sick leave.	
	27		Lecture by Capt. Sladen on Artillery Telephonic Communication. Brigade musketry commenced. 160 mules received from Shirehampton Remount Depot.	
	28		67,000 rds S.A.A. .303 to 2/15th Bn. Lon. Regt. Lt. B.T. Free joined B.T.3. for 2 weeks' course.	
			" 185 " " " 2/14th " " " " " " " 2/15th " " " " " " " 2/16th " " "	

WAR DIARY
or
INTELLIGENCE SUMMARY

(Erase heading not required.)

Army Form C. 2118

Instructions regarding War Diaries and Intelligence Summaries are contained in F. S. Regs., Part II. and the Staff Manual respectively. Title Pages will be prepared in manuscript.

Place	Date	Hour	Summary of Events and Information	Remarks and references to Appendices
No.3. Boyton Camp	April 1916. 29. 30.		1st Essex Battery R.F.A. taken on strength of Brigade. Church Parade.	

C O N F I D E N T I A L.

W A R D I A R Y.

of

H.Q., 60th. (London) Divisional Artillery.

From 4th. May 1916 to 31st. May, 1916.

VOLUME 5.

MAY. 1916

WAR DIARY 60th Divn Artillery, Head Quarters

INTELLIGENCE SUMMARY

Army Form C. 2118.

(Erase heading not required.)

Hour, Date, Place		Summary of Events and Information	Remarks and references to Appendices
9.30 am	4th MAY BOYTON	C.R.A. inspected 2/12th, 2/19th, 2/21st, 2/21st Batteries at manœuvres	CC
10 "	5th " SHERRINGTON	C.R.A. inspected 67 vehicle Div. C. on Road march	CC
9 am	6th " BOYTON CENTRE	C.R.A. visited lines of all BDES and D/A.C.	CC
9.30 am	8th " BOYTON	Signalling Test for all Divn Arty signallers C.R.A inspected stables of 2/7th BDE	CC
9 "	9th " "	Signalling Test concluded	CC
5.30 pm	" " "	Lecture to Anti-Gas mechanics - all officers	CC
9.30 am	10th " CORTON	G.O.C. 60th (Ln) Divn inspected 2 Btys from each BDE at drill and manœuvres	CC
9.30 am	11th " "	C.R.A inspected all BDE Amm. columns	CC
10 am	12th " SHERRINGTON	G.O.C. 60th (Ln) Divn inspected 86 vehicle D.A.C. on route march	CC
9.30 am	15th " CORTON	C.R.A inspected 2/15th and 2/17th BTYS at Drill	C
9.30 —	16th " "	C.R.A inspected 2/16th 2/19th and NEW BTY of 2/6th BDE at Drill	C
2. pm	17th " BOYTON	C.R.A inspect 2/16th BTY at Gun Drill	C
—	18th " "	orders received to nature BDE now composed and reorganise D.A.C. into A and B echelons including a reduction of 10 Officers 265 Other Ranks 310 horses 44 GS wagons and 1 cart Reorganisation completed by bringing extra recruits to each BDE and renumber BDES and BTYS, ex Howitzer Battery becoming as follows:—	
	2/5th { 2/12th 2/13th 2/14th	A/300 B/300 C/300 D/300	300th (Ln) BDE
	LONDON BDE		
	2/8th { 2/21st LONDON BDE		(How?)
	2/6th { 2/15th 2/16th 2/17th	A/301 B/301 C/301	301st (Ln) BDE
	LONDON BDE		(No Howitzer Battery)
	2/7th { 2/18th 2/19th 2/20th	A/302 B/302 C/302 D/302	302nd (Ln) BDE
	LONDON BDE		(How ?)

Page 11

Army Form C. 2118.

WAR DIARY
INTELLIGENCE SUMMARY

MAY 1916 — Head Quarters 60th Divn A.

Instructions regarding War Diaries and Intelligence Summaries are contained in F.S. Regs., Part II and the Staff Manual respectively. Title pages will be prepared in manuscript.

(Erase heading not required.)

Hour, Date, Place		Summary of Events and Information	Remarks and references to Appendices
	MAY 18th (continued)	3/1st Wessex BTY Arrived — A/303	
		3/2nd " " " — B/303 } 303rd (Ln) BDE	
		3/3rd " " " — C/303 }	
		4/60th How. " — D/303 with Bde H.Q.s & 2nd & 3rd/8th BDE	
		The reorganization complete by midnight of May 18th	
10 p.m.	MAY 19th CORTON	All Btys of 302nd, 301st and 303rd BDES practised ambushing during darkness	Ref.
10 a.m.	MAY 20th "	on a fixed scheme	Ref.
3.30 p.m.	MAY 22nd BOYTON	CRA and ADVS inspect horses of "A" relm. D.A.C.	Ref.
7.30 a.m.	MAY 24th SUTTONVENY	Artillery took part in a Divisional Route March under Divisional Arrangements	Ref.
–	MAY 26th SUTTON-VENY	Musketry Practice conducted for all Divn ARTY Units	Ref.
9 a.m.	MAY 27th CORTON	Artillery F.R. Party 302nd Attack Scheme Divisional Arrangements	Ref.
9 a.m.	MAY 28,29,30 LARKHILL	H.Q.,R.H and 303rd BDE moved to LARKHILL CAMP	Ref.
9 a.m.	MAY 29,30th BOYTON	303rd BDE carried out Artillery Practice on LARKHILL RANGES	Ref.
11 a.m.	MAY 31st HEYTESBURY	300th, 301st and 302nd BDES inspected by Maj Gen BRUNKER Inspr R.H and R.F.A	Ref.
		Inspection of 60th (London) Division by His Majesty the King	Ref.
		The Divisional Artillery made great progress during the month and was favourably reported on by Maj Gen BRUNKER and Brig-Gen DRAKE. Its inspection by H.M. King GEORGE, and comments on its appearance and march past on the occasion of the inspection by H.M. King GEORGE. The Divl ARTY is now practically complete in man, horses and equipment.	Ref.

Signed
BRIG. GENERAL.
C.R.A. 60th (LOND.) DIVISION.

WAR DIARY 60th Divl Artillery, Head Quarters.

INTELLIGENCE SUMMARY.

MAY. 1916

Army Form C. 2118.

(Erase heading not required.)

Instructions regarding War Diaries and Intelligence Summaries are contained in F.S. Regs., Part II and the Staff Manual respectively. Title pages will be prepared in manuscript.

Hour, Date.	Place	Summary of Events and Information	Remarks and references to Appendices
9.30. a.m. 4th MAY.	BOYTON	C.R.A inspected 2/12th 2/19th 2/20th 2/21st Batteries at manoeuvre.	
10. a.m. 5th "	SHERRINGTON	C.R.A. inspected 67 vehicles D.A.C. on Route March.	
9. a.m. 6th "	BOYTON, CORTON	C.R.A inspected lines of all BDES and D.I.A.C.	
9.30 a.m 8th "	BOYTON	Signalling Test for all Divl Arty Signallers. C.R.A inspected Stables of 2/7th BDE	
9. a.m. 9th "	"	Signalling Test concluded.	
5.30 p.m = " "	"	Lecture on Anti-gas measures - all officers	
9.30 a.m. 10th "	CORTON	G.O.C 60th (LN) DIVN inspected 2 Btys from each BDE at drill and manoeuvre	
9.30. a.m. 11th "	"	C.R.A. inspected all BDE Amn. columns.	
10. a.m. 12th "	SHERRINGTON	G.O.C 60th (LN) DIVN inspected 86 vehicles D.A.C on route march.	
9.30 a.m. 15th "	CORTON	CRA inspected 2/15th and 2/17th BTYS at Drill	
9.30. " 16th "	"	CRA inspects 2/16th 2/18th and New BTY of 2/6th BDE at drill and manoeuvre	
2 p.m. 17th "	BOYTON	C.R.A. inspects 2/16th BTY at Gun Drill	
18th "	—	orders received to abolish BDE Amn Columns and reorganize D.A.C. into 'A and 'B echelons Initially a reduction of 10 officers 265 other ranks, 310 horses, 44 G.S. wagons and 2 carts. Reorganisation completed by midnight. Orders received to re-group and renumber BDES and BTYS, one Howitzer Battery being scrapped with each BDE. Remembering as follows:—	

$$
\begin{array}{l}
2/5^{th} \\ 2/13^{th} \\ 2/14^{th}
\end{array}
\Big\} \text{LONDON BDE becomes}
\begin{array}{l}
A/300 \\ B/300 \\ C/300 \\ D/300
\end{array}
\Big\} 300^{th} (Ln) BDE
$$

2/8th HOWITZER BDE ... (How 3) " " "

$$
\begin{array}{l}
2/16^{th} \\ 2/16^{th} \\ 2/17^{th}
\end{array}
\Big\} \text{LONDON BDE}
\begin{array}{l}
A/301 \\ B/301 \\ C/301
\end{array}
\Big\} 301^{st} (LN) BDE
$$

(No Howitzer Battery)

$$
\begin{array}{l}
2/7^{th} \\ 2/18^{th} \\ 2/19^{th} \\ 2/20^{th}
\end{array}
\Big\} \text{LONDON BDE}
\begin{array}{l}
A/302 \\ B/302 \\ C/302 \\ D/302
\end{array}
\Big\} 302^{nd} (LN) BDE
$$

2/8th HOWITZER 2/21st ... (How 3)

Page 11

WAR DIARY Head Quarters 60th Divn A
INTELLIGENCE SUMMARY
Army Form C. 2118.

MAY 1916

Hour, Date, Place	Summary of Events and Information	Remarks and references to Appendices
MAY 18th (continued)	3/1st Wessex Bty arrives ⎫	
	3/2nd " " ⎬ 303rd (Ln) BDE	
	3/3rd " " ⎭	
	4/60th Howr " with Bde H.Q's of 3rd 2/8th BDE	
	The reorganization complete by nightfall of May 18th	
10. pm MAY 19th CORTON	All Btys of 300th, 301st and 302nd BDES exercised in entrenching during darkness	RLD
10. am MAY 20th "	on a tactical scheme.	RLD
3.30 pm MAY 22nd BOYTON.	C.R.A and A.D.V.S inspected horses of "A" echelon D.A.C.	RLD
7.30 am MAY 24th SUTTON-VENY	Artillery took part in a Divisional Route March under Divisional Arrangements	RLD
MAY 26th SUTTON-VENY	Musketry Practice concluded for all Divn ARTY units	RLD
—	Artillery took part in an Attack Scheme under Divisional Arrangements	RLD
9 am MAY 27th CORTON	H.Q. R.F.A and 303rd BDE march to LARKHILL CAMP	RLD
9 am MAY 28th,29th,30th LARKHILL	303rd BDE carried out Artillery Practice on LARKHILL ranges	RLD
4 am MAY 29th 30th BOYTON	300th, 301st and 302nd BDES inspected by MAJ.GEN. BRUNKER Inspect. R.H and R.F.A.	RLD
11. am MAY 31st HEYTESBURY.	Inspection of 60th (London) Division by His Majesty the King.	RLD
	The Divisional Artillery made great progress during the month was favourably reported on by Maj.-Genl. BRUNKER and BRIG.-GENL. DRAKE, and complimented on its appearance and march past on the occasion of its Inspection by H.M. King GEORGE.	RLD
	The Divl ARTillery is now practically complete in men, horses and equipment.	RLD

A Dingwall Sackie
BRIG GENERAL
C.R.A. 60th (LOND) DIVISION.

CONFIDENTIAL.

WAR DIARY.

of

H.Q., 60th. (London) Divisional Artillery.

From 1st. June, 1916 to 22nd. June, 1916.

VOLUME 6.

June. 1916

WAR DIARY of H.Q. 60th Divisional Artillery

INTELLIGENCE SUMMARY.

Army Form C. 2118.

(Erase heading not required.)

Hour, Date, Place		Summary of Events and Information	Remarks and references to Appendices
June 1st	CORTON. BOYTON.	Embarkation leave commences.	R.I.P.
" 2nd	SUTTON VENY.	Orders received to return all G.S. wagons and their harness belonging to D.A.C.-Ls ordnance and draw other ordnance.	R.I.P.
" 3rd and 4th	WARMINSTER.	74 G.S. wagons, equipment and harness returned to ordnance	R.I.P.
3.45 pm " 6th	CORTON.	C.R.A. inspects all animals of "B" Echelon. D.A.C.	R.I.P.
2.30 pm " 7th	CORTON	C.R.A. and A.D.R. inspect horses of Batteries	R.I.P.
2 pm " 8th	CORTON	I.G.R. inspects all horses and mules of D/302 Artillery	R.I.P.
" 12th	CORTON. BOYTON.	Embarkation leave finished.	R.I.P.
Noon " 14th	CORTON BOYTON	G.O.C. Division visited all camps	R.I.P.
10.30 am " 15th	SHERRINGTON	C.R.A. inspected "A" Echelon D.A.C. in marching order	R.I.P.
Noon " "	CORTON	C.R.A. inspected 300th and 302nd BDES in stables	R.I.P.
Noon " 16th	BOYTON	C.R.A. inspects 301st and 303rd BDES in stables	R.I.P.
11.30 am " 17th	BOYTON	C.R.A. inspects "A" Echelon D.A.C. in stables	R.I.P.
11.30 am " 19th	CORTON	C.R.A. inspects "B" Echelon D.A.C. in stables, and C/302 BTY in stables.	R.I.P.
11.30 am " 20th	BOYTON	C.R.A. inspects "A" Echelon D.A.C. in stables	R.I.P.
" 21st	CODFORD	The first BDE (303rd) entrains for SOUTHAMPTON for service in FRANCE.	R.I.P.
3.10 pm " 22nd	—	H.Q. 60th DIV. entrains for SOUTHAMPTON for service in FRANCE. Nominal Roll of H.Q. attached.	R.I.P. Appendix I.

Sutton Veny
21.6.16

[signature]
BRIG. GENERAL
C.R.A. 60th (LONDON)

NOMINAL ROLL OF OFFICERS, WARRANT OFFICERS,
N.C.O.'s AND MEN PROCEEDING OVERSEAS WITH
HEADQUARTERS.
60th (LONDON) DIVISIONAL ARTILLERY.

Brigadier General H.A.D.Simpson-Baikie.   C.R.A.
                                 R.A., C.B.
Major H.C.Prance. R.A., D.S.O.   Brigade Major.

Captain W.G.Pison. R.F.A.(T).   Staff Captain.

Captain P.C.Wootton. R.F.A. (T).   A.D.C. to C.R.A.

No.	Rank.	Name.	Peace Unit.
836.	B.S.M.	Hancock, E.V.	"D" Battery, 300th Brigade R.F.A.
887.	Corporal.	Tullett, H.G.	"C" " 300th "
2942.	Bombr.	Waters, F.H.	"C" " 302nd "
1670.	A/Bombr.	S.G.Hofmeyer.	"B" " 300th " Rea
1961.	"	Brooker, E.J.	"B" " 301st "
1895.	Gunner.	Gorham, W.H.	"C" " 301st "
1085.	"	Garrett, F.	"A" " 300th "
2185.	"	Turpin, R.E.	"B" " 302nd "
2194.	"	Dilley, S.J.	"B" " 302nd "
2211.	"	Westlake, F.G.	"A" " 302nd "
2149.	"	Pettitt, G.F.	"B" " 301st "
2748.	Driver.	Honour, E.J.	"A" " 302nd "
2297.	"	Halls, H.W.	"A" " 302nd "
2024.	"	Nosworthy, H.	"A" " 302nd "
2859.	"	Yates, E.	"A" " 302nd "
2203.	"	I'Anson, E.J.	No. 3 Section 60th Divl.Ammn.Col.
1679.	"	Coward, H.F.	No. 3 Section do.

* 55580. Gunner.   Manning, C.B.   R.F.A. (Regular).
                    (Next of kin). Wife. Mrs.C.B.Manning.
                                         17, Navarne St.
                                         Ipswich.

* 178011. Pte.   Seal, V.F.   A.S.C. (M.T.)
                    (Next of kin). Wife. Mrs.Emily Jane Seal.
                                         1, Logan Mews.
                                         Earls Court Road.
                                         Kensington. W.

A T T A C H E D.

| 222. | Corporal. | Coom, T.H. | "C" 303rd Brigade R.F.A. |
| 2794. | Driver. | Young, W.A. | "A" Battery, 302nd Brigade R.F.A. |

21/6/16

June 1916

Army Form C. 2118.

WAR DIARY of H.Q. 60th Divisional Artillery

~~INTELLIGENCE SUMMARY~~

(Erase heading not required.)

Instructions regarding War Diaries and Intelligence Summaries are contained in F.S. Regs., Part II and the Staff Manual respectively. Title pages will be prepared in manuscript.

Hour, Date, Place		Summary of Events and Information	Remarks and references to Appendices
June 1st	CORTON, BOYTON	Embarkation leave commenced	Rep.
" 2nd	SUTTON VENY	Orders received to return all G.S. wagons and their harness belonging to D.A.C-6 Ordnance and draw others overseas	Rep.
" 3rd, 4th	WARMINSTER		
" 5th, 6th	CORTON	74 T.S. wagons equipment and harness returned to ordnance	Rep.
1.30 pm " 7th	CORTON	Inspected all animals of "B" Echelon D.A.C.	Rep.
2 pm " 8th	CORTON	C.R.A. and A.D.R. inspect horses of Batteries	Res
" 12th	CORTON, BOYTON	I.G.R. inspects all horses and mules of Divl. Artillery	Rep.
Noon " 14th	CORTON, BOYTON	Embarkation leave finished	Rep.
10.30 am " 15th	SHERRINGTON	G.O.C. Division visited all Camps	Rep.
Noon "	CORTON	CRA inspected "A" Echelon D.A.C. in marching order	Rep.
Noon " 16th	BOYTON	CRA inspected 302nd and 303rd Bdes in stables	Rep.
11.30 am " 17th	BOYTON	CRA inspected 301st and 303rd Bdes in stables	Rep.
11.30 am " 19th	CORTON	CRA inspect "A" Echelon D.A.C. in stables	Rep.
11.30 am " 20th	BOYTON	CRA inspects "B" Echelon D.A.C. in stables, and C/302 Bty in stables	Rep.
— " 21st	CODFORD	CRA inspects "A" Echelon D.A.C. in stables	Rep.
3.10 pm " 22nd	—	The first Bde (304) entrains for Southampton for service in France H.Q. 60th Divl. Artillery entrains for Southampton for service in France. Nominal Roll of H.Q. attached.	Appendix I.

Sutton Veny
21.6.16

[signature]
BRIG. GENERAL,
C.R.A. 60th (LOND.) DIVISION.

WAR DIARY
H.Q. 60th Divisional Artillery

INTELLIGENCE SUMMARY

Army Form C. 2118.

Instructions regarding War Diaries and Intelligence Summaries are contained in F.S. Regs., Part II. and the Staff Manual respectively. Title pages will be prepared in manuscript.

(Erase heading not required.)

Hour	Date	Place	Summary of Events and Information	Remarks and references to Appendices
6. pm.	June 22nd	Southampton	H.Q.R.A. embarked on H.M.T. "NIRVANA". Sailed 7. pm.	Rep.
7. am.	" 23rd	Le Havre	Disembarked and marched to no. 1. Rest Camp. No casualties en route.	Rep.
6.30. pm.	" 24th	Le Havre	H.Q.R.A. entrained at Point.3. 300th F.A. Bde detrained at St Pol and Petit Houvin.	Rep.
5. pm.	" 25th	Petit Houvin	H.Q.R.A. detrained and marched to billets at FLERS.	Rep.
—	" 25th	—	Advance parties of all Batteries 300th BDE and of 2. BTYS. 303rd BDE (detrained night 24/25th) report to H.Q.R.A. 51st Divn at HERMAVILLE to take over from BTYS. of 38th Divn attached to 51st Divn.	Rep.
6.30 pm	" 25th	St Pol	C.R.A. reported to H.Q. 3rd ARMY, and at 7.15. pm. to H.Q. 17th CORPS.	Rep.
9.45 am.	" 26th	Hermaville	C.R.A. reported to H.Q.R.A. 51st Divn and examined BTY positions of LEFT GROUP 51st DIVn.	Rep.
		Hermaville	Advance parties of Second 2. BTYS. 303rd BDE report to H.Q.R.A. 51st Divn. 301st BDE detrain at ST POL and PETIT HOUVIN. Rain.	Rep
10. pm.	" 27th	Slatargette Ecurie	First Section 300th and 303rd F.A. BDEFS relieve corresponding sections of 38th DA	Rep
10. am.	" 27th	Ecurie	C.R.A. visits BTY positions of CENTRE GROUP 51st DIV ARTY. 302nd F.A. BDE detrain. Heavy Rain.	Rep
8. am.	" 28th	Flers	H.Q.R.A. march to Billets at VILLERS CHATEL.	Rep
10. am.	"	—	C.R.A. visited H.Q.R.A. 51st Divn and XVII corps. Also HQs of 301st and 302. FA BDES	Rep
11. pm.	"	—	Relief of 38th Divn BTYS by 300th and 303rd BDES. Complete. Rain.	Rep
10. am.	" 29th	Ecurie Warlus St Pol	C.R.A. visits BTY positions of RIGHT GROUP 51st Divn	Rep
3.30 pm	"		C.R.A. visits H.Q.R.A. 14th Divn and inspects some BTY positions of 14th Divn in ARRAS. Rep. 60th D.A.C. detrained and to Billets at ST MICHEL-SUR-TERNOISE. Determinement of Div Arty complete	Rep

Appendix. I

H.Q. 60th Divisional Artillery

Army Form C. 2118.

WAR DIARY
or
~~INTELLIGENCE SUMMARY.~~
(Erase heading not required.)

Instructions regarding War Diaries and Intelligence Summaries are contained in F.S. Regs., Part II. and the Staff Manual respectively. Title pages will be prepared in manuscript.

II

Hour, Date, Place	Summary of Events and Information	Remarks and references to Appendices
9 a.m. JUNE. 30th LIGNY ST FLOCHEL	6 officers and 69 Other ranks, taken from BTYS and D.A.C. to form personnel of 3. Medium Trench Mortar Batteries, join at Trench Mortar School.	REP.
9.30 a.m. 30th ST MICHEL-SUR-TERNOISE	CRA visits D.A.C. BTY positions and O.Ps of 300th and 303rd BDES.	REP
" 30th LATTRECOURT?	BDE and BTY Commanders and proportion of Officers, N.C.Os and men of 301st and 302nd F.A. BDES attended to 51st Div WIRTH gun instruction.	REP APPENDIX II.

VILLERS-CHATEL
30.6.16

J Stephen Parker?
Brigadier - General
Cmdg 60th Divl Artillery.

SECRET APPENDIX. I COPY No. 8

51st DIVISIONAL ARTILLERY

OPERATION ORDER No. 26.

25th June, 1916.

RELIEF of 38th by 60th Div: ARTY

1. The Batteries of the 38th Divisional Artillery now in the line will be relieved by Batteries of 60th Divisional Artillery as follows :-

   RIGHT GROUP

   C/121 Relieved by ---------- A/300
   A/121 Relieved by ---------- B/300

   CENTRE GROUP

   B/119 Relieved by ---------- C/300
   A/122 Relieved by ---------- C/303

   LEFT GROUP

   D/120 Relieved by ---------- D/300
   C/120 Relieved by ---------- A/303
   A/119 Relieved by ---------- B/303
   D/122 Relieved by ---------- D/303

2. One Section of each Battery will be relieved on night 27th/28th and the second section on night 28th/29th. The Batteries will be under the Command of the B.C's. of 38th Division until relief is completed.

3. Two Officers, 2 telephonists and 2 linesmen of the relieving Batteries will be attached to the Batteries they are relieving from afternoon of 25th inst., and morning 26th inst.

4. Guns and Howitzers of the Batteries of 38th Divisional Artillery will be left in position stripped of all stores including sights (except the sights of the 4.5" Batteries) and will be taken over by relieving Batteries of 60th Divisional Artillery.
   The Batteries of 60th Divisional Artillery will hand over their guns similarly stripped to the Batteries of the 38th Divisional Artillery at the latters Wagon Lines.
   Memorandum of Examination must accompany the guns.

5. All existing telephone lines will be left in position and will be taken over by relieving units.

6. In-going Batteries will take over from out-going Batteries all Maps, Photos, Plans, Log Books, Target Register, etc.

7. All Batteries of 38th Divisional Artillery will assemble in their respective Wagon Lines as they are relieved, and these 8 Batteries of the 38th Divisional Artillery will rejoin the 38th Division on the morning of 1st July, halting on the 30th June, at OPPY- GIVENCHY-le-NOBLE- VILLERS-SIRE-SIMON.
   All moves to take place after dark on the night 29th/30th June, and 30th June/1st July.

8. Batteries of the 60th Divisional Artillery will take over the Wagon Lines of those Batteries they are relieving on the night of 29th/30th June.

9. The eight Batteries of 38th Divisional Artillery will be/

9. contd.

be rationed up to and for 1st July, by 51st Division.
Marching out strength of men and horses to be reported by Batteries to 51st Divisional Artillery by night of 27th June.

10. The eight Batteries of the 60th Divisional Artillery will be rationed by 51st Division from the 30th June inclusive.

11. All out-going Batteries will march out with their Ammunition Wagons and Limbers full, with 75% Shrapnel and 25% of H.E. for 18-pounders and all H.E. for 4.5" Howitzers.

12. Progress of reliefs will be reported by Group Headquarters, also that the order in para 11, has been complied with.

Acknowledge.

Issued at 4.30 p.m.

L.J. Davidson
Captain,
for Brigade Major,
51st Divisional Artillery.

```
Copy No. 1.  to  51st Division 'G'
         2.  to  51st Division 'Q'
         3.  to  XVII Corps R.A.
         4.  to  Right Group
         5.  to  Centre Group
         6.  to  Left Group
         7.  to  38th Divisional Artillery
         8.  to  60th Divisional Artillery
         9   to  Senior Supply Officer
        10.  to  51st D.A.C.
        11.  to  Retain
        12.  to  Retain.
```

SECRET
No. 2772/A.
HIGHLAND
DIVISION.

C.R.A.
C.R.E.
152nd Infantry Brigade.
153rd Infantry Brigade.
154th Infantry Brigade.
Divisional Train.
60th (London) Division.
----

1. The following units of the 60th Division will be attached for Administration as shown below :-

Unit.	Date of arrival.	Place.	Formation to which attached.	Remarks.
Hd. Qrs. 179th Infantry Brigade.	27/6/16.	ECOIVRES.		Mining Fatigues.
2/13th Ln. Regt.	26/6/16.	MT. ST. ELOY.	152nd Inf. Bde.	
2/14th -do-	25/6/16.	MAROEUIL.	153rd -do-	
2/15th -do-	26/6/16.	MAROEUIL.	153rd -do-	
2/16th -do-	26/6/16.	ECOIVRES.	153rd -do-	
2/17th Ln. Regt.	27/6/16.	ACQ.	152nd Inf. Bde.	
2/18th -do-	"	½ ACQ. ½ MT. ST. ELOY.	152nd -do-	
2/19th -do-				
2/20th -do-				
2/21st Ln. Regt.	28/6/16.	LOUEZ.	154th Inf. Bde.	
2/22nd -do-	28/6/16.	MAROEUIL.	154th -do-	
2/23rd -do-				
2/24th -do-				
Pioneer Bn. 1/12th L.N.L. H.Q. & 2 Cos.	25/6/16.	LOUEZ	1/8th Royal Scots.	
2 Cos.	25/6/16.	ACQ.		
300th Bde. R.F.A.	27/6/16.	LARESSIT & ACQ.	Headquarters, Divl. Artillery.	
303rd Bde. R.F.A.	27/6/16.	ACQ & CAPELLE FERMONT.		
3/3rd F. Co. R.E.	25/6/16.	LOUEZ.	Headquarters Divisional Engineers.	
2/4th F. Co. R.E.	26/6/16.	MAROEUIL		
1/6th F. Co. R.E.	28/6/16.	MT. ST. ELOY.		
No. 2 Co. Train.	26/6/16.	ACQ.	Divl. Train.	
No. 3 Co. "	28/6/16.	HAUTE AVESNES.	-do-	

P.T.O.

(2)

2. All casualties sustained by these units while in the Divisional Area will be reported in the daily casualty wire of the formation to which attached.

         Major,
        D.A.A. & Q.M.G.,
26th June, 1916.   51st (Highland) Division.

C.R.A.
C.R.E.
179th Inf. Bde.
180th do.
181st do.
Pioneer Battn.
Divl. Train.
"G" Branch

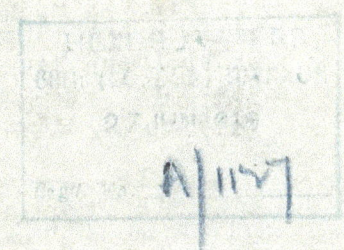

For information and necessary action.

         Major,
        D.A.A. & Q.M.G.,
27th June, 1916.   60th (London) Division.

Secret.

G.740.

60th Division.

Reference para. 2 of XVll Corps Order No. 13 of 20th June.

1. The six 18-pdr. batteries and two 4.5" howitzer batteries 38th Divisional Artillery, now in the line with the 51st Division, will be relieved by a corresponding number of batteries 60th Divisional Artillery.

2. One section per battery 38th Divisional Artillery will be relieved by a section per battery 60th Divisional Artillery on the night 27th/28th June. The balance of each battery 38th Divisional Artillery will be relieved by the 60th Divisional Artillery on the night 28th/29th June.
   The 60th Divisional Artillery will come under the orders of the 51st Division on completion of relief.

3. Advance parties from the two leading Artillery Brigades of the 60th Divisional Artillery will report at the Headquarters 51st Division, HERMAVILLE, on the afternoon of the 25th and morning of the 26th June respectively.

4. From 12 midnight 26th/27th until the relief has been completed VILLERS BRULIN and MINGOVAL will be used temporarily as wagon lines by the 60th Divisional Artillery. The present wagon lines of the 38th Divisional Artillery will be occupied by the 60th Divisional Artillery on the departure of the former.

5. Stripped guns will be exchanged by the batteries of the 38th and 60th Divisional Artilleries.

6. The 51st Division will supply ammunition to the 60th Divisional Artillery until further orders.

7. On relief the personnel of the 38th Divisional Artillery will return to their present wagon lines and the batteries of the 38th Divisional Artillery will rejoin the 38th Division on the morning 1st July, halting on the 30th June at OPPY - GIVENCHY -le-NOBLE- VILLERS-SIRE-SIMON.
   All moves to take place after dark on the nights 29th/30th June and 30th June/1st July.

8. The 38th Divisional Artillery will be rationed up to and for 1st July by 51st Division. Ration strength to be wired to 38th Division.

9. The 60th Divisional Artillery will be rationed by the 51st Division from the 30th June inclusive.

10. Progress of move to be reported to XVll Corps.

H.Q., XVll Corps.
24th June, 1916.

Sd. J. MACKENZIE, Major for
Brigadier General,
General Staff.

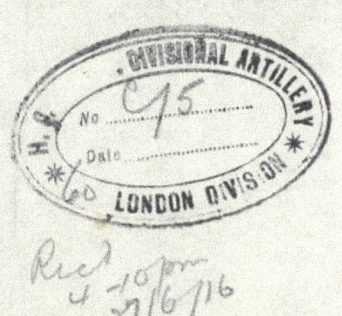

ALC   Q/3/4   SECRET
                                               No. 2167/A
                                               HIGHLAND
                                               DIVISION.

Headquarters,
    60th Division (for information.)
----

1.   When the full number of troops of 60th Division
have arrived in the area for training, their billeting
arrangements will be as follows:-
2 Brigades R.F.A.
        3 Batteries. Wagon Lines at ACQ.
        3   "   "   "   " CAPELLE FERMONT.
        2   "   "   "   " LARESSET.
Field Cos. R.E.
        ½ 3/3rd Field Co. ½ Co............ANZIN.
        ½   "   "   ) 1 Section......ECURIE.
) 1   "   ....MAISON BLANCHE.
        ½ Field Co. MAROEUIL ½ Field Co..MONT ST ELOY.
152nd Infantry Brigade.
        1 Mining Fatigue Bn..............NEUVILLE ST VAAST
        1 Bn. 51st Div. out of line......MONT ST ELOY.
        1 Bn out of line (½ Bn...........MONT ST ELOY.
                         (½ Bn...........ACQ
        1 Bn out of line.................ACQ
153rd Infantry Brigade.
        1 Mining Fatigue Bn (½ Bn.......MAROEUIL
                            (½ Bn.......ANZIN
        1 Bn out of line................ECOIVRES
        1 Bn out of line................Huts at ECOIVRES
                                        and BRAY.
        1 Bn 51st Div. out of line......MAROEUIL
154th Infantry Brigade.
        1 Bn out of line................MAROEUIL.
        1 Bn 51st Div. out of line......ETRUN.
        1 Bn out of line................LOUEZ.
Pioneer Battalion distributed in line ½ with 1/8th
Royal Scots and ½ under C.B. Corps.
2 Cos Div. Train 60th Division.........ACQ and HAUTE AVESNES
/ 3 Sections Field Ambulances (1 Section..ACQ
                              (2 Sections..HAUTE AVESNES

2 Units of 60th Division will be administered as follows:-
        Batteries by C.R.A. 51st Division.
        Field Cos. by C.R.E. 51st Division.
        Infantry by the Brigadier-Generals of Infantry
            Brigades as shown above.
        Pioneer Battalion by O.C., 1/8th Bn Royal Scots.
        A.S.C.   by O.C., 51st Div. Train.
        R.A.M.C.   by A.D.M.S. 51st Division.

                        (Sgd) A. F. G. MOIR.
                              Lieut-Col.
                              A.A. & Q.M.G.
26th June 1916.   51st (Highland) Division.

C. R. A.
C. R. E.
H.Q., 179th Infy. Bde.
H.Q., 180th   "   "
H.Q., 181st   "   "
A. D. M. S.
O.C., Divl. Train, A.S.C.   Q/3/4

                Forwarded for information.

                                            Major.
H.Q., 60th Division.   for D.A.Q.M.G.
27th June 1916.   60th Division.

C/10 Appendix II   SECRET.
                          N⁰ G.1036
                          HIGHLAND
     INSTRUCTIONS   DIVISION.
  regarding the attachment of the
         60th DIVISION
              to
     51st (HIGHLAND) DIVISION.

------------oOo------------

1.   The following troops of the 60th Division will undergo a course of training with the 51st Division:-

   All Infantry Battalions.
   One Field Company & two ½ Companies of R.E.
   Two Companies, Pioneer Battalion.
   All Divisional Artillery.
   Machine Gun Companies.
   Departmental Troops.

2.   The object of the attachment is to initiate the officers and men of the new formations into the routine of trench life, in order that they may profit by experience already gained. The value of the instruction will greatly depend upon the interest and pains taken by the troops in the trenches to make known all details to the new-comers.

3.   The instruction of the Infantry will be carried out in five phases, according to Tables to be issued later.

(a) Individual Instruction.

   During this phase the officers and N.C.Os. will be distributed amongst the companies in the front line. Each officer and N.C.O. will be told off to an "opposite number" and should actually carry out with him all the usual duties of trench warfare. Points to which particular attention should be paid are attached as Appendix "B".

(b) Platoon Instruction.

   During this phase platoons of the new formations will be introduced similarly at the rate of 1 platoon per company in front line. The platoons of the 60th Division will, during this period, work under their own platoon officers, but will be under the command of the O.C. Company to which they are attached.

(c) Company Instruction.

   During this phase the Company will go into the line as such, at the rate of 4 companies to each Brigade, and will work under its own officers. A similar number of companies of the 51st Division will be withdrawn into Support. The companies of the 60th Division will be under the command of the O.C. Battalion to which they are attached.

(d) Battalion Instruction.

   A Battalion takes over a complete sub-sector, a Battalion of the 51st Division being withdrawn into Reserve. The battalion will work entirely under its own officers, but will be under the command of the Brigadier of the 51st Division commanding the Sector.

                                              (e)/

(e)　　　The training for troops in back area is attached as Appendix "A".

4. **Troops not undergoing Training.**

Any troops in the forward area not actually undergoing training will be employed under the C.R.E. on such work as is considered most urgent.

5. **Machine Guns.**

The machine guns of battalions undergoing instruction will go into the trenches at the rate of 50% at a time and will be relieved in the same manner as the infantry.

6. **Artillery.**

(1) **To each Brigade Headquarters.**

1 Brigade Commander with his Adjutant and 2 telephonists.

(2) **To each Battery.**

1 Battery Commander with 1 Subaltern and 2 telephonists, and a small proportion of gun numbers and N.C.Os.

(3) **To each Brigade Wagon Lines.**

1 Officer and 4 N.C.Cs. for instruction in Ammunition supply to gun positions.

(4) **To Divisional Ammunition Column.**

60th D.A.C. Commander and his Adjutant to Headquarters, and 1 Officer and 2 N.C.Cs. to each Nos. 1, 2 and 3 Sections.

It will be arranged that the units to which these officers are attached are those which they will subsequently relieve.

7. **Signals.**

1/3rd of the technical personnel should be attached for a week with the exception of D.Rs. where a smaller percentage would suffice:-

1 Officer and 1/3rd operators and 1/3rd linesmen (mounted and dismounted) of Headquarters and No.1 section to 51st Divisional Signal Co., H.Q., and No.1 section.

1 Officer and 1/3rd Brigade section and Pioneers of each Brigade section.

It is desirable for the officer to remain for a longer period than 1 week.

8. **R.E.**

The C.R.E. 51st Division will issue instructions as regards the accommodation and employment of Field Companies, 60th Division during their attachment.

9. Pioneers./

(3)

9. **Pioneers.**

   Instructions for the distribution and training of the Pioneer Battalion have been issued separately.

10. **Field Ambulance.**

    Under instructions from the A.D.M.S., 51st Division, sections of the 60th Division Field Ambulances will be attached to Highland Field Ambulances for training.

11. **A.S.C.**

    Instructions for the training of the A.S.C. Companies will be issued later.

12. **Headquarters.**

    Every facility will be given to individual members of the Staffs of 60th Division to be attached to the Brigade and Divisional Staffs of the 51st Division in order to make themselves acquainted with the routine.

13. Detailed instructions as regards dates will follow as soon as definite information is received.

Ian Stewart
Lieut.Colonel,
General Staff,
51st (Highland) Division.

27th June 1916.

N.B. Para 8 (d) is subject to the time available for the course of training.

APPENDIX "A".

INSTRUCTIONS FOR TRAINING BATTALIONS OF 60th DIVISION.
IN BACK AREA.

1. **GRENADE TRAINING.** Each Battalion of 60th Division in back area to send 1 Officer and 2 N.C.Os. a Company to Divisional Grenade School, HERMAVILLE, for 6 days training.   Officers and N.C.Os. to be billeted in HERMAVILLE.   2 Courses to be completed.

    Date of commencement of 1st Course will be notified later.

2. **CONSOLIDATION OF CRATERS.** Each Battalion in rest in turn on consecutive days will send 1 Company, or 200 all ranks, in motor busses to AGNIERES, where they will receive instruction in the consolidation of craters under an R.E. Officer of the 51st Division.   The C.R.E. of the Division will make the necessary arrangements for the collection of the necessary materials for the consolidation.

3. **BAYONET FIGHTING.** Each Battalion in rest will send 2 Officers and 4 N.C.Os. who are likely to make efficient Instructors, to the 51st Divisional Gymnastic School for 6 days training.   Officers and N.C.Os. to be billeted in HERMAVILLE.

    Date of commencement of 1st Course will be notified later.

4. **RAPID WIRING.** Two Instructors from the Pioneer Battalion, 51st Division, will be sent to each Battalion in the back area to train them in the organization and drill of wiring parties.

    Date on which these Instructors will be required will be notified later.

G.1036.   APPENDIX "B".

POINTS TO WHICH ATTENTION SHOULD BE DIRECTED DURING TOURS OF INSTRUCTION IN TRENCHES.

Fire Trenches - dimensions, advantages and disadvantages.

Breastworks.

Supporting Trenches - suitable positions for and profile of.

Field of fire - foreground.

Communication trenches - depth and direction of.

Thickness of parapet. - Height of parapet.

Revetments, sandbags, hurdles, wooden frames, etc.

Traverses - dimensions and how made.

Loopholes, steel - (a) for firing through - (b) for observation.

Best positions for machine guns.

Sandbags - uses for.

Attitude and habits of the enemy should be studied.

Distribution of a company in the trenches.

Look-out system and reliefs for.

Action in case of attack.

Position of Company H.Q., & intercommunication between platoons.

Telephones - speaking tubes.

Listening posts.

Spare ammunition reserve, where kept in company's trenches.

Reserve of bombs and hand grenades, periscopes, etc.

One company relieving another in the trenches.

Flooring of trenches.

Construction of dug-outs - (a) in fire trench - (b) in breastwork.

Bridges over small streams with traverse to cover any gap.

Wire entanglements - where placed and various natures of.

Loose wire trips and "chevaux de frise".

"Very" pistols and periscopes - used for.

Latrines in the trenches.

/System.

System of delivery of rations to units and transport of same to the trenches.

Issue of R.E. material to units - how organized and how disposed of by units.

Use of pumps in flooded trenches and system of damming portions that have become waterlogged.

SANITATION MEASURES GENERALLY
FOR TROOPS EMPLOYED ON TRENCH DUTY.

X   Action to be taken before going into the trenches as regards the body and especially the feet, socks, boots and clothing.

X   How to dress for duty in the trenches. Change of socks to be taken.

X   Such exercise as is possible in narrow limits to be taken to encourage corculation.

X   Meal hours - best hours for issue of rum.

X   Lights in the trenches - to be screened. This also applies to fires in braziers.

No singing or loud talking to be allowed in the trenches.

Measures to be taken when about to hand over trenches to another company.

What is done after leaving the trenches.

A bath as soon as possible, in any case feet washed, clean socks and change of underclothing.

Reasonable exercise should be taken by all ranks to keep them fit for marching, in the intervals of trench duty. This is of the utmost importance.

The hours and arrangements for such route marches or walking exercise must, of course, be fixed with due regard to the troops not being exposed to shell fire, and to allow of an adequate proportion being left in billets in case of emergency.

Battalions in billets should, besides a quarter guard on each company's billets, always have one entire company detailed as inlying picquet and held ready to turn out at shortest notice both by day and by night.

X Refers to Winter.

23rd June, 1916.

Vol 2

Confidential

War Diary

of

Headquarters, 60th Divisional Artillery.

from 1st July 1916 to 31st July 1916.

(Volume 7).

1916.

Vol 3

Confidential

War Diary

of

Headquarters, 60th London Divl. Artillery.

From 1st August 1916 to 31st August 1916.

(Volume 8).

Army Form C. 2118.

WAR DIARY
of
INTELLIGENCE SUMMARY.

AUGUST 1916 HQ.R.A. 60TH (LONDON) DIVN

Instructions regarding War Diaries and Intelligence Summaries are contained in F. S. Regs., Part II. and the Staff Manual respectively. Title pages will be prepared in manuscript.

(Erase heading not required.)

Place	Date	Hour	Summary of Events and Information	Remarks and references to Appendices
BERTHONVAL	2nd	11 am	G.O.C. Divn visit C.R.A. Visits Left Group Battery Positions	Ref.
FROM - MARETZ	3rd	9.30 am	C.R.A. visits Right Centre and Left Inf BDE HQs. Left Group Artillery and H.Q. XVII Corps Heavy Artillery	Ref
FORD DE VASE	4th	10 am	G.O.C. Divn visits C.R.A. visits Left and Centre Groups Battery Positions	Ref
ROCLINCOURT	5th	10 am	G.O.C. Divn visits Right Group Bty Position	Ref
NEUVILLE-VITASSE	6th	10 am	C.R.A. visits all Inf BDE HQs and Centre Arty Group	Ref
"	"	10.30 pm	Raid on hostile trenches carried out by 179th Inf. Bde supported by Centre Group Arty. Point bombarded & trapped	App. I Ref
ROCLINCOURT	7th	9.30 pm	Raid on hostile trenches by 181st Inf. BDE supported by Right Arty Group	App II Ref
"	8th	9.15 am	C.R.A & 181 V Inf BDE HQs and Right Arty Group and Gun positions	Ref
MT ST-ELOY	9th	3 pm	H.M. King George visited bombardment by CHANTECY CRATER by Arty Group	Ref
AUX RIETZ	10th	10.30 am	C.R.A. visits Centre and Left Inf BDE HQs and B/302 Bty position	Ref
ABOVILLE	11th	10.30 am	Mine exploded by Centre Sector. Consolidation supported by Centre Arty Group	Ref
ECOIVRES	"	3 pm	Conference under G.O.C. Divn C.R.A. attended	Ref
AUX RIETZ	12th	11 am	C.R.A. visits HQs 179th and 180th Inf BDES. 2" Trench Mortars positions, Centre Group AMF.Q 02, A3 Rep H.Stamp 40 Ref	Ref App II
LA FOLIE	13th	2 am	Raid on hostile trenches by 180th Inf BDE supported by Left Group.	Ref App. II
ECURIE	"	11 am	S.O. visits Right Arty Group and A/300 Battery Position	Ref
ROCLINCOURT	14th	11 am	C.R.A. visits Right Group H.Q. 05 and Heavy T.M. Emplacements. Heavy Rain.	Ref

WAR DIARY or INTELLIGENCE SUMMARY

Army Form C. 2118

H.Q. R.A. 60th (London) DIVL ARTILLERY. August 1916

Place	Date	Hour	Summary of Events and Information	Remarks and references to Appendices
RUCLINCOURT	15th	11 a.m.	C.R.A. visits Right Group H.Q. and Battery Positions	Ref
"	"	5 p.m.	Continued Bombardment of hostile Trenches and Trench Mortars in A.16.c by Div. Arty. Heavy Rain	App 4. Ref
CAMBLIN L'ABBÉ	16th	9.30 a.m.	C.R.A. visits C.R.A. 9th Divn; and wagon lines 300th and 301st BDES at FORESTEL at 4 pm	Ref
NEUVILLE-ST-VAAST	17th	10 a.m.	B.D.E. and left Inf. B.D.E. H.Qs. left group H.Qs and H.Qs of left group Btys. Heavy Rain afternoon	Ref
ACOIVRES	18th	3 p.m.	Conference by M.G.R.A. 3rd Army. Rain during afternoon	Ref
ECURIE ROCLINCT	19th	10 p.m.	C.R.A. to all Inf. BDE camps. Bombardment of hostile CTs during night. Relief been expected	Rain Ref App 5
FERMENT-CAFEUR	20th	2.30am	C.R.A. inspects wagon lines 303rd BDE	Ref
BLAIRCOURT	21st	10 a.m.	C.R.A. visits left Group H.Q. and Btys	Ref
ACRE-DEMIRAUMONT	"	5 p.m.	G.O.C. Divn with C.R.A. & 9th Divn O.R.A. to watch shoot by left group on ORSHANVILLERS SECTOR	Ref
ROCLINCOURT	22nd	10 a.m.	G.O.C. Divn and C.R.A. to Right Group H.Q. C.R.A. to Centre Group H.Qs and Battery Positions	Ref
"	23rd	10.30a	C.R.A. to Centre group front trenches and Battery posns. Bombardment of Enemy Reserve trenches by Divl Arty	App 6 Ref
BERTHONYAL	24th	10 a.m.	C.R.A. visits left group H.Q. C/300 BF position, Field Supply Park at MISTGOY. An Isolated Hun 300th + 301st BDES	Ref
AUX RIETZ	25th	11.30am	C.R.A. G. Centre and left Inf. BDEs	Ref
"	"	3.45pm	Bombardment by Divl Arty of hostile Trenches and Trench Mortars in A.17.c and A.16.a. Rain	App 7. Ref
NEUVILLE	26th	11 a.m.	G.O.C. Divn with C.R.A. to C/303 Bat OP. Rain	Ref
CARENCY	27th	4 p.m.	C.R.A. to Conference at IV Corps H.Q.	Ref
FOND DE VASE	"	5 pm	Conference of Group Commanders. Rain	Ref

WAR DIARY H.Q. R.A. 60th (LONDON) DIVn ARTILLERY

INTELLIGENCE SUMMARY

Army Form C. 2118.

(Erase heading not required.)

Instructions regarding War Diaries and Intelligence Summaries are contained in F.S. Regs., Part II. and the Staff Manual respectively. Title pages will be prepared in manuscript.

Place	Date	Hour	Summary of Events and Information	Remarks and references to Appendices
SOMME	28th	11 a.m.	C.R.A. visits the BOMINE Battery group	R.y.P.
ROCLINCOURT	29th	2 a.m.	Rgn group carried in raid on hostile trenches.	R.y.P.
"	"	10 a.m.	C.R.A. to left Group H.Q. and H.Q. 181st Inf. Bde. Very heavy rain.	R.y.P.
BY RIEZ	30th	11 a.m.	C.R.A. to H.Q. 179th and 180th Inf. Bdes, and to four Fewster and Scalen posts. Rain all day.	R.y.P.
"	"	2.30 a.m.	Left Group co-operated in raid on hostile trenches nr WATLING CRATER. 8 prisoners captured.	R.y.P.
"	31st	6 a.m.	Reorganisation of 60th Divn Arty into 6 gun Batteries completed. 300th F.A. Bde and A/301 Battery abolished and absorbed as follows:— 301st Bde = B/301 + ½ A/301, C/301 + ½ A/301, and D/301 (4 gun How Bty late D/303). 302nd Bde = A/302 + ½ A/302, B/302 + ½ B/300, C/302 + ½ D/300, D/302 (as before 4. guns)(How) 303rd Bde = A/303 + ½ C/300, B/303 + ½ C/300, C/303 + ½ A/300, D/303 (as before 4. guns)(How)	R.y.P.

{ HERMAVILLE
{ 31st August 1916

[signature]
Brig-General
Cmdg 60th Divisional Artillery

SECRET.   APPENDIX I   Copy No. 6.

OPERATION SCHEME No. 1.

(REFERENCE TRENCH MAPS ROCLINCOURT & GIVENCHY 1/10,000).

1. The 179th Infantry Brigade will raid the enemy trenches at A.4.d.5.2. on the evening of Sunday 6th instant.

2. The Artillery will co-operate, engaging targets as shown in attached table.

3. Two 18 pr. Batteries Left Group will carry out a bombardment of hostile trenches about S.28.a.6.1 as a feint to distract the enemy's attention from the actual point to be raided.

4. The following are the arrangements for timing etc:-

   X is the time of the opening of the main Artillery bombardment.
   Our trench mortars will commence wire cutting operations a few minutes before X.
   At X.1 the Feint Bombardment will commence.
   At X.3 Artillery lift, forming a barrage round point to be raided, and raiding party go forward.
   When the Infantry have returned they will send up a shower of green rockets.
   Artillery fire will be maintained on enemy's second line for 10 minutes after this shower of green rockets, and will then cease.
   Batteries who lift their fire at X.3 on to the enemy's support line will "xxxxxxxxxxx continue on the support line until "cease fire".

5. O.C. Centre and Left Groups will meet the Battalion Commander undertaking the raid at H.Q. 179th Infantry Brigade about 4 hours before X on 6th instant to synchronise watches under arrangements to be made direct with G.O.C. 179th Infantry Brigade.

6. The time of X will be notified later.

7. Acknowledge.

                                            R.E.Rance
                                            Major.
                                            Brigade Major.
                                            60th Divisional Artillery.

Issued typewritten at 10-15 a.m. 5th August, 1916.
   Copy No. 1. Centre Group.
     "   " 2. Left Group.
     "   " 3. 179th Infantry Brigade.
     "   " 4. 180th Inf. Bde. (for information)
     "   " 5. War Diary.
     "   " 6. File.

ARTILLERY SCHEME - RAID No. 1.

PHASE 1.

Time.		Battery.	Group.	Target.	Rate of fire.
X.3 to X.8	(a)	1 18 pr.	Centre.	A.10.b.35.65 - A.10.b.35.57.	Section fire 10 seconds
	(b)	1.18 pr.	Centre.	A.10.b.35.57 - A.4.d.35.65.	
	(c)	1 18 pr.	Centre.	A.4.d.35.05. - A.4.d.35.27.	
	(d)	1 18 pr.	Left.	A.4.d.35.27. - A.4.d.42.50.	
	(e)	1 18 pr.	Left.	A.4.d.42.50. - A.4.d.24.75.	
	(f)	1 4.5".	Centre.	A.10.b.35.70. & A.4.d.35.15.	
	(g)	1 4.5".	Left.	A.4.d.52.72. & A.4.d.55.25.	

PHASE 2.

		Target.	Time.	Rate of fire.
(a)		As in Phase 1.	X.3 to 10 minutes after shower of green rockets	X.3 to X.10 Section fire 10 seconds
(b)		A.10.b.60.95 - A.4.d.35.10.		
(c)		A.4.d.35.10. - A.4.d.35.35.		
(d)		A.4.d.35.35. - A.4.d.53.50.		
(e)		A.4.d.60.50. - A.4.d.24.75.		
(f)		1 Section, no change; 1 Section lift from A.4.d.35.15 to A.4.d.32.22.		X.10 to "cease fire" 20 seconds.
(g)		As in Phase 1.		

FEINT BOMBARDMENT.

Time.		Battery.	Group.	Target.	Rate of fire.			Target.	Time.	Rate of fire.
X.1 to X.6.	(h)	1 18 pr.	Left.	S.33.c.6.9. - S.28.a.6.1.	Section fire 10 seconds	(h)		S.28.c.6.9. - S.28.c.8.9½.	X.6 to shower of green rockets	X.6 to X.10 section fire 15 seconds
	(i)	1 18 pr.	Left.	S.28.a.6.1. - S.28.a.7.2.		(i)		S.28.c.8.9½. - S.28.a.9.1.		X.10 to "cease fire" 30 seconds

AMMUNITION. All A.X. and B.X.

Neuville-St-Vaast

been located on a squared
000 scale.
on the trace. Sufficient
own map. A little detail
always given. The trace

Tracing taken from Sheet 51³ N.W.1

of the 1:10,000 map of ROCLINCOURT

Signature _____ Date 3/3/10

SECRET.

APPENDIX II Copy No. 7

OPERATION SCHEME NO. 2.

(REFERENCE TRENCH MAP, ROCLINCOURT. 1/10,000).

1. The 181st Infantry Brigade will raid the hostile trenches about A.23.d.3.7 on the evening of Monday, 7th instant.

2. The Artillery will co-operate, engaging targets as shown in attached table.

3. Two 18 pr. Batteries, Centre Group will carry out a bombardment of hostile trenches about A.16.c.7.5 as a feint to distract the enemy's attention from the point to be raided.

4. The following are the arrangements for timing etc:-

   X. is the time of the opening of the main Artillery Bombardment.
   At X.1. the Feint Bombardment will commence.
   At X.4. the Artillery lift, forming a barrage round the point to be raided, and raiding party go forward.
   A shower of red rockets will be the signal to our raiding party to withdraw. This signal will go up about X.25.
   When our Infantry have completed the withdrawal a shower of green rockets will be sent up.
   This shower of green rockets is the signal to the Artillery to "cease fire".
   Batteries who lift their fire at X.4. on to enemy's support line will continue on the support line until the "cease fire" signal (green rockets) is seen.

5. The Centre Group Howitzer Battery will fire 20 rounds at each of the following points during the afternoon of Monday, 7th instant:-

   A.23.d.15.75.
   A.17.c.17.18.

6. O.C. Right Group will meet the Battalion Commander undertaking the raid about 4 hours before X. on 7th instant in order to synchronise watches, arrangements being made direct through G.O.C. 181st Infantry Brigade.
   Group Commanders are responsible for synchronising the watches of the Batteries of their Group.

7. The time of X. will be notified later.

8. Acknowledge.

R.C.France
Major.
Brigade Major.
60th Divisional Artillery.

Issued typewritten at 10-15 a.m. 5th August, 1916.
   Copy No. 1. Right Group.
   "   "   2. Centre Group.
   "   "   3. R.H.A.
   "   "   4. 181st Infantry Brigade.
   "   "   5. 179th Infantry Brigade.
   "   "   6. War Diary.
   "   "   7. File.

ARTILLERY SCHEME - RAID No. 2.

PHASE 1.

Time.		Battery.	Group.	Target.	Rate of fire.
X.1 to X.5.	(a)	1 18 pr.	Right.	A.25.d.5.5. - A.25.d.4.2½.	Section fire 10 seconds
	(b)	1 18 Pr.	Right.	A.25.d.2½.5. - A.25.d.0½.	
X to X.4.	(c)	1 18 pr.	Right.	A.25.d.5.8. - A.25.c.0½.9½.	
	(d)	1 18 pr.	Right.	A.25.c.0½. - A.25.c.0.1.	
	(e)	5 guns "A" Bty.	M.G.s.	A.25.c.0.5. - A.25.c.4.4.	
	(f)	1 4.5"	Centre.	2 guns. A.25.d.7.5 and 7.4. 1 gun. A.25.d.3.0. 1 gun. A.25.c.9.1.	

PHASE 2.

		Target.	Time.		Rate of fire.
	(a)	As in Phase 1.	X.4 to "cease fire" (green rockets)		X.4 to X.10 Section fire 10 seconds
	(b)	(1 Section A.25.d.4½.5½ - A.25.d.2.5 (1 Section A.25.d.2.9 and 1.9.			
	(c)	A.25.b.1.0. - A.25.a.7½.1.			X.10 to "cease fire" Section fire 20 seconds
	(d)	As for Phase 1.			
	(e)	As for Phase 1.			
	(f)	As for Phase 1.			

PRINT BOMBARDMENT.

		Battery.	Group.	Target.	Rate of fire.	Time.		Target.	Rate of fire.
X.1 to X.5.	(g)	1 18 pr.	Centre.	A.18.c.7.5. - A.18.c.7.8.	Section fire 10 seconds	X.5 to cease fire	(g)	A.18.c.9.2½. - A.18.d.0.5.	X.5 to X.10 Section fire 15 seconds
	(h)	1 18 pr.	Centre.	A.18.c.7.8. - A.18.c.8.7.			(h)	A.18.d.0.5. - A.18.d.1.7.	X.10 to cease fire. Section fire 30 seconds

AMMUNITION. The Section of (b) Battery which enfilades C.T's, will fire 120 "A" in Phase 2.
"A" Battery M.G.s. will 1-clude 120 "A".

O'Meara all A X and BX

use with Artillery Maps.

Hoclincourt

<u>S E C R E T.</u> PRELIMINARY WARNING.

(Reference, Trench Map, ROCLINCOURT.) (Edition 2.C.)
Scale, 1/10,000.

1. A small raid entering the German trenches about A.23.c.9½.7 will take place very shortly.

2. The following targets will be engaged by Batteries as stated:

1st PHASE.

	Battery	Group.	Target.	Paying special attention to
a.	18 Pr.	Right.	A.23.d.5.3. – 2½.5.	2 C.T's. running N.& E.
b.	18 Pr.	Right.	A.23.d.2½.5 – c.9½.7½. – d.½.8½	Projecting point at A.23.d.1.6. whence flanking fire might be brought.
c.	18 Pr.	Right.	A.23.d.½.6 – A.23.c.9½.9½.	(Purposely overlapping b)
d.	18 Pr.	Right.	A.23.c.9½.9½ – A.23.a.6.1½.	3 C.T's. running N.& E.
e.	3 guns "A" Bty.	1st I. R.H.A.	Enfilade trenches A.23.a.0.5½ – A.23.a.4.4.	Junction A.23.a.4.4.
f.	4.5" How.	Centre.	Following C.T. junctions. 2 guns sunken road at A.23.d.7.3½ and 7.4, 1 gun A.23.d.2½.9. 1 gun A.23.a.9½.1.	(All important).

2nd PHASE.

	Battery	Group	Target.	Paying special attention to
a.	18 Pr.	Right.	As in 1st Phase, no change.	As before.
b.	18 Pr.	Right.	1 Section. Support line A.23.d.4½.5½ – 3.6½. 1 Section. C.T's. at A.23.d.2.9. and 1.9.	Junction on road at A.23.d.4½.6. (important).
c.	18 Pr.	Right.	A.23.b.1.0. – A.23.a.8½.1½.–7½.1.	Junction A.23.a.8½.1½.
d.	18 Pr.	Right.	As in 1st Phase, no change.	As before.
e.	3 guns "A" Bty.	1st I. R.H.A.	As in 1st Phase, no change.	As before.
f.	4.5" How.	Centre.	As in 1st Phase, no change.	As before.

3. Batteries should begin to quietly register their targets at once, care being taken not to draw attention to the point.

Major.
Brigade Major.
1st August, 1916.   60th Divisional Artillery.

SECRET.   APPENDIX. III   Copy No. 6

OPERATION SCHEME NO. 3.

(Reference Trench Maps ROCLINCOURT & GIVENCHY 1/10,000).

1. The 180th. Infantry Brigade will raid the enemy trenches at S.28.c.6.9. on the evening of Wednesday 9th. instant.

2. The Artillery will co-operate engaging targets as shown on attached table and plan.

3. The Centre Group will carry out a bombardment of the hostile trenches about A.4.d.3.1. as a feint to distract the enemy's attention from the actual point to be raided.

4. The following are the signals and timing arrangements:-

   The feint bombardment will commence at X - 1.
   X is the time of opening of the main artillery bombardment.
   At X3 the Artillery lift, forming a barrage round the point to be raided, and raiding party go forward.
   When the Infantry have returned they will send up a shower of green rockets.
   This shower of green rockets will be the signal for the Artillery to cease fire.
   Batteries who lift their fire on to the enemy's support line at X3 will continue on the support line until "Cease fire".

5. 4 guns of "Q" Battery R.H.A. are placed under the orders of O.C. Left Group for the purposes of this operation.

6. O.C's Left and Centre Groups will meet the Battalion Commander undertaking the raid, about 4 hours before X on 9th. inst. in order to synchronise watches: arrangements being made direct through G.O.C. 180th. Infantry Brigade.
   Group Commanders are responsible for synchronising the watches of their Batteries.

7. The time of X will be notified later.

8. Acknowledge.

                                    R.L.Hawes
                                    Major.
                                    Brigade Major,
                                    60th. Divisional Artillery.

Copies to:-
   Copy No. 1 Left Group.
          2 Centre Group.
          3 R.H.A.
          4. 179th. Infantry Brigade.
          5 180th. Infantry Brigade.
          6 War Diary.
          7. File.

ARTILLERY SCHEME. RAID NO. 5.

Time.	Battery.	Group.	Target.	Rate of fire.		Time.	Battery. Target.	Rate.
X	3-18 prs. 4 guns "Q" R.H.A. 1st.Indian R.H.A.	Left	Front Barrage. A - B., B - C., C - D., D - E. (under orders of O.C. Left Group.)	X to X3 Section fire 10 secs.	a	X3	Lift to:- A - N., N - K., K - M., M - E.	X3 to X10 Section Fire 10 secs. X10 to "Cease Fire" Section fire 20 Secs.
X	1-4.5"How.	Left	Points F. G. H. & I.	X to X3 points F.& G. Section fire 15 secs. Points H.& I. (B.9. Crater) Section fire 10 seconds.	b	X3	F and G. no change H and I lift to N and P.	X3 to cease fire Section fire 20 seconds.
X	1-4.5"How.	Left.	Points J. K. L. & M.	X to X3. Section fire 15 seconds.	c	X3	No change.	X3 to cease fire Section fire 20 secs.

FEINT BOMBARDMENT.

Time	Battery	Group	Target	Rate of fire		Time	Battery. Target.	Rate.
X - 1	3-18 prs.	Centre	As for raid No. 1. (6th. inst).	X-1 to X.3 Section fire 10 secs.	d	X3	Lift as for raid 1.	X3 to X10 section fire 15 secs. X10 to X15 section fire 30 seconds.
	1-4.5"How.	Centre.	Do Do.	Section fire 15 seconds.	e	X3	Do. Do.	X3 to X15 section fire 30 seconds.

O.C. Centre Group will issue his own orders with regard to the feint bombardment. The Howitzer points fired on during raid No. 1 may be varied (within the area of the feint) on to any points which G.O.C. 179th. Infantry Brigade may desire to have knocked out.
All Guns taking part in the FEINT BOMBARDMENT will cease fire at X15.

Major.
Brigade Major 60th. Div'l. Arty.

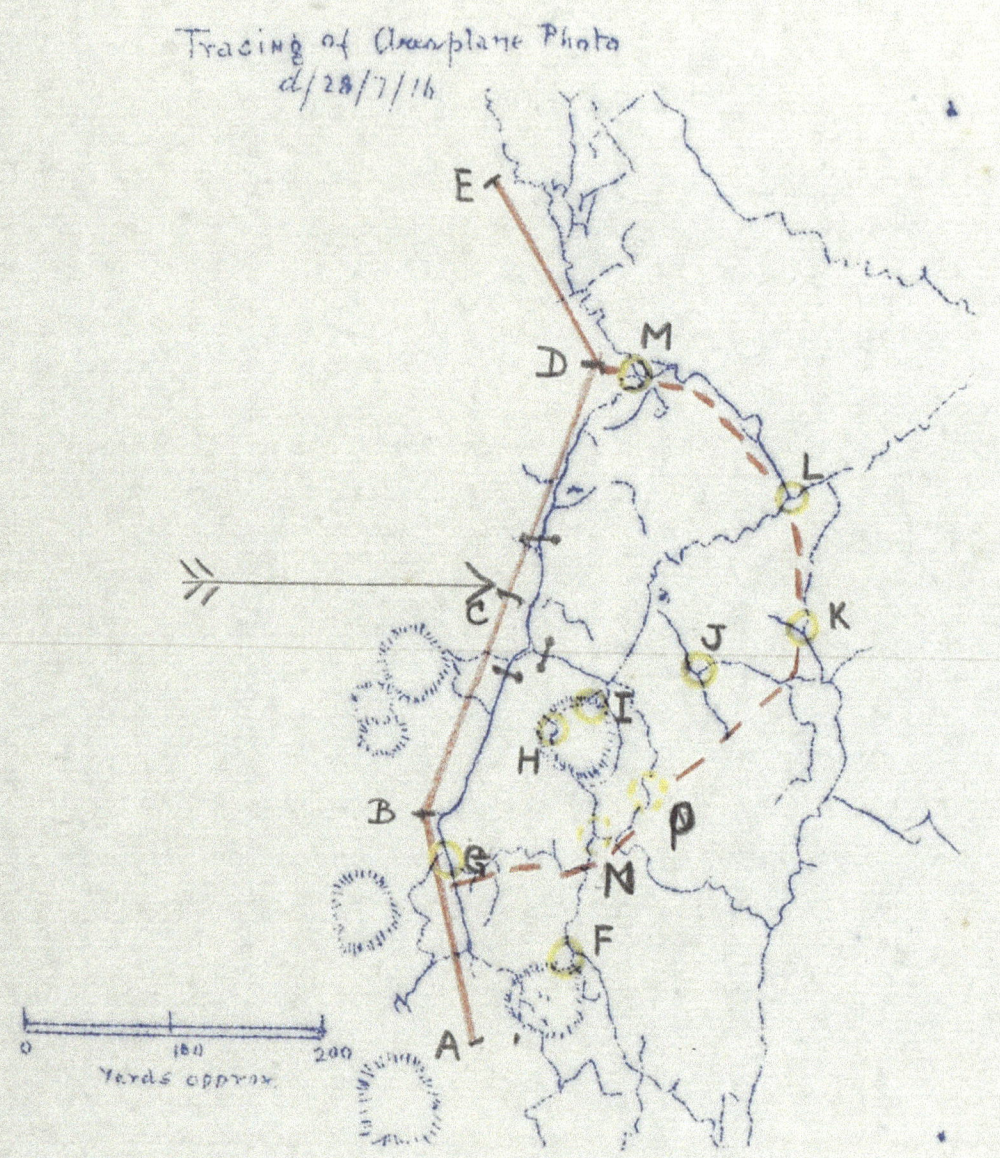

APPENDIX. 4   Copy No. 8

SECRET.

ARTILLERY SCHEME NO. 4.

Reference Plan attached.

1. The 60th. Divisional Artillery will carry out a bombardment of the hostile trenches and T.M. positions in square A.16.b. at 5.0pm. Tuesday 15th. instant, in conjunction with XVIIth. Corps Heavy Artillery.

2. Objects (a) To cause the enemy loss, by enfilade fire on his support and communication trenches (b) to knock out his Trench Mortars located at A.16.b.67.57, A.16.b.57.62 and A.16.b.27.13.

3. Batteries will engage targets as detailed in attached plan.

4. Timing arrangements are as follows:-

Time	Phase	Details
5.0pm - 5.1pm	Phase 1.	18-pdrs. Section Fire 5 secs. All Shrapnel. 4.5" Howitzers, Section fire 10 Seconds. H.E.
5.1pm - 5.2pm	PAUSE.	
5.2pm - 5.3pm	Phase 1 continued.	18-pdrs. Section fire 5 seconds All H.E. 4.5" Hows. Section fire 10 seconds. All H.E.
5.3pm - 5.5pm	PAUSE.	
5.5pm - 5.10pm	Phase II.	Howitzers and selected 18-pdr. Batteries concentrate on T.M. positions. 18-pdrs. Section fire 15 secs. All H.E. 4.5" Hows. Section fire 15 seconds All H.E.
5.10pm	CEASE FIRE.	

---

5. An officer with a watch from each group Headquarters and R.H.A. will meet a Staff Officer at Centre Group Headquarters on 15th. inst. at a time to be notified later to synchronise watches.

6. Trench Mortars will co-operate on hostile front line system between PARIS and ARGYLE Craters, under orders of the D.O.T.M.

7. acknowledge.

R.E.France
Major.
Brigade Major,
60th. Divisional Artillery.

Copies to:-
Copy No.1 1st. Indian R.H.A.
2 Right Group.
3 Centre "
4 Left Group.
5 D.O.T.M.
6 179 Inf.Bde.
7 181st.Inf.Bde.
8 War Diary.
9 File.

SECRET.

ARTILLERY SCHEME NO. 4.

		Phase I. (X to X.1. and X.2. to X.3.)			Phase II. (X.5. to X.10.)	
Battery.	Group.	Time.	Target.	Rate of fire.	Target.	Rate of fire.
(a) A/301	Right	X to X.1.	1 section only. Search between points A and B.	18-pdr. Section fire 5 seconds. 4.5" Hows. " 10 "	(a) Cease fire.	18-pdrs. Section fire 15 secs. Hows. Section fire 15 secs.
(b) B/301	"		Search between points C. and D.		(b) Cease fire.	
(c) C/301	"		Search from E. to F. and from G to H.		(c) Concentrate all guns on point Y.	
(d) B/300	"		Search M – F – H – N.		(d) Concentrate all guns on point Y.	
(e) A/302	Centre.	X.1. & X.2. to X.3.	Search I – C – E – G.		(e) Concentrate all guns pn point Z.	
(f) B/302	"		1 section only. Search from K to L.		(f) Concentrate section on Point Z.	
(g) D/302	"		1 section. Trench mortar point at point Z. 1 section. 2 trench mortars at point Y.		(g) 1 section on Z. continue on Z. 1 section continue on Y.	
(h) Detached section "Q" R.H.A. LA TARGETTE.			Search C.T. from point Y – H – X – LILLE Road at O.		(h) Concentrate section on point Y.	
(i) C/305	Left.		Search between points B and N. 1 section. 2 trench mortars at point Y.		(i) Cease fire.	
(j) D/305	"		1 section. Point X.		(j) Concentrate all guns on point Y.	

NOTE:- All the above 18-pdr. Batteries are selected to obtain absolute enfilade fire in Phase I.

Square A.16.c
Scale 1.5000

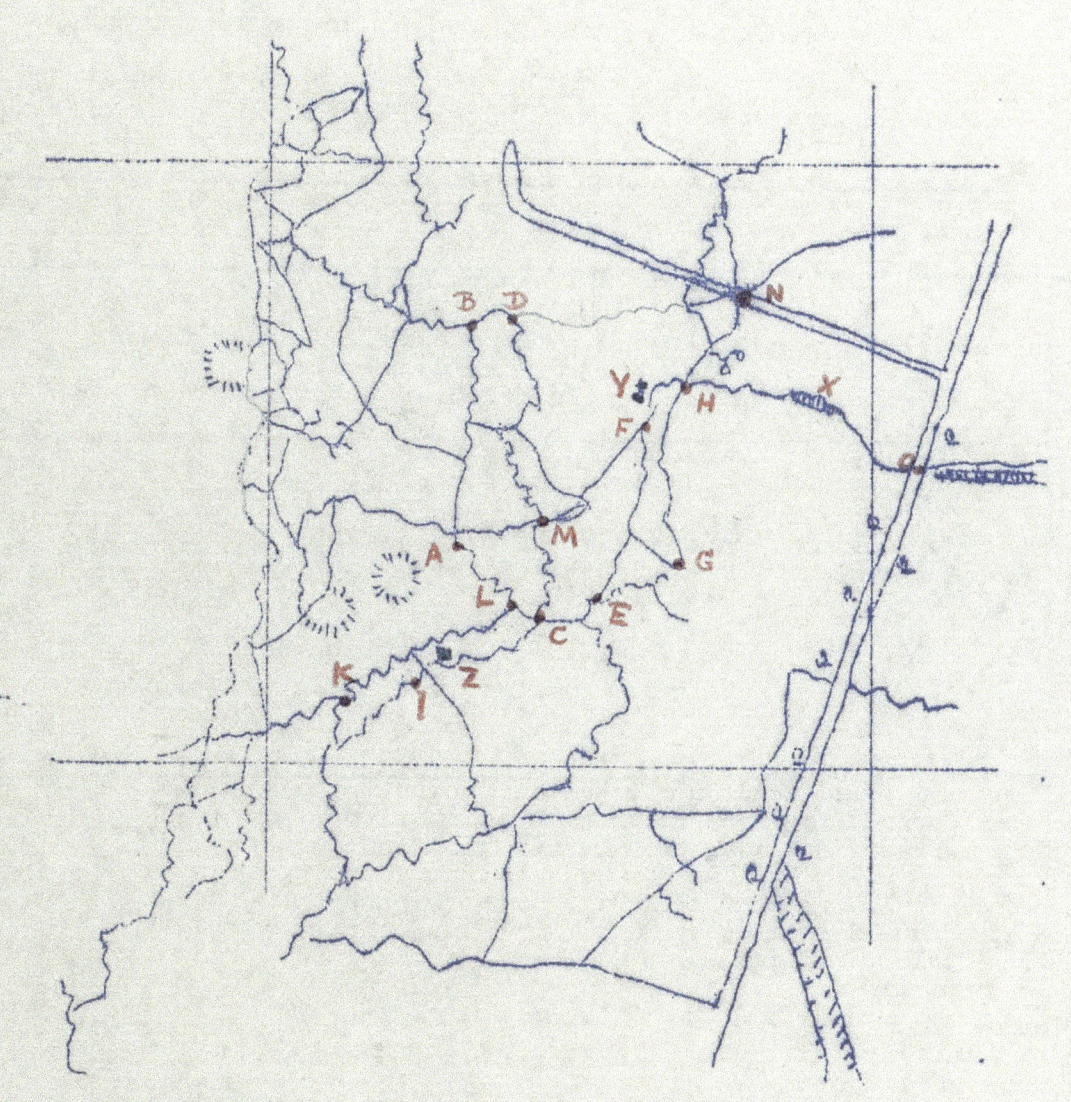

APPENDIX 5

SECRET.   Copy No. 41.

ARTILLERY SCHEME No.5.

(Ref. Trench Map ROCLINCOURT 1/10,000)

1. A relief is expected to be carried out by the enemy opposite our Centre Sector on the night 19th/20th August.

2. The following targets will be engaged by Centre and Right Group Batteries during the night 19th/20th with the object of causing the enemy loss:-

Group.	Battery.	Target.
RIGHT.	A/301.	Enfilade railway in sunken road A.17.b.9.0. - A.12.c.4.7.
	B/301.	Enfilade German 2nd line trenches from A.17.b.3.6. - A.11.d.8.4.
	C/301.	Enfilade A.16.b.7.3. - A.10.d.9.4.
CENTRE. v	A/302.	Enfilade KRAMER AVENUE from A.16.b.4.7. - A.11.d.2.4.
	C/302.	Enfilade EMPEROR AVENUE A.17.b.0.6. - A.12.d.2.$\frac{1}{2}$.
	A/300.	Trench junctions round TREE B.13.c.6.9.
	D/302	Trench junctions A.16.b.7.8. and A.16.b.8.8. and junction of EMPEROR AVENUE with 2nd line at A.17.b.5$\frac{1}{2}$.7. and A.17.b.6$\frac{1}{4}$.7$\frac{1}{2}$.

The first five batteries in above list will search the whole length of their targets at different times, paying special attention to trench junctions.

3. All 18.pr. Batteries will fire 2 rounds a minute and D/302 1 round a minute on the above targets at the following hours:-

				TOTAL.
10.10pm.	to	10.15pm.	(5 minutes)	
10.32pm.	to	10.37pm.	(do)	
11.4 pm.	to	11.9 pm.	(do)	
11.20pm.	to	11.25pm.	(do)	50 minutes.
11.31pm.	to	11.36pm.	(do)	100 rds. per
12.3 am.	to	12.8 am.	(do)	18 pr. bty.
12.15 am.	to	12.16 am.	(1 minute)	
12.52am.	to	12.57am.	(5 minutes)	
1.5am.	to	1.7am.	(2 minutes)	50 rds. per
2.0am.	to	2.2am.	(2 minutes)	4.5" bty.
3.55am.	to	4.0am.	(5 minutes)	
4.31am.	to	4.36am.	(5 minutes)	

4. 18 prs. will use shrapnel only.

5. Watches will be synchronised by the firing of one Green rocket by Right group H.Q. from A.5.central at 9.0pm. and again at 10.0pm.

3. Code name for this scheme will be BELINDA.

[signature]

Brigade Major.
30th Divisional Artillery.

18/8/1916.

Copy No. 1. Right Group.
      2. Centre Group.
      3. 179th Inf. Bde.
      4. 180th Inf. Bde.
      5. 181st Inf. Bde.
      6. Left Group (for information)
      7. R.H.A.   (do.)
      8. H.Q.30th Divn. (do.)
      9. D.O.T.M.
10 & 11. War Diary.
    12. File.

APPENDIX. 6 War Diary

SECRET.   Copy No.

ARTILLERY SCHEME "CHRISTABEL"

(Ref. Trench Maps ROCLINCOURT and GIVENCHY.1:10,000)

(1) The Divisional Artillery will carry out a combined shoot on dug-outs etc. behind enemy lines on Wednesday 23rd.instant.

(2) Targets will be engaged as under:-

Group.	Battery.	Target.	Ammunition.
R.H.A.	4 guns "A"	Trench A.17.b.6½.8.- A.18.a.2.9.	AX
"	4 guns "Q"	Dug-outs S.29.d.8.7.- S.29.d.9½.8.	A
"	2 guns "Q"	Dump at Railway Terminus A.17.d.5.1.	AX
RIGHT.	A/301	Dug-outs in sunken road from A.12.d.6.5. to A.12.d.5.9½.	A
"	B/301	Houses along road A.12.a.4½.0 to A.12.a.5.3.	AX
"	C/301	BOIS CARRÉ B.7.c.4.5½. especially trench along Eastern edge.	A
"	B/300	Trench parallel to railway A.17.b.8½.2.- A.17.b.9.3.	AX
CENTRE.	A/302	Large house and enclosure at S.E. end of THELUS at A.12.b.2.1.	A
"	B/302	Trench A.12.d.5.½.- A.12.d.7.½.	AX
"	C/302	Trench under trees A.12.d.3.7. to A.12.d.6.5.	A
"	A/300	1 Section.BOIS CARRÉ B.7.c.4.5½.especially East end. 1 Section.Dug-outs along LILLE road S.29.b.9.0. - S.30.a.1.5.	A / A

Group.	Battery.	Target.	Ammunition.
LEFT.	A/303	Dug-outs along trench S.23.a.7.1.-S.23.d.0.6.	A
"	B/303	Dug-outs along LILLE road S.29.b.9.0.-S.30.a.1.5.	A
"	C/303	Dug-outs along bank S.30.c.0.7. to S.30.a.7.2.	A
"	C/300	N.W. edge of BONVAL WOOD S.30.c.0.3. to S.30.c.5.5.	A
		Total.	A. 480 AX. 216

(3) All Batteries will fire 3 rounds 'gun-fire' at the following hours:-
5.am. 6.am. 7.pm. 7.35.pm.

(4) O.C. Right Group will fire one red and one green rocket in quick succession from G.3.central at 4.30.am. 23rd.instant.

R. C. Rance
Major.
Brigade Major.
30th Divisional Artillery.

22nd August 1916.

Copies to
no 1. R.H.A
2. Right
3. Centre
4. Left
5. 60 Div
6. 179th ⎫
7. 180th ⎬ for information
8. 181st ⎭
9.⎫ War Diary
10.⎭   11 File

SECRET.   Copy No.

ARTILLERY SCHEME "DELILAH".
(Ref. Trench Map BOULESCOURT—1:10,000)

The Divisional Artillery will bombard Trench Mortar positions at A.13.d.80.60. and A.17.c.15.18. at 3.45 pm. on Friday 25th instant. Targets as under:—

Time.	Group.	Batteries.	Phase 1.				Phase 11.		
			Target.	Ammn.	Rate.	Time.	Target.	Ammn.	Rate.
3.45pm	R.H.A.	Detchd.sectn."Q"	Trench A.13.d.7.3. –A.17.c.3.1.	A	Section fire at 5 seconds.	3.50pm.	Trench Mortars at A.17.c. 15.18.	AX	18 prs.Section fire 10 secs 60 secs. How. Section fire 20 secs.
to	Right.	3.18 prs.Btys.	Trenches, A.16.d.7.0.- A.16.d.7½.3.- A.16.d.7.3.- A.16.d.8.5½.- A.23.a.0.7.- A.17.c.3.1.	A		to	2Btys.Trench Mortar at A.16.d. 80.60. 1 Bty. Trench Mortar at A.17.c. 15.18.	AX	
3.47pm.	Centre.	2.18 pr.Btys. 1.4.5"How.Bty.	Nil.			4.0pm.	one 18 pr.Bty.Trench Mortar at A.17.c.15.18. one 18 pr.Bty.Trench Mortar at A.13.d.80.50. 1 section 4.5"How.Trench Mortar at A.17.c.15.18. 1 section 4.5"How.Trench Mortar at A.16.d.80.60.	AX BX	

(Total Ammn. 168.A. 660.AX. 60.BX.

O.C. Right Group will arrange to synchronize watches of his Batteries.
Centre Group will take the time from the opening of fire by Right Group in Phase 1.

Copies to:- 1.R.H.A.   4&5.War Diary.   8.181st.Inf.Bde for infrm
            2.Right Group.   6.File.   "   "   "
            3.Centre Group.   7.Divl.H.Q.for information.10.D.O.T.M.

Vol 4

Confidential

War Diary

of

Headquarters, 60th Divl. Artillery.

From 1st to 30th Sept. 1916.

(Volume 4).

(I.) September 1916.   WAR DIARY of H.Q. 60th DIVISIONAL ARTILLERY   Army Form C. 2118.
of
INTELLIGENCE SUMMARY.
(Erase heading not required.)

Instructions regarding War Diaries and Intelligence Summaries are contained in F.S. Regs., Part II. and the Staff Manual respectively. Title pages will be prepared in manuscript.

Place	Date	Hour	Summary of Events and Information	Remarks and references to Appendices
	Sept			
MT ST ELOI	1st	10 am	CRA inspected Left ARTY Group H.Q's and B.T.Y. positions of H.Q's 180th INF BDE	R.P. APPENDIX I
FORS DE VAUX	2nd	10 am	CRA visits Centre and Right ARTY Group H.Q's and B/301 & B/302 B.5 positions. Bombardment of hostile T.M's	R.P.
			Captain F.C. WOOTTEN posted from A.D.C. to C.R.A. to B/303 Battery R.F.A. and joined accordingly	R.P.
ETRUN	3rd	"	CRA visits H.Q's 181st Inf BDE and judges turn out and horses Competition of B Echelon D.A.C.	R.P.
MT ST ELOI	4th	9.30 am	CRA reconnoitred for B.T.Y positions in view of possibility of movement of another Divl ARTY in line	R.P.
HERMAVILLE	"	5 pm	Lieut R.G. SOUTHEY arrived from 17th DIV ARTY on appointment as A.D.C. to CRA	R.P.
NEUVILLE St VAAST	5th	11 am	CRA & H.Q's 179th and 180th Inf BDES and to H.Q's Right ARTY Group. Rain all day	R.P.
FORD DENNE	6th	2.30 pm	CRA & H.Q's Centre ARTY Group	R.P. APPENDIX II
—	"	6 am	DIV ARTY maintained weapons barrage fire on all enemy communication trenches from 6 am till midnight	R.P.
NEUVILLE	7th	10-11 am	CRA visits H.Q's 179th and 180th Inf BDES and Centre and Left Sector Trenches	R.P.
"	"	9 pm	"A" and "G" Batteries, 1st Indian R.H.A. BDE withdrawn from action and rejoin 1st Indian Cav. BDE	R.P.
(CAPELLE FERFAICHT & FREMIN CORBIE)	8th	11.30 am 2 pm	C.R.A. inspects wagon lines of 303rd BDE R.F.A. and No. 1 and 3. Section D.A.C.	R.P. APPENDIX III
"	"	6.30 pm	Bombardment of hostile communication trenches and back areas by DIV ARTY throughout the night & various smaller	R.P.
ETRUN NEUVILLE	9th	9.45 am	CRA to H.Q's 179th, 180th and 181st Inf BDE, and to H.Q's Left ARTY. Group	R.P.
FORT GEORGE	"	3 pm	CRA watched practice in rapid concentration of fire on selected targets by DIV ARTY	R.P.
ACHICOURT	10th	9.45 am	CRA to D.T.M.O., H.Q's Right and Centre ARTY Groups, 2/1st Trench Mortar Battery, and front trenches and crater positions Centre and Right Sector	R.P.

WAR DIARY of H.Q. 60th Divisional Artillery

INTELLIGENCE SUMMARY

Army Form C. 2118.

Instructions regarding War Diaries and Intelligence Summaries are contained in F.S. Regs., Part II. and the Staff Manual respectively. Title pages will be prepared in manuscript.

(Erase heading not required.)

Place	Date	Hour	Summary of Events and Information	Remarks and references to Appendices
	Sept.			
NEUVILLE	11th	3 a.m.	Divl ARTY cooperated in two successful raids by 180th and 179th Inf BDES	Rep
		3.30 a.m.		
	11	11 a.m.	CRA visits HQ 180th Inf BDE and left Sector Centre posts. All available men engaged in preparation of	Rep
			gun pits for a Second Divl ARTY in line	Rep
HERMAVILLE	12th	10 a.m.	Conference between BGRA XVII Corps, CRA 30th Div & CRA 60th Div. DTMO	Rep
LIGNY ST FLOCHEL	11	3 p.m.	CRA in demonstration at Trench Mortar School	Rep
BERTINVAL	13th	12.30 pm	CRA inspects work on new BTY positions B'vals left and Centre ARTY Group HQ. Heavy Rain 8.30 pm	Rep
FORT OKLAHOMA	14th	10 a.m.	CRA & HQ's Centl ARTY Group and 180th Inf BDE. Also to left Sector Centre posts. Plans in progress weather colder	Rep
ROCLINCOURT	15th	11 a.m.	CRA visits Right Sector front trenches and Centre posts	Rep
NEUVILLE	16th	11 a.m.	CRA visits Y/60 Trench Mortar Battery and Heavy T.M. emplacements under construction in Left Sector	Rep
NEUVILLE	17th	10.30 am	CRA visits HQ's 179th and 183rd Inf BDES, and 2/60 Trench Mortar Battery	Rep
AGNEZ-LES-DUISANS	18th	10 a.m.	CRA visits CRA 35th Div and HQ 182nd Inf BDE. Heavy Rain all day	Rep
ROCLINCOURT	19th	10.30 am	CRA to HQ Right ARTY BDE and all Right Group Batteries. Heavy Rain all day	Rep
NEUVILLE	20th	11 a.m.	CRA & HQs Centre ARTY Group and to HQ's 179th and 180th Inf BDES. Rain	Rep
ACQ & TARREST RD	21st	10 a.m.	CRA inspects all Battery Wagon Lines	Rep
AUX RIETZ	22nd	11 am	CRA visits 179th Inf TMB HQ's and Centre Sector front trenches and sapes	Rep
ETRUN	23rd	9.45 am	CRA visits HQ XVII Corps Heavy ArMbly, 181st Inf BDE, 2/60 Trench Mortar Battery, and D/303 BTY	Rep
			Guns received curtailing ammunition expenditure of 18 pdrs.	Rep

T2134. Wt. W708—776. 500,000. 4/15. Sir J. C. & S.

Army Form C. 2118.

WAR DIARY of H.Q. 60th DIVISIONAL ARTILLERY

or INTELLIGENCE SUMMARY.

September

(Erase heading not required.)

Instructions regarding War Diaries and Intelligence Summaries are contained in F.S. Regs., Part II. and the Staff Manual respectively. Title pages will be prepared in manuscript.

Place	Date	Hour	Summary of Events and Information	Remarks and references to Appendices
	Sept			
ETRUN NEUVILLE	24th	11.30am	CRA visits H.Qr 179th, 180th and 181st INF BDES	R.J.P
NEUVILLE	25th	11.30am	CRA visits Left Sector Front Trenches and Sapes and D/303 Battery	R.J.P
CAPELLE HERMONT	26th	10.45am	CRA visits wagon lines 303rd ARTY BDE	R.J.P
MT ST ELOI	"	2.30pm	CRA visits Central Trophies Exchange and Heavy ARTY Bureau Exchange	R.J.P
MAZIN	27th	11 am	CRA visits Heavy Artillery Batteries 12", 9.2" Anti Aircraft Battery, A/302 BTY and Centre Group ARTY H.Q.	R.J.P
NEUVILLE	28th	11 am	CRA visits 179th and 182nd INF BDES. New Trench Railway, Heavy TM Bombardment, new battalion. & D/303	R.J.P
ANZIN	29th	3 pm	CRA to Right ARTY Group H.Qs	R.J.P
	30th	11.am	CRA visits H.Qs 179th, 180th, 181st INF BDES, Centre and Left ARTY Groups.	R.J.P

HERMAVILLE
30/Sept/19.16

H. Sampson Walker
Brig. General
Commanding 60th Divisional Artillery

APPENDIX I

War Diary Copy No 1/XI.

ARTILLERY SCHEME GERTRUDE.
(Ref. attached diagram)

(1) The Divisional Artillery will bombard hostile trenches and Trench Mortars in A.i.d. on Saturday, September 2nd as follows:-

Group.	Battery.	Phase I.		Phase II.		Phase III.		Ammn.	Remarks.
		Time.	Target.	Time.	Target.	Time.	Target.		Targets and ammunition to be sub-allotted by Group Commanders.
CENTRE.	3.18pr.Btys.	3.30 - 3.35.	A to E	3.38 - 3.43.	1.Bty.remain on SHEBA. 1.Bty.A to B 1.Bty.E to F	3.45 - 3.50.	P-F-F-D-E	450 AX) per group for 150 BX) whole bombardment.	
	1.4.5"Bty.	3.30 - 3.35.	1 Section area A 1 Section area E	3.38 - 3.43.	1.Section area E. 1.Section area F.	3.45 - 5.50.	1.Section area D. 1.Section area F.		
LEFT and R.H.A.	2.18pr.Btys. 4 guns "Q" R.H.A.	3.30 - 3.35.	E to L	3.38 - 3.43.	K to J	3.45 - 5.50.	H to P		
	1.4.5"Bty.	3.30 - 3.35.	1.Section area G. 1.Section area L.	3.38 - 3.43.	1.Section area J. 1.Section area K.	3.45 - 5.50.	1.Section area H. 1.Section area K.		

(2) The XVII Corps Heavy Artillery will bombard SHEBAS BREASTS from 3 pm. to 3.50 pm.

(3) The D.O.T.M. will arrange to co-operate with all available Trench Mortars on the bombarded front, concentrating especially on SHEBAS BREASTS and areas L and G. The Trench Mortars will commence fire at 3.30 pm.

(4) Watches will be synchronized over the telephone at NOON, 2nd prox. Group Commanders will arrange to synchronize the watches of their Batteries.

(5) Trenches opposite area of bombardment should be cleared by 2.45 pm.

Copies:- (1) Centre group. (2) Left Group. (3) R.H.A. (4) D.O.T.M. (5) XVIIth Corps Heavy Artillery.
(6) 179th Inf.Bde. (7) 181st Inf.Bde. (8) H.Q.60th Division (9 & 10) War Diary (LI) File.

R.C. Grant
Brigade Major.
60th Divisional Artillery.

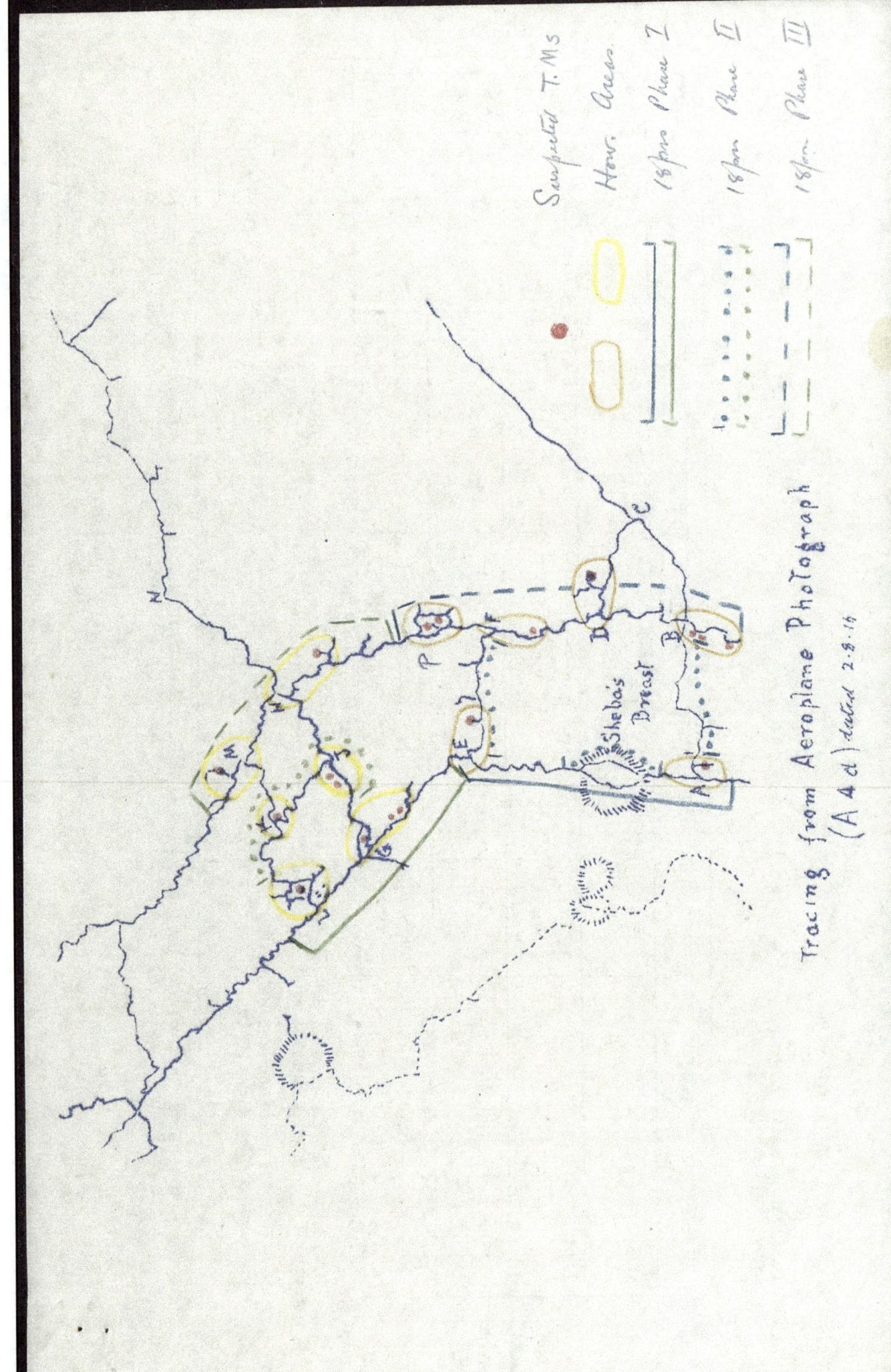

APPENDIX II
War Diary

SECRET.   Copy No. 6

ARTILLERY SCHEME "FLOSSIE."

(1) The Divisional Artillery will maintain an irregular sniping fire on all main enemy communication trenches on 'X' day as under.

(2) Group Commanders will arrange for one section of 18-prs. to engage each of the following Trench junctions :-

Group.	Trench junctions.
RIGHT.	A.24.a.2.9. A.17.d.4.2. A.17.d.4.6. A.17.c.1½.7. A.17.b.3½.8. A.11.d.8.2.
CENTRE.	A.17.a.4.5. A.17.a.4.9. A.13.b.7½.8. A.11.c.1.9¾. A.11.a.1.5. and 0.4. A.5.c.5.5½. A.5.a.9.1.
LEFT.	A.5.a.4.2. A.4.b.8½.5. S.29.c.2.2. S.29.c.2½.4½. S.28.b.6½.0. S.22.d.4½.5. S.22.a.9.4½.

(3) Each Section will fire 10 rounds per hour at irregular intervals on its target during the following periods :-

6 am. to 7 am.	4.30 pm. to 5.30 pm.
7.30am. to 8.30 am.	6.30 pm. to 7.30 pm.
9.30am. to 10.30am.	8.30 pm. to 9.30 pm.
NOON. to 1 pm.	11 pm. to MIDNIGHT.

(4) Each Section will fire a total of 80 rounds, of which as much as possible should be "A".

AMMUNITION :- RIGHT GROUP.   6.Sections=80 X 6 = 480
              CENTRE GROUP. 7.Sections=80 X 7 = 560
              LEFT GROUP.   7.Sections=80 X 7 = 560

                                    Total.   1600

R.C.Ranken
Major.
Brigade Major.
60th Divisional Artillery.

Copies to :- (1) Right Group. (2) Centre Group.
(3) Left Group. (4) 1st Indian R.H.A. (5) 60th Division.
(6 & 7) War Diary. (8) File.

Secret APPENDIX III Copy No 6

ARTILLERY SCHEME. "GERTIE."
(Ref. Trench Map. MOEUVRECOURT 1:10,000)

An enemy relief is expected opposite our Left on the night 8/9th inst.
The Divisional Artillery will assist as follows :-

Time.	Group.	Battery.	Target.	Ammunition.
a 6.30 pm.	Left.	1.How.Bty.	1.Section Railway Bridge T.26.a.3.0½.	
			1.Section Railway Bridges T.13.d.8.4. (Section Salvoes on each)	12 BX
- 7 pm.	(as in a)		Repeat a.	12 BX
b 7.15 pm.	Left.	1.How.Bty.	(1.Section Cross Roads S.18.c.9.2. (1.Section Road junction T.25.a.6.9.	8 BX
		1.How.Bty.	(1.Section Cross Roads T.19.c.1½.4½. (1.Section Cross tracks S.30.b.9.3.	8 BX
		1.18-pr.Bty.	Tracks and road round S.30.b.9.3.	18 A
		1.18-pr.Bty.	Roads round S.30.a.6½.2½.	18 A
		1.18-pr.Bty.	Tracks and trench from CHAMP POURRI WOOD to S.25.b.6½.9.	18 A
	Centre.	1.How.Bty.	1.Section Road junction S.30.a.6½.2½.	
			1.Section Road junction S.29.d.3.2.	8 BX
- 8 pm.	(as in b)		Repeat b	8 BX or 18 A per Bty.
c 10.10pm. to 10.40pm.	Left.	1.18-pr.Bty.	Search COMMUNE C.T. (STAUBWASSER WEG)	
		1.18-pr.Bty.	Search FOLLY C.T. (ARTILLERIE WEG)	
		1.18-pr.Bty.	Search BONVAL C.T. (PRINZ ARNOLF GRABEN)	45 A per Battery.
	Centre.	1.18-pr.Bty.	Search DUMP AVENUE (especially junction at S.29.c.2.2.)	
		1.18-pr.Bty.	Search GRENADIER GRABEN.	
		1.18-pr.Bty.	Search BALLOON AVENUE. (Irregular sniping fire - Enfilade where possible)	
d 11 pm. to 11.2 pm.	Left Centre.	18-prs. and 4.5"Hows.	Bombardment of hostile support line between NEUVILLE - THELUS road and North Divisional Boundary by all guns and howitzers on ordinary Barrage frontages and points. (Note. Our Outpost line will NOT) (be cleared and enemy front line) (will not be fired on.)	20 AX per 18-pr.Bty. 20 BX per 4.5"How.Bty.
- 11.30 pm. to 11.32 pm.	(as in d)		Repeat d	as in d
- 11.40 pm. to midnight.	(as in c)		Repeat c	25 A per Bty.
- 12.15 am.	(as in b)		Repeat b	18 A per 18-pr.Bty. 8 BX per How.Bty.
- 12.30 am.	(as in b)		Repeat b	18 A per 18-pr.Bty. 8 BX per How.Bty.
- 1.15 am.	(as in a)		Repeat a	12 BX

ARTILLERY SCHEME "G E R T I E" (contd)

Time.	Group.	Battery.	Target.	Ammunition.
1.25 am.	Left Centre	all 4.5" How.Btys.	Final salvo by all Howitzer batteries on Battalion Commander's Dug-out at S.29.c.2½.5.	4 HX per Bty.

G O D S A V E T H E K I N G.

R.C.Rance
Major.
Brigade Major.
60th Divisional Artillery.

6th September 1916.

Copies to :-
    (1)   179th Infantry Brigade.
    (2)   180th   do.   do.
    (3)   H.Q. 60th Division.
    (4)   Centre Group.
    (5)   Left Group.
(6 & 7)   War Diary.
    (8)   File.

CONFIDENTIAL.

WAR DIARY

of

HEADQUARTERS, 60th. DIVISIONAL ARTILLERY.

From:- 1st. October 1916.   To:- 31st. October 1916.

VOLUME 10.

WAR DIARY H.Q. 60th Divisional Artillery

INTELLIGENCE SUMMARY

October

Place	Date	Hour	Summary of Events and Information	Remarks and references to Appendices
			attack	
NEUVILLE ST VAAST	1st	10 a.m.	CRA visits HQ 179th INF BDE, Front Trenches Centre Sector, and HQ Centre ARTY Group	Ref.
"	2nd	2 a.m.	Left ARTY Group supported raid by 180th INF BDE. Trenches entered but no prisoners captured	Ref.
FOND RE JULIE	"	11 a.m.	CRA visits Centre and Left ARTY BDE HQs. Rain all day	Ref.
ETRUN, etc.	3rd	10.30 a.m.	CRA visits HQ 179th, 180th, 181st INF BDEs and Left ARTY Group. Rain morning	Ref.
ETRUN, ROCLINCOURT	4th	11 a.m.	CRA visits HQ 181st INF BDE. Right ARTY Group HQ, Front Trenches Right Sector, and 2/60 T.M.B'y.	Ref.
LARESSET	5th	11 a.m.	CRA visits Wagon lines 301st and 303rd F.A. BDES. B/2 Major proceeds on 7 days leave to England	Ref.
ECOIVRES	6th	9.30 a.m.	CRA to HQ XVII Corps Heavy Artillery. 179th and 181st INF BDES and Centre Sector Trenches	Ref.
AUX RIETZ, etc.	7th	10 a.m.	CRA to HQrs. 29th DIV ARTY, XVII Corps H.A., 179th and 180th INF BDES, Centre Group BTYs and Left Group HQ	Ref.
LIGNY ST FLOCHU	8th	10.30 a.m.	CRA to Trench Mortar School	Ref.
"	"	2.30 p.m.	CRA to HQrs 14th DIV ARTY and HQ Right Group ARTY	Ref.
ROCLINCOURT	"	8.45 p.m.	Right Group 60th Div ARTY cooperated with 35th DIV ARTY in successful bombardment of hostile trenches	
"	"	—	Combined with gas projection by 35th Div.	Ref.
AUBIGNY	9th	9.15 a.m.	CRA to HQ XVII Corps ARTY, HQs 179th and 180th INF BDES, C.Os and Left ARTY Group	Ref.
LA TARGETTE	10th	11 a.m.	CRA to HQrs 179th INF BDE, Left Sector Trenches and HQ Centre ARTY Group	Ref.
NEUVILLE ST VAAST	11th	3 a.m.	Enemy attempt raid on Trenches between LES TILLEULS and NEUVILLE ST VAAST but failed to enter our Front line	Ref.
"	"	11 a.m.	CRA to HQ 180th INF BDE. Reconnaissance for additional Battery Positions in case of attack from the North	Ref.

Army Form C. 2118.

WAR DIARY
of H.Q. 60th Divisional Artillery
INTELLIGENCE SUMMARY.
(Erase heading not required.)

Place	Date	Hour	Summary of Events and Information	Remarks and references to Appendices
	6th October			
HERMAVILLE	12th	9 a.m.	Staff Captain proceeds on 7 days leave to ENGLAND. B/M Major returns.	Ref?
ECOURT St	13th	9.30 a.m	CRA to HQ XVII Corps H.A. 179th, 190th and 181st Inf. Bdes and D.T.M.O.	Ref?
FEND DE VASE	14th	10 a.m	CRA to HQ and all B/y positions. Cinder ARTY Group, and to HQ XVII Corps H.A.	Ref.
ROCLINCOURT	15th	3 a.m.	Right ARTY Group co-operated in raid by 181st Inf. BDE. Hostile trenches entered. No prisoners	Ref?
ROCLINCOURT — VIMY	16th	8.30 a.m.	Bombardment of hostile Trench Mortar positions, which have recently caused damage and loss.	
			XVII Corps H.A. fired from 8.30 am – 11.30 am and from 1.30 pm – 4.30 pm. The 60th Divl ARTY from	
			10.30 am – 11.45 am and from 3.30 pm – 4.45 pm, being employed chiefly in cutting the fire of W/60	
			Heavy Trench Mortar Battery, which opened fire for the first time. Present Heavy T.M. ammunition	
			found to be defective and dangerous	Ref?.
HERMAVILLE	17th	10 a.m.	CRA proceeds on 7 days leave to ENGLAND. Lt Col C.H. BAYLEY. D.S.O. assumes	
			duties of CRA.	Ref?
AUBIGNY	"	5.30 p.m	Conference on ARTY employment under B.G.R.A. XVII Corps. CRA and B/y attended	Ref?
ECOIVRES	18th	9.45 a.m	CRA to HQ XVII Corps H.A.	Ref?
	"	Noon	88th Siege Battery placed under tactical control of 60th Div ARTY. Heavy Rain	Ref?.
SAVY	19th	10 a.m	CRA to Ordnance workshops. Lt Col H.H. DRAKE assumed duties of CRA vice Lt Col H. BAYLEY	Ref?
"	"		Staff Captain returns from leave.	Ref?

Army Form C. 2118.

WAR DIARY
of HQ. 60th Divisional Artillery
INTELLIGENCE SUMMARY.
Part II

Instructions regarding War Diaries and Intelligence Summaries are contained in F.S. Regs., Part II. and the Staff Manual respectively. Title pages will be prepared in manuscript.

(Erase heading not required.)

Place	Date	Hour	Summary of Events and Information	Remarks and references to Appendices
	October			
SAVY	20th	4.30 p.m.	519th (How) Battery discontinued on posting to 60th Div Arty and to billets in A.C.Q.	Rep
FOND PÉVASE	"	2 p.m.	M.G.R.A. 1st Army inspects Centre Group Battery Position	Rep
ECON. MORRIEN	21st	11.30 a.m.	ACRA to Centre Arty Group HQrs, and to HQrs 179th and 181st INF BDES. From.	Rep
LA TARGETTE	22nd	11 a.m.	ACRA to 180th INF BDE HQ and HQrs Left Group BTS.	Rep
"	"		519 (How) BTY posted to 20th BDE (A/301) and brought into action during evening, over tactical orders that	Rep
"			of Left BDE Group	
LA TARGETTE	23rd	11 a.m.	2nd CAN Divnl. M/301 RTY Relief of 60th Divn Infantry by 3rd CANADIAN BTYS commenced.	Rep
ACQ LARGESET	24th	11 a.m.	2nd CRA assis begin trans. CRA and ADC return from leave. Rain all days.	Rep
—	25th	8 p.m.	88th Siege RTY reverts to Control of VIIth Corps H.A. Rain all day	Rep
HERMAVILLE	26th	10 a.m.	Command of the front passes to G.O.C. 3rd CANADIAN DIVISION.	Rep
"			CRA visits HQs, 7th and 9th Canadian INF BDES, all Centre Group BTYS, A/301, B/303, and Left Group HQs.	Rep
ECOIVRES, etc	27th	10 a.m.	CRA visits HQ XVIIth Corps H.A., 50th H.A. Group D/301 and C/301 BTYS and wagon lines at LARGESET.	Rep
BRULEMONT HQ	28th	10.30 a.m.	CRA visits HQ Right Arty Group B/301 and C/301 BTYS, and BTY wagon lines at ACQ.	Rep
MARCEUIL	29th	10.15 a.m.	CRA visits CRE D.O.T.M. HQrs 7th Canadian BDE. M/303 and C/303 BTYS. Rain till 3 p.m.	Rep
CHAPELLE PERMONT	30th	Noon	CRA Bring BTY wagon lines at CHAPELLE PERMONT, H.R.H. Duke of CONNAUGHT visits 3rd Canadian Divl H.Q. at 2.30 p.m.	Rep
HERMAVILLE	31st	2 p.m.	HQ 60th Div ARTY move to AUBIGNY.	Rep

S. Aubigny
31st October 1916.

W. McBride
Brig. General
Commanding 60th Divisional Artillery

Army Form C. 2118.

WAR DIARY
of H.Q. 60th (London) Divn Artillery

INTELLIGENCE SUMMARY.

(Erase heading not required.)

Instructions regarding War Diaries and Intelligence Summaries are contained in F.S. Regs., Part II. and the Staff Manual respectively. Title pages will be prepared in manuscript.

July

Place	Date	Hour	Summary of Events and Information	Remarks and references to Appendices
MONT ST ELOY	1st	9.30 am	C.R.A. visits H.Q. Arty Group, Battery Positions and O.P's of 57th Divn Arty	Rep.
FOND DE VASE	2nd	10 am	" " Centre "	Rep, also centre Inf Bde H.Q.
ANZIN	4th	10 am	" " Right "	Rep. Heavy rain
ECURIE	5th	11 am	" " Right INF BDE and Right Sectn Trenches	Rep.
NEUVILLE ST. VAAST	6th	10.30 am	" " Left INF BDE and Left Sectn Trenches. Three 2" T.M. Batteries joined from T.M. School	Rep.
HERMAVILLE	7th	9.30 am	" " 51st Divn Arty H.Q. D.A.C. and all wagon lines of BTYS	Rep.
—	—	—	Half personnel of 2" T.M. BTYS attached to 51st Divn T.M.S. for instruction	Rep.
HAUTE CLOQUE	8th	10.30	C.R.A. visits Artillery School. Lieut-Col. GREATHED, Cmdg 308th F.A.B. invalided home	Rep. Appendix
AGNY ST FLOCHEL	9th	10 a.	C.R.A. visits T.M. School. Orders received for Relief of 51st DIV ARTY nights 14/15th, 15/16, 16/17 July	Rep Appx B
ECOIVRES	"	3.30 p	C.R.A. visits H.Q. XVII Corps, Heavy Arty 4 p.m. Divisional Conference	Rep
LA TARGETTE	10th	10 pm	Relief of personnel of "RICHARDS" Battery (Heavy French Mortar) commenced by men of 60th D.A.C.	Rep.
FOND DE VASE	11th	11.45 am	Conference of Group Commanders at Centre Group H.Q.	Rep.
AUBIGNY	13th	6 pm	C.R.A. to conference XVII Corps H.Q.	Rep.
HERMAVILLE	14th	9 am	R.A. H.Q. move from VILLERS CHATEL to HERMAVILLE	Rep.
"	"	5.30 pm	Orders recd to complete entire relief of 51st Div Arty during night 14/15th July. All 51st Div being withdrawn	Rep Appendix B
"	15th	2 am	Relief of 51st Div Arty by 60th Div Arty complete	Rep.
"	"	10 am	C.R.A. accompanied G.O.C. Divn round Trenches	Rep.

Army Form C. 2118.

WAR DIARY of HQ 60th (London) Div¹ Artillery
INTELLIGENCE SUMMARY.
(Erase heading not required.)

Instructions regarding War Diaries and Intelligence Summaries are contained in F. S. Regs., Part II. and the Staff Manual respectively. Title pages will be prepared in manuscript.

July

Place	Date	Hour	Summary of Events and Information	Remarks and references to Appendices
WARLUS	16th	11:30am	CRA visits CRA 4th Div. 2.pm. Heavy T.M. Exhibition at LIGNY ST-FLOCHEL	Rep.
MT ST ELOY	"	6.pm	Conference Group Commanders	Rep.
	17th	9:30 am	CRA visits BTY wagon lines. Rain.	Rep.
NEUVILLE	18th	11 am	CRA visits CRHQ and LEFT INF BDE CMDRS. Heavy Rain.	Rep.
EIRON	19th	3.pm	CRA visits RIGHT INF BDE CMDR and O.C. Right Arty Group	Rep.
NEUVILLE SV.	20th	4.pm	Bombardment of German Trenches and Trench Mortar positions in conjunction with XVII Corps Heavy Arty	Rep.
ANZIN	"	-	B/300 and B/301 BTYS heavily shelled	Rep.
ACQ. LAMBERT	21st	9:30 am	CRA visits wagon lines 300th and 301st F.A. Bde. D.O.T.M. and CRA XVII Corps Heavy Arty.	Rep.
	"	-	Officer of Special Works Park R.E. visited Battery positions. C/300 BTY heavily shelled	Rep.
	"	1 am	"A" and "Q" Batteries 1st Indian R.H.A. Bde. brought into action on 60th Div² front. (Bde in C/. Col CHARLTON)	Rep.
FND DE VASE	22nd	6:30 am	CRA visits Right and Centre Groups HQ's and BTYS. Rain.	Rep.
ECURIE	23rd-3:30pm	Bombardment of German trenches and trench Mortar positions near 21462 R³ in conjunction with Heavy Arty.	Rep. Appendix C
BERTHONVAL	24th	10 am	CRA visits Left Group HQ and BTYS.	Rep.
ECURIE	25th	9:30 am	CRA and B.M. selecting sites for Heavy T.M's and Single 15 pr. B.L.C. Guns for close defence	Rep.
	26th	2:55 am	Enemy Sprang mine in left Sector. S.O.S. signal rec'd. No infantry action	Rep.
	"	10 am	CRA selecting Heavy T.M. sites	Rep.
	"	9:12 pm	M² sprang mine in left sector. Left Group Arty barrages German trenches	Rep.

WAR DIARY of H.Q. 60th Divl Artillery
INTELLIGENCE SUMMARY

Army Form C. 2118.

July

Place	Date	Hour	Summary of Events and Information	Remarks and references to Appendices
CAMBLAIN	27th	11 am	C.R.A. visits C.R.A. 37th Div ARTY. 2-3 pm T.M. Schl. LIGNY ST FLOCHEL.	
ECURIE	28th	9.30 am	C.R.A. selects site for Heavy T.M. in right sector. Inspects Centre Group ATY position.	C.R.A.
			Canvas commences at LIGNY ST FLOCHEL for Heavy Trench Mortar Bty. W/60. 1 Officer from 60th Div Infantry.	Rep
		2.15 pm	Officers from 60th Divl Arty N.C.Os from XVII Corps Heavy Arty. Remaining personnel from 64 Divl HQR.	Rep
	"	10 pm	Enemy spring mine in left sector at 10 pm. No infantry action.	Rep
ECORIE	29th	5 pm	Bombardment of enemy trenches and trench mortar positions in conjunction with Heavy Artillery	Rep APPENDIX "D"
VIMY RIDGE	30th	11/10 am	Small enemy attack on crater post in left sector. S.O.S. sent and attack dispersed.	Rep
—	"	Noon	C.R.A. visits HQ Bde Crops Centre and left Section; left Arty group HQ and Bty positions. HP	Rep
	31st	10 am	C.R.A. visits D.A.C.	
FOSSE DROUEG	"	2.45 pm	M.G.R.A. 3rd Army inspects Centre Group Battery Positions	

Howard Such Lee
Mg-General
Cmdg 60th Divisional Artillery

APPENDIX. A

RELIEF 51ˢᵗ DIV.

SECRET.   Copy No. 4

60th DIVISION ORDER No. 1.

10th July 1916.

(1)   The 60th Div. will relieve the 51st Div. in the line during the period 11th to 17th July.

(2)   The relief of the Infantry will be carried out in accordance with the attached tables. Reliefs are to be completed by 6 a.m., 14th inst. Bde. Commanders will take over Command of Sectors on completion of relief during the night of 13th/14th July.
        Guides from Units to be relieved will be provided and the time and place where they will meet relieving troops will be arranged between Bde. Commanders.

(3)   The Artillery reliefs will be carried out on nights 14th/15th, 15th/16th and *16th/17th under arrangements between the two B.G's., R.A. concerned.
        *16ᵗʰ/17ᵗʰ
        Six 18 pdr., and two 4.5" Howitzer Battys., 51st Div. are remaining in the line.   FREVIN CAPELLE
        The D.A.C. will move to Capelle Ferment on the 17th under the orders of the C.R.A.

(4).   T.M.Battys. (Light & Medium) will relieve those of the 51st Div. during the nights 11th/12th and 12th/13th under arrangements to be made between Bde. Commanders concerned.

(5)   The Fd. Cos. R.E. will relieve the Fd. Cos. R.E., 51st Div. on the 12th and 13th July under arrangements between C.R.E's concerned.

(6)   Bde. M.G.Cos. will relieve those of the 51st Div. during the nights 12th/13th and 13th/14th under arrangements to be made between Bde. Commanders concerned.

(7)   The 1/12th L.N.Lancs. R. will concentrate at Maroeuil and Louez on the 11th. On the 13th one Co. will relieve one Co. 1/8th Royal Scots in each Sector. The H.Q. and remaining Co. of the Bn. will be in Louez.

(8)   The Field Ambs. will relieve those of the 51st Div. under arrangements between the A.D's.M.S. concerned. They will be located as under:-

            2/4th Fd. Amb..........Ecoivres.
            2/5th & 2/6th Fd. Ambs..Haute d'Avesnes.

        The San. Sec. will move to Hermaville on the 14th under the orders of the A.D.M.S.

(9)   The Mob. Vet. Sec. will relieve the Mob. Vet. Sec. of the 51st Div. on the Arras - St. Pol road, half mile S. of Aubigny on the 15th inst. under the orders of the A.D.V.S.

(10)   The Train will move as follows, under the orders of the A.Q.M.G.:-

            Det. No. 1 Co., Nos. 2 and 4 Cos. to Haute d'Avesnes.
            No. 3 Co.   to Acq.

-2-

(11) A List of Trench Stores handed over will be given to incoming Units. A List showing permanent, Brigade and Regimental Stores is attached. (App. "B").

(12) The 51st Div. is leaving behind the following personnel. Arrangements are to be made for their rations and quartering:-

For 24 Hours.

    1 Off. and 1 N.C.O. with each Medium T.M.Batty.
    2 Off. and 2 N.C.O's with each Light T.M.Batty.
    1 Off. (per Bde.) with each Bde. M.G.Co.
    1 man (per gun relieved) with each Bde. M.G.Co.

For 3 days.

    1 Off. and 3 Linesmen with   H.Q. Sec. Signal Co.
              3   "   with each Bde. Sec. Signal Co.
    1 Off. and 8 N.C.O's with each Bn.

(13) The 152nd Inf. Bde. and No. 4/Co., 51 Div. Train, will be billetted in Acq and Ecoivres and will be administered by this Div.   H.Q. at Ecoivres.
    2 Bns. of this Bde. will relieve the 2/15 and 2/16 London Regiments respectively on the night of the 12th/13th July.

(14) Orders as regards the adminstration of Units in the Div. Area, other than those belonging to the 51st or 60th Divs. will be issued later.

(15) On arrival in the line, refilling points will be as under:-

    Acq. - 180th Inf. Bde. (including Bde. M.G.Co, 180 Light and Y Medium T.M.Battys.), 1/6th Fd. Co. R.E., 2/4th Fd. Amb. and No. 3 Co., Div. Train.
    Haute d'Avesnes.- All other Units of the Div.

(16) The Command of the Front remains in the hands of the G.O.C., 51st Div. until 10 a.m., 14th July.

(17) 60th Div. H.Q. will be established at Hermaville at 10 a.m., 14th July.

(18) Acknowledge

H.Q., 60th Div.
10th July 1916.

                                    Lieut-Colonel.
                                    General Staff.

Copies issued at........
    to:-

No.			No.	
1.	179 Inf. Bde.		12.	A.D.C.
2.	180 " "		13.	A.D.V.S.
3.	181 " "		14 &	
4.	C.R.A.		15.	17 Corps.
5.	C.R.E.		16.	14th Div.
6.	"A".		17.	2nd Div.
7.	A.D.M.S.		18.	51st Div.
8.	Signals.		19.	War Diary.
9.	1/12 L.N.Lancs. R.		20.	File.
10.	Div. Train.		21.	Camp Commandant.
11.	Div. Supply Col.			

Appendix A.1
RELIEF 57TH DIV

SECRET.   Copy No. 23

51st (HIGHLAND) DIVISION.

OPERATION ORDER No. 61.

Reference Map:-   8th July 1916.
 LENS 11. 1/100,000

1.   The 60th Division will relieve the 51st Division in the line during the period 11/17th July.

2.   The relief of the Infantry will be carried out in accordance with Table "A" attached. Relief to be completed by 6 a.m., 14th inst. ✕Instructions as regards handing and taking over of trench stores are republished for information.
            Brigadiers of 60th Division will take over Command of Brigade Sectors during the night 13/14th July on completion of the relief.

3.   The Artillery reliefs will be carried out on nights 14/15th, 15/16th and 16/17th July, under arrangements to be made between B.Gs. R.A., 51st Division and 60th Division.
            Six 18-pdr. and two 4·5" Howitzer Batteries 51st Divisional Artillery will remain in the line under the Command of G.O.C. 60th Division until further orders.
            On relief the 51st Divisional Artillery, less the above mentioned Batteries, will be withdrawn to the billeting areas shewn on the attached plan.

4.   The C.R.E., 51st Division will arrange that all special work now being carried on under him by the R.E. and Pioneers of the 60th Division is closed down by the night of the 11th inst.

5.   The Field Coys.R.E., 51st Division, will be relieved by Field Coys. R.E., 60th Division, as follows:-

    1/1st High.Fd.Co.R.E.   by   2/4th London Fd.Co.R.E.
    1/2nd High.Fd.Co.R.E.   by   3/3rd London Fd.Co.R.E.
    2/2nd High.Fd.Co.R.E.   by   1/6th London Fd.Co.R.E.

            Reliefs to take place on 12th and 13th July, under arrangements to be made by C.R.Es. of Divisions.

6.   The 1/12th Loyal North Lancs (Pioneers) will be withdrawn from the line on the 11th, and concentrated at HAROEUIL. On the 13th, 1 Company 1/12th Loyal North Lancs, will move into each Sector of the line, and take over from the 1/8th Royal Scots (Pioneers). On relief the 1/8th Royal Scots will withdraw to ECOIVRES.

✕ Will be issued later   17

(2)

7. The 152nd Infantry Brigade, 51st Division, will be billetted in ACQ and ECOIVRES, and will take over mining fatigues from the 60th Division before completion of relief. Headquarters at ECOIVRES.

This Brigade will be administered by the 60th Division.

The two Battalions not employed on mining fatigues will be in Corps Reserve.

8. On relief the 51st Division (less 1 Infantry Brigade and 8 Batteries) will move to billets as shewn in March Table (Table "B") and billetting plan.

51st Division Headquarters will be at VILLERS CHATEL.

9. Trench Mortar Batteries (Light and Medium) will be relieved during the nights 11/12th and 12/13th under arrangements to be made between the Brigadiers concerned.

The 51st Division will leave 1 Officer and 1 N.C.O. with each 2" Battery, and 2 Officers and 2 N.C.Os. with each Stokes Battery of the 60th Division for 24 hours after relief.

10. Brigade Machine Guns will be relieved under arrangements to be made between Brigadiers concerned during nights 12/13th and 13/14th.

1 Officer in each Brigade of 51st Division and 1 man of each gun relieved, will remain for 24 hours with the 60th Division Machine Gun Companies.

11. The O.C. 51st Divisional Signal Co. will arrange to leave with the Signal Co., 60th Division:-

With Headquarters Section - 1 Officer.
                              3 Linesmen.

With each Bde. Section   - 3 Linesmen.

These details will remain with the 60th Division for 3 days after completion of the relief.

12. The 51st Divisional Grenade School and Physical Training School will close down on 12th inst., and will be handed over to 60th Division on 13th inst. The Gas School will close on the 13th inst., and be handed over on 14th inst.

13. Mobile Vet. Section will move to TINQUES on 15th inst.

14. Divisional Train (less 4th Company which remains in ACQ) will move to TINQUES under orders of D.A.Q.M.G.

/15

(3)

15.   Field Ambulances will be relieved under arrangements to be made by A.Ds.M.S. of 51st and 30th Divisions.
      Field Ambulances of 51st Division will move to new area under orders of D.A.Q.M.G.

16.   On arrival in Back Area Refilling Point for all units will be at TINQUES.

17.   The Command of the front will pass to G.O.C. 30th Division, at 10 a.m. 14th July.

                    D Baird Major
                 for Lieut.Colonel,
                     General Staff,
                     51st (Highland) Division.

Issued at 8.30 p.m.

Copy No. 1   152nd Infantry Bde.
        2   153rd Infantry Bde.
        3   154th Infantry Bde.
        4   C.R.A.
        5   C.R.E.
        6   "A".
        7   A.D.M.S.
        8   Signals.
        9   Divl. Train.
       10   8th Royal Scots.
       11   Divl. Supply Col.
       12   Divl. Amm. Col.
       13   A.D.C. for G.O.C.
       14   A.D.V.S.
       15   XVII Corps.
       16   " "
       17   14th Division.
       18   2nd Division.
       19   30th Division.
       20   War Diary.
       21   File.
       22   Camp Commandant.

APPENDIX A

WAR DIARY

SECRET   Copy No... 7

60th. (LONDON) DIVISIONAL ARTILLERY.

OPERATION ORDER NO. 1

11th July, 1916.

1. The 60th Division will relieve the 51st Division during the period July 11th - July 17th. The Infantry relief will be completed by 6 a.m. 14th. instant.

2. The 301st. F.A.Brigade will relieve 255th Brigade (less B/256th. Battery).
   The 302nd. F.A.Brigade will relieve 255th. Brigade.

3. The first sections of all batteries 301st and 302nd Brigades will carry out their relief on the night July 14/15th. The second Sections on the night 15/16th.

4. The Battery Commander, 4 numbers 1, and 2 telephonists of each Battery 255th and 256th Brigades will remain in action till 9 a.m. 17th July, at which hour the command passes to group and Battery Commanders 60th Division.

5. The wagon lines of 255th and 256th Brigades will be clear by 2 p.m. 16th July.
   The 301st Brigade will take over the wagon lines of 256th Brigade, the D.A.C. will take over wagon lines of 255th Brigade.
   Wagon lines of 301st Brigade will move up complete on 16th July, sending on a small advance party to arrive at their new wagon lines by 11 a.m.
   The D.A.C. will move up on July 17th.

6. The wagon lines of the 302nd Brigade will move to ACQ on July 14th. arriving by 10.30 a.m.
   Guns and Howitzers of the 302nd Brigade will be handed over on that date to 255th Brigade at the latter's wagon lines in PREVIN CAPELLE.

7. Guns of the 301st Brigade will be handed over to the 256th Brigade at the latter's wagon lines in LAMBERT on July 14th. Teams returning to their own wagon lines that day.

8. Guns will be taken over stripped (except 4.5" sights) and a corresponding number of stripped guns handed over to 51st Division.

9. Memoranda of examination will be handed over with guns.

10. On arrival in the line, the refilling point for the Divisional Artillery will be at HAUTE AVESNES.

11. Reports to BERNAVILLE after 9 a.m. 17th. July.

R.C.Rawe
Major.
Brigade Major,
60th Divisional Artillery.

Copy No.1. 300th. F.A.Brigade.
     2. 301st.   Do.
     3. 302nd.   Do.
     4. 303rd.   Do.
     5. D.A.C.
     6. 51st Divisional Artillery.
     7. War Diary.
     8.   Do.
     9. File.

APPENDIX A.3

RELIEF

SECRET

51st DIVISIONAL ARTILLERY   COPY No. 4

OPERATION ORDER No.27

12th July, 1916.

Reference Map.
LENS. 11. 1/100,000

1.   The 60th Division will relieve the 51st Division in the line during the period 11th/17th, July.

2.   The following units of 51st Divisional Artillery will be relieved by the 60th Divisional Artillery :-

     255th Brigade R.F.A. by- 302nd Brigade R.F.A.
     256th Brigade R.F.A.(less D/256) by - 301st Brigade R.F.A.
     Headquarters, 260th Brigade R.F.A. by - Headquarters,
                                              303rd Brigade R.F.A.

     One Section of each above Batteries will be relieved on night 14th/15th.
     The remaining Sections night 15th/16th.
     The Sections on relief will march to their respective Wagon Lines.
     Battery Commanders, Nos.I, the senior telephonist and another telephonist per Battery will remain with the relieving Batteries until 9 a.m., on morning of 17th July, at which hour the Command passes to Group and Battery Commanders of 60th Division.
     The remaining Batteries will remain in their present positions until further orders, and will come under the Command of C.R.A., 60th Division at 9 a.m., on 17th July.

3.   Guns and Howitzers of Batteries being relieved will be left in position stripped of all stores including sights (except the sights of 4.5" Howitzers) and will be taken over by relieving Batteries of 60th Divisional Artillery.
     Batteries of 60th Divisional Artillery will hand over their guns similarly stripped to the Batteries of 51st Divisional Artillery at the latter's wagon lines. Memoranda of Examination must accompany the guns.

4.   All existing telephone lines will be left in position and will be taken over by relieving units.

5.   Out-going units will hand over to relieving units all Artillery Map Boards, Photos, Local Plans, Log Books, Target Registers, etc.
Maps will not be handed over, except a few of the new 1/50,000 Sheet NEUVILLE ST VAAST, if the in-coming units have not sufficient.

6.   All Ammunition less sufficient to fill limbers and wagons in the proportion of 75% Shrapnel and 25% H.E. in the case of 18-pounders and 100% H.E. in the case of 4.5" Howitzers will be handed over to incoming Batteries.

7.   Out-going units will march to the new area on 16th inst., in accordance with attached March Table.
     Billetting parties will meet the Staff Captain at the

2/-

- 2 -

the Cross Road ¼ mile South of S of SUR in ST MICHEL SUR TERNOIS at 11 a.m., on that date.

Each Battery must leave behind a rear party under an officer to ensure that the billets are left thoroughly clean.

8.   In-coming units will take over the wagon lines from out-going units on 16th inst.

9.   Special instructions will be issued as to drawing of rations.

10.   The Command of the Divisional Artillery in the line will pass to C.R.A., 60th Division at 9 a.m., on 17th inst.

At that hour the 51st Divisional Artillery office will close at HERMAVILLE and open at ROELLECOURT.

11.   Progress reports will be rendered by Brigade Commanders immediately each relief is completed.

                          Major, R.A.
                          Brigade Major,
Issued at 9 a.m.   51st Divisional Artillery.

Copy No. 1. to 51st Division 'G'
       2. to 51st Division 'Q'
       3. to XVII Corps R.A.
       4. to 60th Divisional Artillery
       5. to 255th Brigade R.F.A.
       6. to 256th Brigade R.F.A.
       7. to 258th Brigade R.F.A.
       8. to 260th Brigade R.F.A.
       9. to 51st D.A.C.
      10. to 51st Division Signals.
      11. to Senior Supply Officer.
      12. to Staff Captain
      13. to Diary
      14.   Retained
      15   Retained.

SECRET.   APPENDIX B   COPY No: 4.

51st (HIGHLAND) DIVISIONAL ARTILLERY.

OPERATION ORDER No: 28.

RELIEF

14th July, 1916.

The whole of the 51st Divisional Artillery will be withdrawn from action to-night.

The Batteries being relieved by Batteries of 60th Division will leave their stripped guns in position, and take over guns from 60th Division in exchange at the Battery Wagon Lines.

The remaining batteries will take their guns out of the line.

On withdrawal from the line all batteries will march to their Wagon Lines.

Battery Commanders, No's.1 and telephonists will withdraw with their Batteries.

Group Commanders of RIGHT and CENTRE Groups will be relieved by Group Commanders of 60th Division when the relief of the Batteries of 255th and 256th Brigades has been completed.

The LEFT Group Commander will be relieved at 9 p.m.

Batteries not being relieved by Batteries of 60th Division will hand over their ammunition, Artillery map-boards, target registers, etc., to the nearest battery of 60th Division.

Brigades *and D.A.C.* will march from their Wagon Lines at 6 a.m. tomoroow, destination will be notified later.

Major, R.A.
Brigade Major, 51st Divisional Artillery.

Issued at 5-0 p.m.

Copy No. 1 to 51st Division "G".
2 to 51st Division "Q".
3 to XVII Corps R.A.
4 to 60th Divisional Artillery.
5 to 255th Brigade, R.F.A.
6 to 256th Brigade, R.F.A.
7 to 258th Brigade, R.F.A.
8 to 260th Brigade, R.F.A.
9 to 51st D.A.C.
10 to 51st Division Signals.
11 to Senior Supply Officer.
12 to Staff Captain.
13 to Diary.
14 retained.
15 retained.

APPENDIX "C"

S E C R E T.

COMBINED BOMBARDMENT.

(Ref. Trench Map ROCLINCOURT 1:10,000).

1. A combined bombardment against Hostile Trench Mortars will be carried out on Sunday, 23rd. instant, in conjunction with the XVII Corps Heavy Artillery.

2. Targets are allotted as under:-

Battery.	Group.	Target.
One 18-pr. Battery.	Right.	Front line. A.22.b.5½.3. to A.22.b.3.5. LILLE ROAD. (inclusive).
One 18-Pr. Battery.	Right.	A.22.b.3.5. LILLE ROAD (exclusive) to A.22.b.2.6.
One 4.5" How. Battery.	Centre.	Points:- A.22.b.5.3½. A.22.b.4½.5. A.22.b.5.5½. A.22.b.3½.6.

3. The Heavy Artillery will fire on points A.16.d.68.75 and A.22.b.45.85.

4. Ammunition allotted:-

   18-Pounders. 150 rounds per Battery.
   4.5" Hows.   50   Do.   Do.

5. The bombardment will commence at 3.30 p.m. and will be intensive for the first minute. Thereafter fire will be regulated, so as to make the bombardment last for 40 minutes, concluding at 4.10 p.m.

6. Watches will be synchronised at 2.30 p.m. 23rd. instant.

R.G.France
Major,
Brigade Major,
22nd. July 1916.   60th. Divisional Artillery.

Copies to:- Right Group.
            Centre   "
            181st. Infantry Brigade.
            XVII Corps Heavy Artillery.

APPENDIX "D"
War Diary

SECRET.

ARTILLERY SCHEME.

(Ref. Trench Map ROCLINCOURT 1:10,000).

1. A combined bombardment against hostile Trench Mortars will be carried out on Thursday 27th. instant, in conjunction with the XVII Corps Heavy Artillery.

2. Targets are allotted as follows:-

Battery.	Group.	Target.
One 18-pr. Battery.	Right.	1 Section. Trench A.16.c.7½.8½ to A.16.c.9½.8.
		1 Section. Trench A.16.c.9½.3. to A.16.d.1.8. (Paying special attention to the Northern portion A.16.d.½.7. - A.16.d.1.8.)
One 18-pr. Battery.	Centre.	Trenches A.16.c.9½.8. - A.16.c.9½.1. and A.16.d.1.8. - A.16.b.1.1.
One Section (detchd) 18-pounder.	R.H.A.	A.16.c.9.9. - A.16.d.½.7.
One 4.5" How. Battery.	Centre.	Points:- A.16.c.9½.8. A.16.d.½.7. A.16.d.1.8.

3. Ammunition allotted :-

    18-pr. Batteries.   200 AX per Battery.
    R.H.A. Section.   50 AX
    4.5" Howitzers.   40 BX and PF.

4. The D.O.T.M. will arrange to bomb the hostile front line trenches behind ARGYLE CRATER during the Artillery bombardment.

5. The bombardment will be intensive for the first minute. Thereafter fire will be regulated so as to make the bombardment last for 20 minutes.

6. Time of commencement and hour for synchronising watches will be issued later.

                                     R.C. PRANCE.

Copies to:-   Major.
  1st. Indian R.H.A.   Brigade Major,
  Right Group.   60th. Divisional Artillery.
  Centre Group.
  179th. Inf. Bde.   H.Q.R.A. XVII Corps.
  181st. Inf. Bde.   D.O.T.M.
  H.Q. 60th. Divn.   War Diary
                      File.

Confidential

Vol 6

War Diary

of

Headquarters 60th Divl Artillery.

from 1st to 30th Nov. 1916

(Volume 11.)

WAR DIARY OF H.Q. 60th DIVN ARTILLERY.

INTELLIGENCE SUMMARY.

(Erase heading not required.)

Army Form C. 2118.

November 1916

Place	Date	Hour	Summary of Events and Information	Remarks and references to Appendices
	Nov.			
AUBIGNY	1st	—	Orders received to reorganize Divnl ARTY into 4 gun BTYS, and to withdraw 60th D.A.C. and personnel of W/60 Trench Mortar Bty to rejoin 60th DIVn in 4th ARMY area, marching on 3rd inst.	REF. APP. I
" "	2nd	—	MGRA 1st ARMY visited CRA. Rain	Re. APP. II REF.
MARŒUIL	3rd	10 a.m.	W/60 Trench Mortar BTY (less mortars) proceeds direct by motor lorry to rejoin DIVn	REF
FREVIN CAPELLE	"	—	60th D.A.C. proceeds by march route to rejoin DIVn. Artery before arrival of relieving units, to reorganize into 3 BDE AMn COLUMNS and D.A.C. according to "War Establishment" SALONIKA.	REF. IV
NEUVILLE ST-VAAST	"	11.45 pm	Germans bombard 3rd CANADIAN DIVn Trenches (C.2) for ½ hour, causing a few casualties.	REF.
AUBIGNY	4th	11 a.m.	Bde Major 56th DIV ARTY arrives and commences to take over.	REF
"	"		A/301. BTY (late 519th BTY- HOWITZER) withdrawn from action. Rain	REF
"	5th	Noon	All 60th DIV ARTY wagon lines (less gun limbers and teams) withdrawn from action to BONNIÈRES area. 56th DIVn ARTY arrive and occupy wagon lines.	APP. VI REF
"	"	4 p.m.	60th Divl teams take up 56th Divl guns into action, withdrawing all 60th Divl guns. A/300 and D/300 BTYS to CAMBLIGNEUL, B/300 BTY to HERMAVILLE, these 3 BTYS ceasing to form part of Divl ARTY or reorganization. A/300 ordered to join 5th DIVn, B/300 as instructional BTY at 1st ARMY ARTY SCHOOL at AIRE, D/300 (late 519th BTY) to LAHORE DIVn when ready to move. Detachments, officers etc of 60th DIV ARTY than 56th DIVn guns night 5th/6th Nov.	REF APP. III, IV REF. APP. V REF

WAR DIARY "H.Q. 60th DIV.l ARTILLERY.

Army Form C. 2118.

November 1916

Place	Date	Hour	Summary of Events and Information	Remarks and references to Appendices
	Nov			
AUBIGNY	6th	9. a.m	Wagon lines march to billets in BOUBERS area	REF. APP VII
"	"	"	Guns and gun limbers to ETREE WAMIN area	REF. APP VIII
"	"	10. a.m	Detachments 56th DIV ARTY arrive and take over; detachments 60th DIV ARTY remaining with 56th DIV till 5. p.m, when they are withdrawn by motor lorry to ETREE WAMIN area, leaving 1 officer and 2 telephonists per BTY as rear party. Personnel of 2" Trench Mortars remain in action, relief not having arrived.	
"	"	5 pm	C.R.A. 56th DIVn assumes command	REF.
BOUBERS etc	7th	9. a.m	Wagon lines to billets in ETREE WAMIN area	REF.
NEUVILETTE	"	5. pm	Rear parties 60th DIV ARTY withdrawn by motor lorry to ETREE WAMIN area, where the DIVn ARTILLERY is concentrated (less D.A.C and W/60 BTY) on night 7th/8th Nov.	REF. APP IX
AUBIGNY	"	7.30 a.m	Bde MAJOR R.A. to ETREE WAMIN.	REF.
"	8th	10.a.m	C.R.A., STAFF CAPT. R.A, and A.D.C. drive by car to AILLY-LE-HAUT-CLOCHER to divest the reorganisation of D.A.C., leaving Lt COL H DRAKE in command of 60th DIV ARTY when rested at ETREE WAMIN throughout day of 8th inst.	REF.
ETREE- WAMIN	9th	8.30 a.m	DIV ARTY march to OCCOCHES area	REF. APP X & XI
OCCOCHES	10th	8.15 a.m	DIV ARTY march to rejoin 60th DIV in reorganisation area, S.E of ABBEVILLE, and billeted night 10th/11th onwards at BELLOY, BOURDON, and BETHENCOURT, with H.Q.s at AILLY.	REF. APP XII

WAR DIARY of H.Q. R.A. 60th Division. Army Form C. 2118.

INTELLIGENCE SUMMARY

(Erase heading not required.)

November 1916.

Place	Date	Hour	Summary of Events and Information	Remarks and references to Appendices
AILLY-LE-HAUT-CLOCHER	Nov 11th	Noon	Bde Amm Columns and nucleus of S.A.A. Sections join Arty Bdes	Ref.
			C.R.A. visits all Arty Bdes and remounts at ABBEVILLE. Draft of 77 other ranks arrive from base Ammunition in all echelons adjusted to 50% of shrapnel and H.E.	Ref.
AILLY	12th	-	162 horses arrive for Div Arty from Remount	Ref.
"	13th	11 am	G.O.C. Div'n visits D.A.C. and Arty Bdes	Ref.
LONGPRÉ	14th	-	Entrainment of Division commenced, the whole Div'n being entrained at LONGPRÉ - Details in Appendix	Ref. App XII APP XIV APP XV
			122 riding horses received from Remount. Div Arty now complete in horses up to Part VII War Establishment as regards light Draught horses, and up to Part XII (SALONIKA) as regards Riding, Mules and Pack Transport to complete establishment to be drawn at SALONIKA	App. VII
AILLY	15th	-	Entrainment continued	Ref.
LONGPRÉ	16th	-	398 Arty Drivers received direct from England. Entrainment continued	Ref App XII & XIII
"	17th	-	Entrainment continued. 312. R.G.A. gunners (draft) arrived	Ref.
"	18th	-	Entrainment continued	Ref App XIII & XIV
"	19th	-	Entrainment continued. R.A.H.Q. Staff and horses and Bde Majr R.A. entrained & left for MARSEILLES	Ref.
	20 & 21st	-	Entrainment continued	Ref App XV & XVI
MARSEILLES	22nd	4 a.m.	R.A.H.Q. Staff under Bde Major arrive MARSEILLES. Entrainment of Div Arty continued	Ref App XXII & XXIII
			Camp. Entrainment of Div Arty continued	

WAR DIARY of H.Q. 60th DIVn ARTILLERY.
INTELLIGENCE SUMMARY.

November. 1916

Army Form C. 2118.

Place	Date	Hour	Summary of Events and Information	Remarks and references to Appendices
AILLY	22nd	-	C.R.A. Staff Capt. and A.D.C. leave for MARSEILLES, arriving 24th	Ref.
LONGPRÉ	24th	-	Entrainment of 60th Div ARTY concluded	Ref. APP XXIV v XXV
MARSEILLES	25th	11 am	C.R.A. visits camps VALENTINE, FOURNIER, and CARCASSONE, and inspects units of DIV ARTY	Ref.
"	26th–30th	-	Entrainment of 60th Division for SALONIKI continues under direct orders of Base Commandant.	Ref.
"		-	Entrainment continues. Inspection of Camps. Draft of 31 Gunners received	Ref.

Dec 26th 1916.

[signature]
Brig. General.
Cmdg 60th Divisional Artillery.

APPENDIX. I

R.4 "A"

SECRET.   First Army No. G.S.468.

Canadian Corps.

Reference attached O.B.1849 of the 31st. October, para 8 (b), the re-organisation of the Divisional Artillery of the 60th. Division will be carried out as follows, and not as therein stated:-

As soon as the 60th. Divisional Artillery have been relieved in the line, a section will be withdrawn from each of the 3-18-pr. Batteries of the 302nd. and 303rd. Brigades; these 6 sections will be organised as two 6 gun Batteries, the sections from the 302nd. Brigade forming A/300 and those from the 303rd. Brigade B/300.

These two Batteries A/300 and B/300, together with A/301 (4.5' How) will be withdrawn from the 60th. Division and attached as follows:-

    A/300 and B/300 to XI Corps.
    A/301 to Lahore Divisional Artillery.

Canadian Corps will report to First Army the date that A/300 and B/300 will be ready to move to XI Corps area, and the date A/301 moves to Lahore Divisional Artillery.

2. The 60th. Divisional Artillery will then leave the First Army area with 301st., 302nd., and 303rd. Brigades re-organised each as three 4 gun 18-pr. batteries and one 4 gun Howitzer Battery.

3. The Divisional Ammunition Column will re-organise after rejoining the 60th. Division.

4. Please pass the attached copies of O.B. 1849 to the C.R.A. 60th. Divisional Artillery for his information.

                (sd) O.H.L.Nicholson, Major G.S.
                     for Major General
                 General Staff, First Army.

First Army,
1st. November 1916.
                         Canadian Corps G.382
3rd. Canadian Division.   1st. November 1916.

To be passed to 60th. Div. Arty., for action in accordance with above.
Acknowledge.

                (sd) A.C.CRITCHLEY Major G.S.
                   for B.G.G.S. Canadian Corps.

                3rd. Canadian Division.
                    G.156.

C.R.A., 60th. Divl. Arty.

Passed in accordance with Minute 2.

                (sd) F.L.ARMSTRONG. Major G.S.
                 for Lieut. Col. General Staff
1/11/16.   3rd. Canadian Division.

APPENDIX II

S E C R E T. Copy No. 1.

(THIRD) ARMY ORDER No. 87.

Ref. Map. LENS 1/100,000. 1st November, 1916.

1. The 60th Divisional Ammunition Column and personnel Heavy Trench Mortar Battery will be transferred from the First Army to join its Division in the Fourth Army area, and will come under the orders of the Third Army from midnight the 2nd/3rd November.

2. The 60th Divisional Ammunition Column and personnel Heavy Trench Mortar Battery will move in accordance with the attached march table.

3. ACKNOWLEDGE.

(Sgd) J.J.C. Fuller.
Major.
General Staff, Third Army.

Issued at 5 p.m.

Copy No. 1 to 60th Divl. Ammn. Col.
```
    xxxxxxxx
        2    First Army.
        3    Fifth Army.
        4    Fourth Army.
        5    VIth Corps.
        6    VIIth Corps.            P.T.O.
    7 - 8    G.
    9 - 11   Q.
       12    A.
       13    P.M.
       14    D.D. of Signals.
       15    War Diary.
```

MARCH TABLE 60th Divisional Ammunition Column & Personnel Heavy T.M. Battery. Issued with Third Army Order No. 97 dated 1st November, 1916.

Unit.	Date.	From.	To.	Route.	Remarks see below.
60th Divl. Ammn. Col. & Personnel Heavy T.M. Batty.	3rd Nov.	FREVIN- CAPELLE) MAROEUIL)	HERMAXXXXX ETREE - WAMIN & WAMIN.	HERMAVILLE - AVESNES LE COMTE. HABARCQ - AVESNES LE COMTE.	*
do.	4th Nov.	ETREE- WAMIN & WAMIN.	OCCOCHES (N.BANK.)	BEAUDRICOURT - IVERGNY - LE SOUICH BOUQUEMAISON - HTE VISEE - HEM.	+
do.	5th Nov.	OCCOCHES. (N.Bank)	No. 6 area Fifth Army.		§

REMARKS.

* Head not to pass LE CAUROY before 3 p.m.

+ To be clear of BOUQUEMAISON by 12 noon.

§ Under orders of Fifth Army.

SECRET.   APPENDIX III
                                                    Copy No. 7

60th. DIVISIONAL ARTILLERY.

OPERATION ORDER No. 2.

1. The 60th. Divisional Artillery will be relieved by the 56th. Divisional Artillery on the 5th., 6th., and 7th., November; all guns and howitzers being withdrawn on the night 5/6th.

2. Orders as to relief of Trench Mortars will be issued later.

3. Guns and Howitzers of the 60th. Divisional Artillery will be removed, and will not be handed over to the incoming Division.

4. Aiming Posts, will be left in position, and incoming Units will hand over an equivalent number at the Wagon Lines under arrangements to be made by the Battery Commanders concerned.

5. Right and Left Groups will hand over the forward 15-pr. guns at A.28.d.2.8. and A.3.b.3.5. to their relieving Groups on the morning of the 6th.   15-pr. range tables will be handed over with the guns.
   Detachments of 60th. Divisional Artillery will explain the working of the 15-pr. before withdrawing.   15-pr. wagons and limbers will be handed over at the wagon lines.

6. All Ammunition at Gun Positions will be handed over to the 56th. Division at 12 noon on the 6th. after which hour the accounting and supply of Ammunition will be carried out by the 56th. Division.
   Receipts (with a note as to condition) will be obtained for all ammunition handed over.

7. Arrangements for relief are as follows:-

   5th MORNING. Billeting parties, 60th. Divisional Artillery proceed to new area.
   Advanced parties 56th. Divisional Artillery arrive LARESSET 9.30 a.m. and AUBIGNY at 9a.m.

   AFTERNOON. (a) All Ammunition Wagons, spare horses, etc., of 60th. Divisional Artillery march to new area, leaving only gun limbers at present wagon lines.

   301st. Field Artillery Brigade to
   302nd.   Do.   Do.
   303rd.   Do.   Do.

   Time and routes will be issued later.

   Do. (b) 56th. Divisional Artillery Batteries arrive at wagon lines of unit which they are relieving and take over.
   56th. Divisional Ammunition Column arrives 60th. Divisional Ammunition Column wagon lines (vacant).

   EVENING. (c) 60th. Divisional Artillery teams and limbers take up all guns and howitzers of Batteries, 56th. Divisional Artillery, bringing back all guns and howitzers of 60th. Divisional Artillery on completion of relief.
   A/300 and B/300 will be withdrawn complete the same night.
   Complete detachments, officers, Telephonists, etc. of 60th. Divisional Artillery will remain in action with the 56th. Division guns and howitzers throughout the night 5/6th.

6th. MORNING. (a) Detachments of 56th. Division will arrive by motor lorry about 10 a.m. Arrangements for guides will be issued later.
   Guns and Howitzers of 60th. Divisional Artillery will march from present wagon lines to new area.

EVENING. (b) Detachments of 60th. Division will be withdrawn by motor lorry about 5 p.m., and taken direct to new area.

7th.   One officer and two telephonists will remain with each Battery and Group Headquarters 56th. Divisional Artillery till dusk, and will then rejoin their Batteries in the new area.
   60th. Divisional Artillery will be concentrated in new area by midnight 7th/8th.

8. All units of 60th. Divisional Artillery will march out with their full complement of ammunition.

9. All trench stores, camouflage canvas, kite boards, registration books, aeroplane photographs, panoramas, and all documents relating to the present area will be handed over to the incoming Units and receipts obtained.

10. All secret and trench maps, and all other maps - with the exception of LENS 11 and ABBEVILLE 14 scale 1/100,000 - will be handed over to incoming units.

11. The command of Groups and Batteries will pass to 56th. Divisional Artillery Units on completion of relief at 5 p.m. on the 6th.
   Completion of reliefs to be reported by wire to this office.

12. The hour at which the command will pass from C.R.A. 60th. Division to C.R.A. 56th. Division will be notified later.

13 Acknowledge.

Major.
Brigade Major,
60th. Divisional Artillery.

4th. November 1916.

Copies to:-

No. 1 Right Group.
   2 Centre Group.
   3 Left Group.
   4 D.O.T.11.
   5 3rd. Canadian Division.
   6 C.R.A., 56th. Division.
   7 & 8 War Diary.
   8 File.

APPENDIX IV

OPERATION ORDER No. 37   Copy No. 12.

BY BRIGADIER GENERAL R.J.G.ELKINGTON, C.M.G.

COMMANDING 56th DIVNL. ARTILLERY:

November 4th 1916.

Reference 1/100,000 LENS Map.

1. 56th Divisional Artillery will continue the march tomorrow November 5th to Wagon Lines at ACQ, CAPELLE-FERMONT, LARESSET and FREVIN-CAPELLE.

2. For the purposes of relief of 60th Divisional Artillery the 56th Divisional Artillery will be formed into three groups and the 18-pdr Batteries will consist of 6 guns.
Groups as follows:-

RIGHT GROUP:

    Commanding - Lieut-Colonel E.C.POTTINGER

        282nd Brigade H.Q.   ) 2, 18-pdr Bties.
) (6-gun Bties.)
        282nd Brigade R.F.A.   ) 1, 4.5" How. Bty.

CENTRE GROUP:

    Commanding - Lieut-Colonel L.A.C.SOUTHAM.

        280th Brigade H.Q.   ) 3, 18-pdr Bties.
)   (6-gun Bties)
        280th Brigade R.F.A.   )
) 1, 4.5" How. Bty.
    and 93rd Battery R.F.A.   )
        made up to 6 guns.   )

LEFT GROUP:

    Commanding - Lieut-Colonel C.C.MACDOWELL.

        281st Brigade H.Q.   )
) 3, 18-pdr Bties.
        281st Brigade R.F.A.   ) (6-gun Bties.)
)
    and 109th Battery R.F.A.) 1, 4.5" How. Bty.
        made up to 6 guns.   )

3. The 282nd Brigade complete will march to Wagon Lines to the North of LARESSET, via LE CAUROY - AVESNES-LE-COMTE - HABARCQ.
    H.Q. and the present 18-pdr Batteries of 280th Brigade R.F.A. to Wagon Lines North of LARESSET, route as above.
    93rd Battery made up to 6 guns, to Wagon Lines at ACQ, via LE CAUROY - AVESNES-LE-COMTE - TILLOY-LES-HERMAVILLE.
    D/280 Battery to Wagon Lines at ACQ, route as for 93rd Battery.
    109th Battery made up to 6-guns to ACQ, route as for 93rd Battery.
    The 281st Brigade R.F.A. complete less Brigade H.Q. will march to Wagon Lines at CAPELLE-FERMONT via LE CAUROY - AVESNES-LE-COMTE - TILLOY-LES-HERMAVILLE.
    56th D.A.C. will march to FREVIN-CAPELLE via LE CAUROY - AVESNES-LE-COMTE - TILLOY-LES-HERMAVILLE.
    Hdqrs.Coy., 56th Divnl.Train, A.S.C., will march to HAUTE-AVESNES via LE CAUROY - AVESNES-LE-COMTE and TILLOY-LES-HERMAVILLE.

3. (continued)

The 93rd and 109th Batteries will be clear of the Cross Roads at ETREE-WAMIN Station by 7-45 am.
The 281st Brigade R.F.A. will pass this point at 8-0 am.
The 280th   "   "   "   "   "   "   at 8-30 am.
the 282nd   "   "   "   "   "   "   at 9-0 am.
The 56th Divnl.Ammn.Col.   "   "   "   "   at 9-30 am.
H.Q.Coy.56th Divnl.Train will be clear of ETREE-WAMIN by 7-15 am or will march in rear of the Divisional Artillery as preferred by the O.C., H.Q.Company.

4.   H.Q. 283rd Brigade R.F.A. will for the present be attached to the RIGHT GROUP.

5.   Advanced parties of Batteries going to LARESSET should be at the Wagon Lines at 9-30 am.
Advanced parties of remaining Batteries and D.A.C. to be at 60th Divisional Artillery Headquarters at AUBIGNY at 9-0 am.
Advanced party from H.Q. Coy. 56th Divnl. Train should be at HAUTE-AVESNES by 10-0 am to take over billets from H.Q.Coy., 60th Divnl. Train.

6.   Group Headquarters will march to-morrow morning as follows:-

RIGHT GROUP - to Wagon Lines at LARESSET.
CENTRE GROUP- "   "   "   "   "
LEFT GROUP   - to Wagon Lines at ACQ.

and will proceed to Forward Headquarters (positions to be notified later) at night.

7.   56th Div.R.A.,H.Q. will close at REBREUVE at 9-30 am 5th Nov. & be established at AUBIGNY at 10-30 am same day.

BRUCE MACMIN,

Captain,
for Brigade Major,R.A.,
56th Division.

4-11-16.

Copy No.1, to 280th Brigade R.F.A.
      2, to 281st Brigade R.F.A.
      3, to 282nd Brigade R.F.A.
      4, to 283rd Brigade R.F.A.
      5, to 56th Divnl.Ammn.Col.
      6, to H.Q.Coy.56th.Div.Train.A.S.C.
      7, to 56th Division.
      8)
      9)
     10) to 60th Division.
     11)
     12, to 60th Divisional Artillery.
     13, to Canadian Corps.
     14, to IVth Corps.
     15, to First Army.
     16, to Third Army.
     17, to Fifth Army.

APPENDIX V

SECRET.

First Army No. G.S.468.

Canadian Corps.

That part of First Army No. G.S.468 of the 1st Inst. relating to the disposal of B/300 18-pr. Battery is cancelled.

B/300 Battery will now procced to the First Army Artillery School at AIRE as Instructional Battery, as soon as convenient after it has been relieved in the line by a battery of the 56th Divisional Artillery. This battery will stay at the school until the beginning of December by which time it is hoped that a Horse Artillery Battery will have arrived to replace it, when it will probably join XI Corps.

A/300 18-pr. Battery will march direct to XI Corps as soon as relieved, under arrangements to be made direct between Canadian and XI Corps.

Canadian Corps will report when A/300 Battery leaves to join XI Corps, and what day B/300 Battery can reach the School at AIRE.

First Army.
4th Novr.1916.

(sd) J. BUND. Lt. Col.
for Major General.
General Staff, First Army.

---------2---------

CANADIAN CORPS.
G.382/1
4th November 1916.

3rd Canadian Division.

Forwarded in continuation of Canadian Corps G.382 dated 1st instant - to be passed to 60th Divisional Artillery for action and repart.
Acknowldege.

Copy to G.O.C.,R.A.
D.A.& Q.M.G.

(sd) J.G. DILL. Major, G.S.
for B.G., G.S.
Canadian Corps.

---------3---------

3rd Canadian Division
G.156/1

C.R.A.,60th Divl. Arty.
A. & Q.

Passed in accordance with Minute 2 for action and report.
Acknowledge.

(sd) F.LOGAN ARMSTRONG,
Lt. Col. General Staff
3rd Canadian Divn.

5th Novr.1916.

To C.R.A., 60th Divl Artillery.
   A.& Q.
   A. P. M.

G.226   5/11/16.

Following received from Canadian Corps AAA begins AAA
Reference Canadian Corps G.382/1 dated 4th November
moves will be carried out as follows AAA B/300 Battery
on 7th November to PERNES via TINQUES CHELERS - MONCHY-BRETON
VALHOUN AAA On 8th Novr to AIRE via FERFAY and STHILAIRE
AAA A/300 Btty on 7th Novr. via HERSIN - NOEUXLES MINES-
BETHUNE to LOCON where it will join 5th Divisional
Artillery AAA ends.

From 3rd Canadian Divn.
7.30 p.m.   (sd) F.LOGAN ARMSTRONG.
                                         Major, G.S.

"A" Form. Army Form C. 2121.
MESSAGES AND SIGNALS.

TO
Canadian Corps
C.R.A. 60th Divisional Arty.
A. & Q.

Sender's Number.	Day of Month.	In reply to Number.	A A A
G.241	6-11-16.		

300   300

Move of PLOVER and BEETLE, postponed 24 hours

as transport not yet arrived AAA Addsd. Canadian

Corps reptd. C.R.A. 60th Divn. and A.& Q.

From Place: 3rd Canadian Division
Time: 6-50 p.m.

Lt.Col. G.S.

SECRET.

APPENDIX VI

COPY No. 7

60th DIVISIONAL ARTILLERY.

OPERATION ORDER NO.3.

Wagon Lines of 60th Divisional Artillery (less gun limbers) will march tomorrow, 5th instant to the ETREE WAMIN are as follows:-

Unit.	Starting time.	From.	To.	Route.
(a) 301st Bde.	11.15 a.m. at ½ hour intervals to clear by NOON.	LARESSET	PETIT BOURET SUR CANCHE and REBREUVE.	HABARCQ - AVESNES LE COMTE - ETREE WAMIN.
302nd Bde.	(12.15 p.m.) (12.30 p.m.)	LARESSET	REBREUVIETTE	as in (a)
(b) 302nd Bde.	11 a.m. 11.15 a.m.	ACQ		HERMAVILLE - IZEL LES HAMEAU - MAGNICOURT SUR CANCHE.
303rd Bde.	C/303. 11.30 am. Noon at ½ hour intervals to clear by 12.30 p.m.	ACQ	WAMIN and ETREE WAMIN	as in (b)
		CAPELLE FERMONT.		
H.Q. Coy. 60th Train.	10.45 a.m.	HAUTE AVESNES.	BROUILLY and ROZIERE.	as in (a)

2. A guide from each battery and Brigade Headquarters will meet Train wagons at Cross Roads S.W. of First E. in ETREE WAMIN at 5 p.m. to lead wagons to their billets.

3. Billetting parties will meet Staff Captain R.A. at REBREUVIETTE Church at Noon 5th instant.

4th November 1916.

(signature)
Major. Brigade Major.
60th Divisional Artillery.

Copies to :- No.1. Right Group, No.2. Centre Group, No.3. Left Group, No.4. 56th Divisional Artillery,

SECRET.　　　　　　　　　　　　　　　　　　　　　Copy No................

APPENDIX VII.

19

60th DIVISIONAL ARTILLERY.

OPERATION ORDER NO. 4.

1. Wagon lines of 60th Divisional Artillery (less gun limbers) will march tomorrow, 6th instant to the BOUBERS area as follows :-

Unit.	Starting time.	From.	To.	Route.	Remarks.
301st Bde.	8 a.m. at 10 minute intervals.	BOFFLES and FORTEL.	CONCHY SUR CANCHE and MONCHEL.		To be clear of present area by 9 a.m. and
302nd Bde.	8 a.m. at 10 minute intervals.	NOEUX and VILLERS L'HOPITAL.	VACQUERIE LE - BOUCQ (North of PETIT FORTEL)		PREVENT-AUXI-LE-CHATEAU Road to be clear by 11 a.m.
303rd Bde.	7.45 a.m. at 10 minute intervals.	BONNIERES	BOUBERS-SUR-CANCHE and LIGNY-SUR-CANCHE.		do.
Train.	according to refilling arrangements.	BONNIERES	AUDROMETZ		present area must be cleared by 9 a.m.

2. Units will send on billetting parties and arrange their own accommodation within the areas allotted above.

3. Wagon lines will move on the 7th to the ETREE WAMIN area under orders to be issued later. The Divisional Artillery will be concentrated in this area on that day.

C. Essame.

Major, Brigade Major.
60th Divisional Artillery.

Copies to :- No 1 +2. Knight Group H.Q. + Wagon lines   No 4. 60 Divl. Train
                  3+4 Sept   "   "   "   No 8. 3rd Canadian Divn.
                  5+6 Conrm   "   "   "   No 9. Lid.

APPENDIX VIII

SECRET.

Copy No:..............

60th DIVISIONAL ARTILLERY.

OPERATION ORDER No. 5.

1. Guns and Howitzers of 60th Divisional Artillery will/withdraw from their present Wagon lines tomorrow, the 6th instant, and march to the ETREE WAMIN area, as follows :-

Unit.	Starting time.	From.	To.	Route.	Remarks.
(a) 301st Bde.	8.45 a.m. at 5 minute intervals to 9 a.m.	LARESSET	PETIT BOURET SUR GANCHE and REBREUVE.	HABARCH -AVESNES LE COMTE ETREE WAMIN.	ETREE WAMIN
(a) 302nd Bde.	9.5 a.m. and 9.10 a.m.	LARESSET	.REBREUVIETTE.	as in (a)	not to be
(b)	9 a.m. and 9.5 am.	ACQ	WAMIN and ETREE WAMIN.	HERMAVILLE-AVESNES LE COMTE- ETREE WAMIN.	entered before
303rd Bde.	C/303. 9.15am. 9 a.m.) 9.5 am) 9.10am.)	ACQ CAPELLE FERMONT.		as in (b) as in (b)	NOON.

2. Guns and Howitzers will remain in the ETREE WAMIN area on the 7th instant, where they will be joined by Wagon lines from the BOUBERS area.

Major. Brigade Major.
60th Divisional Artillery.

SECRET.

APPENDIX IX

Copy No..........

60th DIVISIONAL ARTILLERY.

OPERATION ORDER NO. 6.

1. Wagon lines of 60th Divisional Artillery (less gun limbers) will march tomorrow, 7th Instant to the ETREE WAMIN area, where they will join the remainder of their batteries.

Unit.	Starting time.	From.	To.	Route.	Remarks.
301st Bde.	9.45 a.m.	CONCHY SUR CANCHE and MONCHEL.	PETIT BOURET SUR CANCHE and REBREUVE.	Direct via FREVENT.	No Unit to pass through FREVENT before 10 a.m.
302nd Bde.	9.45 a.m.	VACQUERIE LE-BOUCQ	REBREUVIETTE		
303rd Bde.	9.45 a.m.	BOUEERS-SUR-CANCHE and LIGNY SUR CANCHE	WAMIN and ETREE WAMIN.		
Train.	9.45 a.m.	AUDROMETZ	BROUILLY and ROZIERE.		

2. Units will send on advance parties to find the positions of their gun billets in above villages, and to lead Units in on arrival.

3. The 60th Divisional Artillery will remain in above area on 8th instant.

Major. Brigade Major.
60th Divisional Artillery.

6th November 1916.

Copies to :- No.1. Right Group, No.2. Centre Group, No.3. Left Group, No.4. 60th Divisional Train,
No.5. 3rd Canadian Division, No.6. 56th Divisional Artillery, No.7.& 8. War Diary,
No.9. File.

SECRET.   Copy No.

OPERATION ORDER NO. 7.   APPENDIX X

(1) The 60th Divisional Artillery (less D.A.C. and Trench Mortars) will move tomorrow 9th inst, and billet for the night 9th/10th in "A" area 5th Army as follows :-

Unit.	Starting Point.	Starting Time.	From.	To.	Route.	Remarks.
(a) 301st Bde & E in LA COUTURE.	Road junction ½ mile North of	9 a.m.	PETIT BOURET SUR-CANCHE and REBREUVE.	BEAUVOIR LA COUTURE RIVIERE	BOUQUEMAISON R of BARLY-OUTREBOIS-FROHEN LE GRAND.	
(b) 302nd Bde & H.Q.R.A.	as in (a)	9.30 a.m.	REBREUVIETTE	BEALCOURT and ST ACHEUL	as in (a)	
(c) 303rd Bde & Detachment Signal Coy.	Cross Roads S.W. of first E in ETREE WAMIN	9.30 a.m.	WAMIN and ETREE WAMIN	OUTREBOIS (South of river)	BEAUDRICOURT IVERGNY- LE SOUICH-HTE VISEE	
(d) H.Q.Coy Div.Train.	as in (a)	10 a.m.	BROUILLY and ROZIERE	OCCOCHES (South of river)	LA COUTURE - BOUQUEMAISON - NEUVILLETTE	

REMARKS

"A" area is not to be entered before 10 a.m.
All troops to be West of DOULLENS-FREVENT road by NOON.

(2) Units will send on billetting parties to make their own arrangements for billetting.

(3) Refilling Point, Chateau at OCCOCHES.

(4) H.Q.R.A. will be at BEALCOURT.

(5) The Divisional Artillery will march South in the morning of the 10th instant to No. 6 area Fourth Army.

                                                 Major.
                                          Brigade Major.
8th November 1916.   60th Divisional Artillery.

Copies to :- Nos.1. Right Group, Nos.2. Left Group, Nos.3. Centre Group.
           No.4. H.Q.Coy Div.Train. Nos.5 H.Q. 61st Division.
           Nos.6&7. War Diary. Nos.8. File.

SECRET.

APPENDIX XII

Copy no.

60th DIVISIONAL ARTILLERY.

OPERATION ORDER NO.6.

(Reference LENS Map 11,
AMIENS " 17)

(1) The 60th Divisional Artillery (less D.A.C. and Trench Mortars) will continue the march tomorrow, the 10th instant, and will billet for the night 10th/11th as follows :-

Unit.	Starting Point.	Starting Time.	From.	To.	Route.
303rd F.A.Bde. and Detachment Signal Coy.	Branch roads ½ mile S.E. of S. in OUTREBOIS	8.15am	OUTREBOIS	BELLOY-SUR-SOMME.	BERNAVILLE-DOMART EN PONTIEU-ST LEGER LES DOMART -ST OUEN- BETHEN COURT
302nd F.A.Bde. and H.Q.R.A.	T of BEALCOURT	8.45am.	BEALCOURT	BOURDON	do
301st F.A.Bde.	S.W. end of BEAUVOIR RIVIERE	9.10am.	BEAUVOIR RIVIERE	BETHENCOURT -ST-OUEN.	do
Coy H.Q./Divl Train.6	Cross roads S. of OCCOCHES.	9.45am.	OCCOCHES.	YZEUX.	do

(2) BETHENCOURT-ST-OUEN will not be entered before 12.30 pm.

(3) H.Q. 60th Divisional Artillery will be at AILLY-LE-HAUT-CLOCHER (Ref map ABBEVILLE 14)

(4x) Billetting accommodation must be arranged for Brigade Ammunition Columns.

R.C.Pierre

Major.
Brigade Major.
60th Divisional Artillery.

9th November 1916.

Copies to :- Nos 1. Right Group, No.2.Left Group,No.3. Centre Group,
No.4.Divisional Train. Nos.5&6 War Diary.No.7.File.

APPENDIX XI

SECRET.   COPY NO. 1

THIRD ARMY ORDER NO. 89.

Ref. Map. LENS 1/100,000.   5th November 1916.

1. The 60th Divisional Artillery (less D.A.C. personnel of Heavy Trench Mortar Battery, two 18-pounder Batteries and one 4.5" How. Battery) will be transferred from the First Army to join its Division in the Fourth Army by march route and will come under the orders of the Third Army from midnight 5th/6th November.

2. The 60th Divisional Artillery will move in accordance with the attached march table.

3. Accommodation Tables for billets in the BOUBERS and ETREE WAMIN areas are attached.

4. Supply Railhead on 7th, 8th and 9th November will be at FREVENT.

5. ACKNOWLEDGE.

J.F.C. Fuller Maj.
General Staff Third Army.

Issued at :- 8.45 pm

Copy No. 1. 60th Divl Arty.   No. 8-9. G.
         2. 60th Division.   10-12. Q.
         3. First Army.   13. A.
         4. Fifth Army.   14. P.M.
         5. Fourth Army.   15. D.D. of Signals.
         6. VIth Corps.   16. War Diary.
         7. VIIth Corps.

MARCH TABLE 60th Divisional Artillery.   Issued with Third Army Order No. 89 dated 5th Nov. 1916.

Unit.	Date.	From.	To.	Route.	Remarks.
Wagon Line 30th Divl. Artillery.	6th Nov.	BONNIERES BOFFLES FORTEL BEAUVOIR.	BOUBERS Area.	BONNIERES - FORTEL.	To clear BONNIERES by 9 a.m. To clear FREVENT - AUXI LE CHATEAU Road by 11 a.m.
--do--	7th Nov.	BOUBERS Area.	ETREE WAMIN Area.	LIGNY SUR CANCHE FREVENT - ETREE WAMIN.	Not to cross FREVENT before 10 a.m.
Remainder of 60th Divl. Arty. (less D.A.C. Heavy T. Personnel 2.18 pr. Battys 1.4.5" How. Betty.).	6th & 7th Novr.	First Army Area.	ETREE-WAMIN Area.	Any roads East & exclusive of ST POL - FREVENT Road.	On 6th Novr. the ETREE WAMIN area will not be entered before 12 noon.

Further orders will be issued later.

SECRET. Copy No. 1

THIRD ARMY ORDER No. 90.

Ref. Map LENS 1/100,000.   6th November, 1916.

In continuation of Third Army Order No. 89.

1. The 60th Divisional Artillery (less Divisional Ammunition Column, Heavy Trench Mortar personnel, two 18- pounder batteries and one 4.5" How. Battery) will march to rejoin their Division in the Fourth Army Area in accordance with the attached March Table.

2. A representative of the 60th Divisional Artillery will report to Headquarters IV Corps DOMART EN PONTHIEU on or before the 8th to arrange billets for the night of the 9th/10th November in A. Area Fifth Army.

3. ACKNOWLEDGE.

Issued at :- 3 p.m.

General Staff, Third Army.

```
Copy No. 1. to 60th Div. Arty.
        2. "  60th Division.
        3. "  First Army.
        4. "  Fifth Army.
        5. "  Fourth Army.
        6. "  61st Division.
        7. "  VI Corps.
        8. "  VII Corps.
     9-10. "  G.
    11-13. "  Q.
       14. "  A.
       15. "  P.M.
       16. "  D.D. of Signals.
       17. "  War Diary.
       18. "  IVth Corps.
```

60th Divisional Artillery March Table.   Issued with

Third Army Order No. 90 dated 6th November 1916.

Unit.	Date.	From.	To.	Route.	Remarks.
60th Divisional Artillery (less D.A.C. Heavy T.M. personnel, two 18-pdr. Batteries and one 4.5" How. battery.	9th Novr.	ETREE WAMIN area	A. area Fifth Army. (about OCCOCHES & OUTREBOIS south bank).	Any roads between GND BOURET - BOUQUE-MAISON - NEUVILLETTE - BARLY - OUTREBOIS road and ETREE WAMIN - BEAUDRICOURT - IVERGNY - LE SOUICH - HTE VISEE road both inclusive.	To be WEST of the DOULLENS - FREVENT road by noon.
-do-	10th Novr	A. area Fifth Army	Fourth Army under orders of Fourth Army.		

"A" Form.   Army Form C. 2121.
MESSAGES AND SIGNALS.

TO: 60th Divisional Artillery,
A. & Q. 3rd. Canadian Division.
A.P.M.

Sender's Number.	Day of Month	In reply to Number	
G.235	6-11-16		AAA

The following received from Canadian Corps AAA
Begins AAA. The moves ordered in Canadian Corps
G.456 forwarding First Army G.S.468 dated 4th.
~~will take place 24 hours sooner than ordered~~
AAA Under arrangements made by ~~SOPPER~~ moves to
ETREE WAMIN will be carried out on 6th. and 7th.
~~inst. AAA Ends.~~

3rd Army.

From: 3rd. Canadian Division.
Place:
Time: 12.45 p.m.

Lt.Col
G.S.

SECRET.

First Army.No. G.S. 468.

Canadian Corps.

The 60th Divisional Artillery (less Divisional Ammunition Column and personnel of Heavy Trench Mortar Battery, which are moving to join the 60th Division on 3rd November, and less two 18-pounder Batteries and one 4.5" How. Battery, which are remaining temporarily under the First Army) will be transferred from 1 Canadian Corps to join the 60th Division in the Fourth Army area.

2. The transfer will be carried out by march route as shown below :-

Date.	March.	Administered by.
9th November	Under orders of Third Army to ETREE - WAMIN area.	Third Army.
10th November.	Under Orders of Third Army to MEZEROLLES area.	Third Army.
11th November.	Under orders of 4th Army to No. 6 area.	Fourth Army.

3. The full complement of ammunition will be carried.

4. Acknowledge by wire.

(sd) O.H.L.NICHOLSON, Major, G.S.
Major General.
General Staff, First Army.

First Army.
2nd November, 1916.

Canadian Corps. G.456.
5th November, 1916.

- 3 -

3rd Canadian Division.
G.221.

C. R. A. 60th Div'l Arty.
A. P. M. 3rd Canadian Divn.
A. & Q.   "

For your information.

[signature]
Lt. Colonel.
General Staff,
3rd Canadian Division.

5-11-16.

APPENDIX XLII

SECRET

Q/5885   Z.Q 1345/69

60th Division.

With reference to Q/5885, dated 10.11.16.

Please hold the following Units ready to entrain on dates as stated.

The numbers as shown should be adhered to as far as possible, any surplus numbers called for by the A.D.R.T.IV to fill up the train should be supplied, and reported in detail to this office as soon as possible.

The entraining station will be LONGPRE for all troops, horses, wagons etc., LONGUEAU for Motor Transport.

Entrain 15th November.

	Units.	Offi-cers.	Other ranks.	Horses.	Four wheel-ed	4 wheel-ed limb'd	Two wheel-ed	Guns.
	Advanced party.	3	1					
	H.Q. Div. R.E.	3	59	102	12	6		
(2/4)	1 Field Company R.E.	7	237	25				
(2/4)	1 Field Ambulance.	11	409	67	3			
(179th)	H.Q. Infantry Brigade.	7	40	20				
"	2 Infantry Battns.	80	1072	48				
(302nd)	2 Batteries R.F.A.	10	280	270	2	16	4	8
"	1 Bde.Ammn.Column.	3	108	135	2	16	2	
"	1 H.Q. Bde. R.F.A.	5	49	48	1	1	3	
(179th & 180th)	2 T.M.Batteries L.	8	92					
		137	3147	715	20	39	9	8

Entrain 16th November.

	Units.	Offi-cers.	Other ranks.	Horses.	Four wheel-ed	4 wheel-ed limb'd	Two wheel-ed	Guns.
(302nd)	x2 Batteries R.F.A.	2	40		2	16	4	8
(181st)	1 T.M.Battery L.	4	46					
(179th)	1 Secn.Div.Sig.Coy.	1	27	10				
	1 S.A.A. Section.	3	255	25				
		10	368	35	2	16	4	8

x Portion of 2 Batteries R.F.A.

G.H.Q.   Sgd. C.P.Higginson. Lt. Col.
November 10th 1916.   for Quartermaster General.

C.R.E.   -----------
A.D.M.S.   /399/7
C.R.A.
179th Inf. Bde.
180th Inf. Bde.   For information.
181st Inf. Bde.
-----------   The Units to be detailed are noted in the
Signal Coy.   margin.
Camp Commandant.

60th Divl. H.Q.   Major.
11. 11. 16.   D.A.A.& Q.M.G.

Q/5885.

60th Division.

In addition to troops already detailed to entrain on the 16th, Q.5885, dated 10.11.16, the following troops will also entrain:-

Entrain 16th November.

Units.	Officers.	Other Ranks.	Horses.	4 Wheeled Limb'd.
2 Batteries, R.F.A. less 2 Officers, 40 men and all Max Vehicles.	8	240	270	
Divisional Ammunition Column.	3	120	190	60

G.H.Q.
12.11.1916.

(sd) C.P. HIGGINSON, Lt.Col.
for Quartermaster General.

C.R.A.
O.C. Train. } for information
Q.

For necessary action in continuation of my minute S/399/7 of 11th inst. forwarding copy of G.H.Q. Q 5885/ZQ 1345/69, dated 10th inst.

12th November 1916.

Major.
D.A.A. & Q.M.G.

60th Divn.

Q.D.519.   11th Novr.

In addition to troops already detailed in Q.5885 of 10th Nov. to entrain for Marseilles on the 15th Nov. two battns. of Infantry and 50 4-wheeled vehicles of D.A.C. will also entrain on that date AAA.

                            Q.M.G.   G.H.Q.

                 2.   A/1611/32.

C.R.A.
H.Q. 179th Inf.Bde.
O.C.Train
Q.
G.

For information and necessary action.

11.11.1916.

                          Major.
                     D.A.A. & Q.M.G.

SECRET

C.R.A.
H.Q., 179th Infantry Brigade.
H.Q., 180th Infantry Brigade.
A.D.M.S.
~~S.S.~~
"A"
"G"

        The attached Tables of Entrainments are forwarded for your information and necessary action

"Q"
13/11/16

Captain.
for D.A.Q.M.G.

APPENDIX XIV
S/399/7

S E C R E T.

60th DIVISION — ENTRAINMENTS.

LONGPRÉ to MARSEILLES.

TRAIN.	DATE.	UNIT.	To be at Station.	Train depts.	Type train.	Off.	O.R.	Horses.	Mules Vehicles. 4 whl. 2 whl.		Lewis guns.	Hotchkiss T.Mortars.	
	NOVBR.												
1st	14	2/4 Fd.Ambce. D.A.C.(part)	3.15 p.m. do.	6.17pm do.	T.C. "	11 1	409 20	67 —	3 11	— 12	— —	— —	— —
2nd	14	2/15 Bn.Ldn.R.(Pt) D.A.C.(part)	6.30pm do.	9.27pm do.	T.P. "	23 1	250 30	24 —	1 28	— 10	8 —	— —	— —
3rd	15	2/4 Fd.Co.RE.(14) 302nd B.A.C.	9.30pm do. —	12.27am do.	T.C. "	7 3	237 108	25 136	1 2	2 18	— —	— —	— —
4th	15	1 By.302 F.A.Bde. 179 T.M.Btty. 180 -do- H.Q.179 Inf.Bde.	3.30am do. do. do.	6.27am do. do. do.	T.C. " " "	5 4 4 8	140 46 46 40	135 — — 21	1 — — —	26 — — —	— — — —	— — — —	8 8 — —
5th	15	1 By.302 F.A.Bde. H.Q. 302 do. 2/15 Bn.L.R.(Part)	6.30am do. do.	9.27am do. do.	T.C. " "	5 5 4	140 49 50	135 48 —	1 1 —	26 5 —	— — —	— — —	8 — —
6th	15	2/13 Bn.L.R. 2/15 Bn.L.R.(Part)	9.30am do.	12.26pm do.	SPECIAL "	39 4	930 ½ 220	24 —	— —	— —	8 —	— —	— —
7th	15	2/14 Bn.L.R. 2/15 Bn.L.R.(Part)	3.15pm do.	6.17pm do.	SPECIAL "	39 4	930 ½ 220	24 —	— —	— —	8 —	— —	— —
8th	15	2/16 Bn.L.R. 2/15 Bn.L.R.(Part)	6.30pm do.	9.27pm do.	SPECIAL "	39 4	930 ½ 220	24 —	— —	— —	8 —	— —	— —

"Q" 60th Division
NOVEMBER 13th 1916.

S E C R E T.

60th DIVISION — ENTRAINMENTS.
LONGPRE to MARSEILLES.

TRAIN.	DATE.	UNIT.	To be at Station.	Train depts.	Type train.	Off.	O.R.	Horses (Chevaux)	Vehicles 4 whl.	Vehicles 2 whl.	guns Lewis.	T.Mortars (Hanseaux)
1st	NOVBR. 14	2/4 Fld.Ambce. D.A.C.(part)	3.15 p.m. do.	6.17pm do	T.C. "	11 1	409 20	67 —	3 11	— 12	— —	— —
2nd	14	2/15 Bn.Ldn.R.(Pt) D.A.C.(part)	6.30pm do.	9.27pm do.	T.P. "	23 1	250 30	24 —	28 —	— 10	8 —	— —
3rd	15	2/4 Fld.Co.RE.(14) 302nd B.A.C.	9.30pm —	12.27am do.	T.C. "	7 3	237 108	25 136	— 2	— 18	— —	— —
4th	15	1 By.302 F.A.Bde. 179 T.M.Btty. -do- H.Q.179 Inf.Bde.	3.30am do do do	6.27am do. do. do.	T.C. " " "	5 4 4 8	140 46 46 40	135 — — 21	1 — — —	26 — — —	— — — —	— 8 8 —
5th	15	1 By.302 F.A.Bde. H.Q. 302 do 2/15 Bn.L.R.(Part)	6.30am do do do	9.27am do do do	T.C. " " "	5 5 4	140 49 50	135 48 —	1 1 —	26 5 —	— — —	— — —
6th	15	2/13 Bn.L.R. 2/15 Bn.L.R.(Part)	9.30am do	12.26pm do	SPECIAL "	39 4	930 220	24 —	— —	— —	8 —	— —
7th	15	2/14 Bn.L.R. 2/15 Bn.L.R.(Part)	3.15pm do	6.17pm do	SPECIAL "	39 4	930 220	24 —	— —	— —	8 —	— —
8th	15	2/16 Bn.L.R. 2/15 Bn.L.R.(Part)	6.30pm do	9.27pm do	SPECIAL "	39 4	930 220	24 —	— —	— —	8 —	— —

APPENDIX XV

S E C R E T.   Copy No...3........

60th DIVISIONAL ARTILLERY.
OPERATION ORDER NO. 9.

1. The following Units of the Divisional Artillery will move to the entraining station (LONGPRE) on the 14th and 15th instant, as follows :-

Unit.	Starting point.	Starting time.	Route.
1st portion D.A.C.	Cross roads just W. of P. in PONT REMY.	12.45 p.m.	LIERCOURT - FONTAINE.
2nd portion D.A.C.	do.	4 p.m.	do.
302nd Bde Ammn. Col.	Cross roads BOURDON	6.45 p.m.	HANGEST - CONDE.
B/302 Btty.	do.	1 a.m.	do.
H.Q., 302nd Bde & C/302 Btty.	do.	4 a.m.	do.

                                                   Major.
                                             Brigade Major.
                                    60th Divisional Artillery.

13th November 1916.

Copies to :- No.1. 302nd Bde.
               No.2. D.A.C.
               No.3. War Diary.
               No.4. File.

SECRET.

To 302nd F.A.Bde.
D.A.C.

Portions of the 302nd Brigade and D.A.C. will entrain on the 14th and 15th instant, as follows :-

Unit.	Off.	O.R.	Horses.	4 wheel.	2 wheel.	Train No.	Departs LONGPRE.	
D.A.C.(part)	1	20	-	11	12	First Train.	6.17pm. 14th inst.	Train also carries 2/4th Fd.Ambulance
D.A.C.(part)	1	30	-	28	10	2nd Train.	9.27pm. 14th inst.	Train also carries part of Inf. Bttn.
302nd Bde Ammn.Column.	3	108	136	2	18	3rd Train.	12.27am. 15th inst.	Train also carries 2/4th Fd.Coy. R.E.
1.Battery 302nd Bde. B/302	5	140	135	1	26	4th Train.	6.27am. 15th inst.	Train also carries H.Q. Inf. Bde, 2 Stokes Mortar Batty.
1 Battery 302nd Bde and C/302	5	140	135	1	26	5th Train.	9.27am. 15th inst.	Train carries part of Inf. Bttn.
H.Q. 302nd Bde.	5	49	48	1	5	do.	do.	

NOTES.

(a) Trains 1 and 2 are intended to take majority of transport of one Section D.A.C. with sufficient gunners for loading and unloading.

(b) G.S. wagons are shown as 4 wheel vehicles. Limbers wagons guns etc, are shown as 2 two wheeled vehicles.

(c) Train 3. is intended to take B.A.C.complete (exclusive of S.A.A.Section). Figures in "2-wheeled" column should read "34". The figure "18" has been queried, and result will be notified.

(d) Journey to MARSEILLES takes about 45 hours.

(e) Information has been received that an additional portion of the D.A.C. will entrain on the 15th. Details not yet received.

R.Crane
Major.
Brigade Major.
60th Divisional Artillery.

12th Novr.1916.

APPENDIX XVI

SECRET.

60th Division Order No 11.

Copy No ___6___

November 15th. 1916

Ref. Map LENS Sheet 11, ABBEVILLE Sheet 14, & AMIENS Sheet 17. 1/100,000.

1. The Division will continue to move Southwards on 16th & 17th November, in accordance with attached programme of entrainment and Schedule "A".

2. All units of the Division not mentioned in the attached programme of entrainment will remain in their present billets.

3. Acknowledge.

Issued at ___11 am___

C.A. Bolton Captain GS
for Lieut. Colonel,
General Staff.

Copies to

A.D.C. for G.O.C.
179th Inf. Bde.
179th M.G. Coy.
180th Inf. Bde.
181st   ,,   ,,
C.R.A.
C.R.E.
"A"
A.D.M.S.
Signals.

60th Amn. Sub-Park.
Div. Train.
Div. Supply Column
A.D.V.S.
Camp Commandant.
IVth Army.
XVth Corps.
War Diary.
File.

SECRET.   TABLE OF PERSONNEL, ANIMALS & VEHICLES
proceeding on the 16th & 17th Nov.

16th November.

No. of Train.	Type of Train.	Time of Departure.	Unit.	Officers	Other Ranks	Animals	4 wheeled	2 wheeled
9th.	T.C.	10-27 a.m.	Part One Batty. 302nd.R.F.A.Bde. Det.Div.Amn.Col.	4. 1.	120. 60.	135. 95.	1.	26. 30.
10th.	T.C.	2-17 p.m.	Part One Batty. 302nd.R.F.A.Bde. Det.Div.Amn.Col.	4. 2.	120. 60.	135. 95.	1.	26. 30.
11th.	T.P.	5-27 p.m.	Part of above two Batteries 302nd. R.F.A.Bde. 181st.T.M.Batty. No.2.Sec.Div.Signals. *Small Arms Section* Amn.Col.	2. 4. 1. 3.	40. 46. 27. 255.	— 10. — 25.	— — — —	— — — —

*Det. of a Bn. 180th.Inf.Bde.of approx. strength.

17th November.

No. of Train.	Type of Train.	Time of Departure.	Unit.	Officers	Other Ranks	Animals	4 wheeled	2 wheeled
12th.	T.C.	10-27 a.m.	Det.Div.Amn.Col. Det.3/17th.Lond.R.	3. 5.	100. 5.	255. —	— —	56. —
13th.	Special	2-17 p.m.	Det.Div.Amn.Col. Det.2/17th.Lond.R.	2. 5.	140. 5.	370. —	— —	— —
14th.	T.C.	5-27 p.m.	Det.Div.Amn.Col. Det.2/17th.Lond.R.	2. 2.	200. 100.	— 84.	— —	36. 20.
15th.	Special	9-27 p.m.	179th.M.G.Co. Det.Div.Train. Det.2/17th.Lond.R.	19. 10. 2. 10.	608. 182. 50. 340.	— 10. 92. —	— — — —	— — — —

	1st.Class.	Covered Trucks.	Flat Trucks.	Brake Vans.
	1.	33.	14.	2.
	1.	24.	23.	2.
	1.	47.	—	2.

Types of Trains. T.C. = Type combatant, composed of ....
T.P. = Type Pure, composed of ....
Special = composed of ....

SECRET.

PROGRAMME OF MOVEMENT.

16th November, 1916.

UNIT.	Starting point.	Time of start.	Route to Station.	Entraining Stn.	Time due at Stn.	Time of departure of train.
Pt.of I Btty. 302 Bde, R.F.A.	BOURDON Cross Roads.	5-30 a.m.	HANGEST-sur- SOMME - CONDE.	LONGPRE	7-27 a.m.	10-27 a.m.
Det. Divl. Amn. Col.	Cross Roads just W. of PONT REMY	4-30 a.m.	LIERCOURT- FONTAINE.	"	"	"
Pt.of I Btty. 302 Bde, R.F.A.	BOURDON Cross Roads.	9-15 a.m.	HANGEST-sur- SOMME - CONDE.	"	11-17 a.m.	2-17 p.m.
Det. Divl. Amn. Col.	Cross Roads just T.of P. of PONT REMY.	8-15 a.m.	LIERCOURT- FONTAINE.	"	"	"
Rendr.of above 2 Battys.302nd Bde, R.F.A.	BOURDON Cross Roads.	Those portions must go with remainder of their Batteries to the Station and remain there until due for entrainment.	"	"	2-27 p.m.	5-27 p.m.
181 T.M.Batty.	Cross Roads BRUCAMPS.	12-15 p.m.	VAUCHELLES-les- DOMART-La FOLIE- L'ETOILE-CONDE.	"	"	"
No.2 Sec.Div. Signal Coy.	Cross Roads just S.W. of B.of BELLAN- COURT.	11-20 a.m.	PONT REMY- LIERCOURT- FONTAINE.	"	"	"
Small Arms Sec. Amn. Col. ※ or ※	BOURDON Cross Roads.	12-30 p.m.	HANGEST-sur- SOMME - CONDE.	"	"	"
Det.of a Batt. 180 Inf. Bde.						

※ If the S.A. Section, Ammunition Column is available, it will proceed, otherwise the detachment of a Battalion, 180th Inf. Bde. will move. Instructions will be issued as soon as possible as to which is to go by the train. The time of starting and route will be arranged by the 180th Inf. Bde., should their detachment go, and the Divisional H'qrs must be informed.

(1)

SECRET.

PROGRAMME OF ENTRAINMENT.

17th November, 1916.

Unit.	Starting point.	Time of start.	Route to station.	Entraining Stn.	Time due at Stn.	Time of departure of train.
Det. Divl. Ammn. Col.	Cross Roads just W. of P of Pont REMY.	5-0 a.m.	LIERCOURT-FONTAINE.	LONGPRE.	7-27 a.m.	10-27 a.m.
Det. 2/17th Bn, Lond. R. ⁂	Road Junction in BUSSUS BUSSUEL leading to AILLY.		AILLY-le-HAUT CLOCHER-LONG.	"	"	"
Det. Divl. Ammn. Col.	Cross Roads just W. of P of PONT REMY.	9 a.m.	LIERCOURT-FONTAINE.	"		
Det. 2/17th Bn, Lond. R. ⁂	Road Junction in BUSSUS BUSSUEL leading to AILLY.		AILLY-le-HAUT CLOCHER-LONG.	"	11-17 a.m.	2-17 p.m.
Det. Divl. Ammn. Col.	Cross Roads just W. of P of PONT REMY.	12 noon.	LIERCOURT-FONTAINE.	"		
Det.Divl. Train.	Road junction Eastern end of YZEUX.	12-15 p.m.	BOURDON-HANGEST-sur-SOMME-CONDE.	"	2-27 p.m.	5-27 p.m.
Det. 2/17th Bn, Lond. R.	Road Junction in BUSSUS BUSSUEL leading to AILLY.	11-40 a.m.	AILLY-le-HAUT CLOCHER-LONG.	"	"	"
Det. 2/17th Bn, Lond. R. 179 M.G. Coy.	Road Junction just N. of V of VAUCHELLES.	2-15 p.m.	PONT REMY-LIERCOURT-FONTAINE.	"	6-27 p.m.	9-27 p.m.
Det. Divl. Train.	Road junction Western end of YZEUX.	3-40 p.m.	BOURDON-HANGEST-sur-SOMME-COND.	"	"	"

⁂ These parties can move under Bde. arrangements but must arrive at entraining station 1½ hours before departure of train.

S E C R E T.   Following amendments to   COPY NO.......
SCHEDULE "A" AND PROGRAMME OF ENTRAINMENT 16th.Nov.1916.
Issued with 60th.Div.Order.No.11 are to be inserted in all copies.

SCHEDULE "A".

10.9th.Train first line 5 Officers 140 other ranks instead of 4 Officers 120 other ranks.
          third line 1   ,,   40   ,,   ,,   ,,   1   ,,   60   ,,   ,,
    16th.,, first line 5 ,,   140   ,,   ,,   ,,   4   ,,   120   ,,   ,,
          third line 1   ,,   40   ,,   ,,   ,,   2   ,,   60   ,,   ,,
    11th.,, first line Det.Div.Amn.Col. instead of "part of above 2 Batteries 302nd.R.F.A.Bde.
          consisting of 1 Officer 40 other ranks, NO animals, NO 4 wheeled vehicles, 60.-2 wheeled.
          INSTEAD OF:... 2 Officers 40   ,,   ,,   NO ,,   2-4 ,,   ,, ,,   84.-2   ,,

PROGRAMME OF ENTRAINMENT.
16th.November.1916.

UNIT.	STARTING POINT.	TIME OF START.	ROUTE TO STATION.	ENTRAINING STATION.	TIME DUE AT STN.	TIME OF DEPARTURE OF TRAIN.
Det.Divl. Amn.Col.	Cross Rds just W. of P of PONT REMY.	12 Noon.	LIERCOURT—FONTAINE.	LONGPRE.	2-27 p.m.	5-27 p.m.
					-do-	-do-

INSTEAD OF:-

Remdr.of BOURDON } These portions must go with -do-   -do-   -do-
above 2. cross Rds.} the remainder of their
Battys.   } Batteries to the Station
302nd.Bde.   } and remain there until due
R.F.A.   } for entrainment.

                                            [signature]
                                            Captain.G.S.
                                            for Lieut.Col.
                                            General Staff.

APPENDIX XVII

SECRET.   Copy No..........

60th DIVISIONAL ARTILLERY.
OPERATION ORDER No.10.

1. The 302nd Brigade and 60th Divisional Ammunition Column will continue entraining on the 16th and 17th instant as in attached Schedule "A".

2. Units will march to the entraining Station, as follows:-

Date.	Unit.	No. Train.	Starting point.	Starting Time.	Route.
16th. (a)	A/302 Bty.	9	BOURDON cross roads.	8.30 a.m.	HANGEST - CONDE.
" (b)	Detachment D.A.C.	9	Cross roads just West of P in PONT REMY.	4.50 a.m.	LIERCOURT - FONTAINE.
" (c)	D/302 Bty.	10	as in (a)	9.15 a.m.	as in (a)
" (d)	Detachment D.A.C.	10	as in (b)	9.15 a.m.	as in (b)
" (e)	Detachment D.A.C.	11	as in (b)	11.30 a.m.	as in (b)
17th. (f)	Detachment D.A.C.	12	as in (b)	5 a.m.	as in (b)
" (g)	Detachment D.A.C.	13	as in (b)	9 a.m.	as in (b)
" (h)	Detachment D.A.C.	14	as in (b)	Noon.	as in (b)

3. Advance parties of 1 Officer and 2 N.C.O's will arrive at the station ½ hour before their Units are due to arrive to mark off trucks etc.

15th November 1916.

Major.
Brigade Major.
60th Divisional Artillery.

Copies to :- No.1. A/302 Btty. No.2. D/302 Btty. No.3. O.C.,D.A.C.
No.4&5. War Diary. No.6. File.

SECRET.   SCHEDULE "A".

Date.	Train No.	Unit.	Offs.	O.R.	Horses.	4 Whld.	2 Whld.	Departs LONGPRE.	Remarks.
16th.	9	A/302 Bty.	5	140	135	1	26	10.27am	Battery complete.
	"	Detachment D.A.C.	1	40	95	-	30	"	
16th.	10	D/302 Bty.	5	140	135	1	26	2.17pm	Battery complete.
	"	Detachment D.A.C.	1	40	95	-	30	"	
16th.	11	Detachment D.A.C.	1	40	-	-	60	5.27pm	Train also carries Stokes Mortar & Infy. Detachment.
17th.	12	Detachment D.A.C.	3	100	255	-	56	10.27am	Train also carries detachment of 2/17th. Lon. Regiment.
17th.	13	Detachment D.A.C.	2	140	376	-	-	2.17pm	Do.
17th.	14	Detachment D.A.C.	2	200	-	-	36	5.27pm	Do.

NOTES:-

(a) G.S. Wagons are shown as 4-Wheeled vehicles.
Guns, limbered wagons, etc., are shown as two 2-Wheeled Vehicles.

(b) Halts Repas will be provided at the following stations:-
1 hour at MONTEREAU.   9 hours from LONGPRE.
½   "   " MACON.   12 "   "   MONTEREAU.
1   "   " PIERRELATTE.   9 "   "   MACON.

(c) PIERRELATTE to MARSEILLES takes 8 Hours.

APPENDIX XVIII

G/S.427.

A.D.C. for G.O.C.	Div. Train.
179 M.G.Co.	Div. Supply Column.
180 Inf.Bde.	A.D.V.S.
181 Inf. Bde.	Camp Commandant.
C.R.A.	IVth Army.
C.R.E.	XVth Corps.
"A".	War Diary.
A.D.M.S.	File.
Signals.	

              and 19th
Units will entrain on 18th/November 1916 in accordance with attached Schedule "A" and Programme of Entrainment.

Acknowledge.

C.A.Bolton.
Captain.
General Staff.
60th Division.

16/11/16.

SECRET
COPY NO. 5
SCHEDULE "A".

Table of Personnel, Animals and Vehicles proceeding on the 18th and 19th November 1915.

No. of Train.	Type of Train.	Time of Departure.	Unit.	Officers.	Other Ranks.	Animals.	Vehicles 4	Vehicles 2	Vehicles —
18th November 1915.									
16	T.C.	10.27 a.m.	H.Q. Div. R.E.	1	57	102	12	12	
			Det. 1/6 Fd. Co. R.E.	3	120				
			Part of 301 R.F.A. Bde.						20
17	Special.	2.17 p.m.	Amn. Col.	2	60	90			
			2/19 Lond.R.	39	958	24			
			Rem. 1/5 Fd. Co. R.E.	3	115	23			
			Det. 2/5 Fd. Amb.	3	130				
18	T.C.	5.27 p.m.	Rem. 301 R.F.A. Bde.	1	48	45	2	14	
			Amn. Col.	8	289	67	3		
			Rem. 2/5 Fd. Amb.	5	200	53		34	
			Det. Div.Train.	7	40	20			
19	Special.	9.27 p.m.	E.Q. 180 Inf. Bde.	39	958	24			
			2/20 Lond.R.						
19th November 1915.									
20	T.C.	10.27 a.m.	H.Q. 301 R.F.A. Bde.	5	49	48	1	5	
			One battery 301 R.F.A. Bde.	5	140	135	1	26	
			H.Q. Div. R.A.	2	117	23		4	
21	T.C.	5.27 p.m.	One battery 301 R.F.A. Bde.	5	140	135	1	26	
			Det. 35th Cas. Clearing Stn.	11	81				
			X.60 T.M.Battery.	2	23				
			H.Q. Div. Sig. Co.	1	59	35	2		

	1st Class.	Covered Trucks.	Flat Trucks
	1.	33.	14.
	1.	24.	23.
	1.	47.	

Types of Trains.
    T.C. = Type Combatant, composed of .....
    T.P. = Type Parc, composed of .....
    Special. = Composed of .....

SECRET.

COPY NO. 5

PROGRAMME OF ENTRAINMENT.

Ref. Map: LENS Sheet 11. AMIENS Sheet 17.
ABBEVILLE Sheet 14. 1/100,000.

18th November 1916.

Unit.	Starting Point.	Time of Starting.	Route to Station.	Entraining Station.	Time due at Station.	Time of departure of train.
H.Q. Div. R.E.	AILLY LE HAUT CLOCHER Crossroads.	5.5 a.m.	LONG - LE CATELET.	LONGPRE.	7.27 a.m.	10.27 a.m.
Det. 1/6 Fd. Co. R.E.	Crossroads BUSSUEL.	4.10 a.m.	AILLY - LONG - LE CATELET.	"	"	"
Part 301 R.F.A. Bde. Amm. Col.	Road junction just N. of BELLOY sur SOMME.	4.30 a.m.	BOURDON - HANGEST - CONDE.	"	"	"
2/19 Lond.R.	AILLY LE HAUT CLOCHER					
Rem. 1/6 Fd. Co R.E.	Crossroads BUSSUS.	10.30 a.m.	LONG - LE CATELET.	"	12.17 p.m.	2.17 p.m.
	Crossroads BUSSUEL.	9.25 a.m.	AILLY LONG - LE CATELET	"	"	"
Det. 2/5 Fd. Amb.	BUSSUEL.	9.25 a.m.		"	"	"
Rem. 301 R.F.A. Bde. Amm. Col.	Road junction just N. of BELLOY sur SOMME.	11.30 a.m.	BOURDON - HANGEST - CONDE.	"	2.27 p.m.	5.27 p.m.
Rem. 2/5 Fd.Amb.	Crossroads BUSSUS BUSSUEL.	11.40 a.m.	AILLY - LONG - LE CATELET.	"	"	"
Det. Div.Train.	(To be arranged by O.C. Div.Train.)					
H.Q. 180 Inf.bde.	Road junction S.E. end of GORENFLOS.	4.10 p.m.	BRUCAMPS - VAUCHELLES - LA FOLIE L'ETOILE CONDE.	"	6.27 p.m.	9.27 p.m.
2/20 Lond.R.	Crossroads VAUCOURT BUSSUS.	3.50 p.m.	AILLY - LONG - LE CATELET.	"	"	"

19th November 1916.

Unit.	Starting Point.	Time of Starting.	Route to Station.	Entraining Station.	Time due at Station.	Time of departure of train.
H.Q. /301 R.F.A. Bde.	Road junction just N. of BELLOY sur SOMME.	4.30 a.m.	BOURDON - HANGEST - CONDE.	"	7.27 a.m.	10.27 a.m.
One Btty. 301 R.F.A. Bde.	Road junction S. End of AILLY.	4.30 a.m.	"	"	"	"
H.Q. Div. R.A.	Road junction just N.W. of BELLOY.	5.40 a.m.	"	"	"	"
One Batty. 301 R.F.A. Bde.	AILLY LE HAUT CLOCHER.	11.30 a.m.	LONG - LE CATELET.	"	2.27 p.m.	5.27 p.m.
Det. 35 Cas. Clearing Station.	Crossroads.	12.40 p.m.	"	"	"	"
H.Q. Div. Sig. Co.	"	12.45 p.m.	"	"	"	"
X.60 Fld. Batty.	BOURDON Crossroads.	13.30 p.m.	HANGEST JC...	"	"	"

The following u.T. will also entrain on the 19th November 1916. Orders will be issued, as regards these, later.

```
                              Drivers.    Lorries.
Det. 35th Cas. Clearing Stn.     8          13.
Rem. 60th Amm. Sub. Park.       30          12.
Det. 60th Div. Supply Col.      40          13.
```

SECRET. G/S.427/2.

A.D.C. for G.O.C.   Div. Train.
179 M.G. Co.   Div. Supply Column.
180 Inf. Bde.   A.D.V.S.
181 Inf. Bde.   Camp Commandant.
C.R.A.   IVth Army.
C.R.E.   XVth Corps.
"A".   35 Cas. Clearing Stn.
A.D.M.S.   War Diary.
Signals.   File.

The attached is to be substituted for Programme of Entrainment for 18th and 19th November 1916 issued with G/S. 427 of the 16th, and the other programme is to be destroyed.

C.A. Bolton.

Captain.
General Staff.
60th Division.

17/11/16.

SECRET.

PROGRAMME OF ENTRAINMENT.

Ref. map: LENS Sheet 11. AMIENS Sheet 17. 18th November 1916.
ABBEVILLE Sheet 14. 1/100,000.

COPY NO..........

Unit.	Starting Point.	Time of Starting.	Route to Station.	Entraining Station.	Time due at Station.	Time of departure of train.
H.Q. Div. R.E.	AILLY LE HAUT CLOCHER Crossroads	5.5 a.m.	LONG - LE CATELET.	LONGPRE.	7.27 a.m.	10.27 a.m.
Det. 1/6 Fd. Co. R.E.	Crossroads BUSSUS BUSSUEL.	4.10 a.m.	AILLY - LONG LE CATELET.	"	"	"
Part 301 R.F.A. Bde. Amn. Col.	Crossroads W. of BETHENCOURT.	7.30 a.m.	FLIXECOURT GONDE.	"	"	"
2/19 Lond.R.	AILLY LE HAUT CLOCHER Crossroads.	9.20 a.m.	LONG - LE CATELET.	"	11.17 a.m.	2.17 p.m.
Rem. 1/8 Fd. Co. R.E.	Crossroads BUSSUS BUSSUEL.	8.25 a.m.	AILLY - LONG LE CATELET.	"	"	"
Det. 2/5 Fd. Amb.	"	8.25 a.m.	"	"	"	"
Rem. 301 R.F.A. Bde. Amn. Col.	Crossroads W. of BETHENCOURT.	11.30 a.m.	FLIXECOURT - GONDE.	"	2.27 p.m.	5.27 p.m.
Rem. 2/5 Fd. Amb.	Crossroads BUSSUS BUSSU..	11.40 a.m.	AILLY - LONG LE CATELET.	"	"	"
Det. Div. Train.	(To be arranged by O.C. Div. Train.)		BRUCAMPS - VAUCHELLES			
H.Q. 180 Inf.Bde.	Road junction S.E. end of GORENFLOS.	4.10 p.m.	LA FOLI - L'ETOILE GONDE.	"	6.27 p.m.	9.27 p.m.
2/20 Lond.R.	Crossroads VAUCOURT BUSSUS.	3.50 p.m.	AILLY - LONG-LE CATELET.	"	"	"

***** 19th November 1916. *****

H.Q. 301 R.F.A. Bde.	Crossroads 7. of BETHENCOURT.	4.30 a.m.	FLIX COURT - GONDE.	"	7.27 a.m.	10.27 a.m.
One Battery 301 R.F.A. Bde.	"	4.30 a.m.	"	"	"	"
H.Q. Div. R.A.	Road junction 5. end of AILLY.	6.0 a.m.	LONG - LE CATELET.	"	"	"
One Btty. 301 R.F.A. bde.	Crossroads 7. of BETHENCOURT.	11.30 a.m.	FLIXECOURT - GONDE.	"	2.27 p.m.	5.27 p.m.
Det. 35 Cas. Clearing Station.	AILLY LE HAUT CLOCHER Crossroads.	12.40 p.m.	LONG - LE CATELET.	"	"	"
H.Q. Div. Sig. Co.	"	"	"	"	"	"
X. 60 T. Battery.	Crossroads just W. of P in PORT REMY.	12.45 p.m.	LIERCOURT - COTTAIN.	Noon.		

The following M.T. will also entrain on the 19th November 1916. Orders will be issued as regards those, later.

	Drivers.	Lorries.
Det. 35 Cas. Clearing Station.	6	3
Rem. 60th Amn. Sub. Park.	30	12
Det. 60th Div. Supply Column.	40	16

SECRET.   APPENDIX XIX

Copy No.

60th DIVISIONAL ARTILLERY.

OPERATION ORDER NO.11.

1. The 60th Divisional Artillery will continue entraining on the 18th and 19th November, 1916 in accordance with attached Schedule "A".

2. Units will march to the entraining LONGPRE, as follows:-

Date.		Unit.	Starting Point.	Starting time.	Route.
18th Nov.	(a)	Part of 301st Bde Am. Col.	Road junction just N.W. of BELLOY.	4-30 a.m.	BOURDON - HANGEST - CONDE.
18th	(b)	Remainder 301st Bde. Am. Col.	do.	11-30 a.m.	do.
19th	(c)	H.Q. 301st Bde, and D/301 Bty.	do.	4.30 a.m.	do.
19th	(d)	C/301 Bty.	do.	11.30 a.m.	do.
19th	(e)	H.Q., R.A.	Road junction S. end of AILLY.	6 a.m.	LONG-LE CATELET.
19th	(f)	X/60 T.M. Battery.	Cross roads just W. of P in PONT REMY.	Noon.	LIERCOURT-FONTAINE.

3. The office of H.Q.,R.A. will remain open at AILLY-LE-HAUT-CLOCHER until further orders.

R.France
Major.
Brigade Major.
60th Divisional Artillery.

17th November 1916.

Copies to :- No.1. 301st Brigade, No.2. D.O.T.M.
No.3&4. War Diary. No.5. File.

SECRET.   SCHEDULE "A"

Date.	Train No.	Unit.	Offs.	O.R.	Horses	4 Whld.	2 Whld.	Departs LONGPRE.	Train also carries.
18th.	16.	Part 301st Bde Amm. Column.	2	60	90	–	20	10.27am.	H.Q., and detachment R.E.
18th	18.	Remainder 301st Bde. Amm. Col.	1	48	45	2	14	5.27pm.	Det. Div. Train and Field Ambulance
19th	20.	H.Q., 301st Bde.	5	48	48	1	5	10.27am.	Nil.
"	"	D/301 Btty.	5	140	135	1	26		
"	"	H.Q.Div.R.A.	2	17	23	–	4		
19th	21	C/301 Btty.	5	140	135	1	26	5.27pm.	H.Q.Signal Coy. & Det. Cas. Clearing Station.
"	"	X/60 T.M.Bty.	2	23	–	–	–		

NOTES.

(a.) G.S.Wagons are shown as 4-wheeled vehicles. Guns, Limbered wagons etc. are shown as two 2-wheeled vehicles.

(b) Halte Repas will be provided at the following stations :-
    1 hour at MONTEREAU.   9 hours from LONGPRE.
    ½ " " MACON.   12 " " MONTEREAU.
    1 " " PIERRELATTE.   9 " " MACON.

(c) PIERRELATTE to MARSEILLES takes 8 hours.

R C Rance
Major.
Brigade Major.
60th Divisional Artillery.

17th November 1916.

APPENDIX XX

SECRET. COPY NO. 4

G/S.428.

A.D.C. for G.O.C.   Div. Train.
180 Inf. Bde.   Div. Supply Column.
181 Inf. Bde.   A.D.V.S.
C.R.A.   Camp Commandant.
C.R.E.   IVth Army.
"A".   XVth Corps.
A.D.M.S.   35 Cas. Clearing Stn.
Signals.   War Diary.

Units will entrain on 20th and 21st/November 1916 in accordance with attached Schedule "A" and Programme of Entrainment. The times of starting are provisional, on the understanding that previous trains leave up to scheduled time. They will be adhered to, unless orders to the contrary are issued.

Acknowledge.

C A Bolton
Captain.
General Staff.
60th Division.

18/11/16.

SECRET.   COPY No......
                    Table of Personnel, Animals & Vehicles
                    proceeding on the 20th/21st November 1916.   SCHEDULE A.

20th November 1916.

No. of Train.	Type of Train.	Time of Departure.	Unit.	Officers.	Other Ranks.	Animals.	Vehicles 4 W.	Vehicles 2 W.
22	Special.	10.27 a.m.	2/18 Lond.R.(less 1 Co. & Det.)	26	693	-	-	-
23	T.C.	5.27 p.m.	180 M.G. Co. (less Det.)	8	178	10	-	-
			302 S.A.A. Sec. Amn. Col.	3	255	25	-	-
			No. 2 Sec. Div. Sig. Co.	1	27	10	-	-
			No. 1 Sec. Div. Sig. Co.	2	71	45	4	-
			One Battery 301 R.F.A. Bde.	5	140	135	1	26
			Det. Div. Train.	1	24	20	-	8
			Det. 2/18 Lond.R.	10	10	-	-	-
			Det. 180 M.G. Co.	4	4	-	-	-

***** November 21st 1916. ******

No. of Train.	Type of Train.	Time of Departure.	Unit.	Officers.	Other Ranks.	Animals.	Vehicles 4 W.	Vehicles 2 W.
24	T.C.	10.27 a.m.	One Battery 302 R.F.A. Bde.	5	140	135	1	26
			Det. Div. Train.	4	150	49	-	13
25	T.C.	5.27 p.m.	One Battery 303 R.F.A. Bde.	5	140	135	1	22
			Det. Div. Train.	4	150	49	-	13

Types of Trains. T.C. = Type Combatant, composed of..........
                  T.P. = Type Parc, composed of..............
                  Special. = Composed of....................

	1st Class.	Covered Trucks.	Flat Trucks.
	1	33	14
	1	24	23
	1	47	-

SECRET.   COPY NO..........

PROGRAMME OF ENTRAINMENT.

Ref. Map: L.H.S Sheet 11. AMIENS Sheet 17.
ABBEVILLE Sheet 14. 1/100,000.

20th November 1916.

Unit.	Starting Point.	Time of Starting.	Route to Station.	Entraining Station.	Time due at Station.	Time of departure of train.
2/18 Lond.R. (less Dets.)	Road junction S.E. end of GORENFLOS.	5 a.m.	BRUCAMPS - VAUCHELLES - LA FOLIE - L'ETOILE - CONDÉ.	LONGPRÉ.	7.27 a.m.	10.27 a.m.
180.M.G. Co. (less Det.)	"	"	"	"	"	"
No. 2 Sec. Div. Sig. Co.	"	5.5 a.m.	"	"	"	"
302 S.A.A. Sec. Amm. Col.	BOURDON Crossroads.	5.10 a.m.	"	"	"	"
No. 1 Sec. Div. Sig. Co.	Crossroads AILLY LE HAUT CLOCHER.	5.45 a.m.	HANGEST - CONDÉ.	"	"	"
One Battery 301 Bde. R.F.A.	Crossroads S.W. end of BETHENCOURT.	12.10 p.m.	LONG - LE CATELET. FLIXECOURT - CONDÉ.	"	2.27 p.m.	5.27 p.m.
Det. Div. Train.	(To be arranged by O.C., Div. Train).	12 noon.		"	"	"
Det. 2/18 Lond.R.	(These parties can proceed to the station under arrangements of the 180th Inf. Bde.)					
Det. 180.M.G.Co.	(They must be at Station 1½ hours before train is due to start.					

21st November 1916.

Unit.	Starting Point.	Time of Starting.	Route to Station.	Entraining Station.	Time due at Station.	Time of departure of train.
One Battery 304 Bde. R.F.A.	Road junction just W. of BELLOY sur SOMME.	4.40 a.m.	BOURDON - HANGEST - CONDÉ.	LONGPRÉ.	7.27 a.m.	10.27 a.m.
Det. Div. Train.	(To be arranged by O.C., Div. Train.)			"	"	"
One Battery 303 Bde. R.F.A.	Road junction just W. of BELLOY sur SOMME.	11.40 a.m.	BOURDON - HANGEST - CONDÉ.	"	2.27 p.m.	5.27 p.m.
Det. Div. Train.	(To be arranged by O.C., Div. Train.)			"	"	"

APPENDIX XXI

SECRET.   Copy No......5......

60th DIVISIONAL ARTILLERY.

OPERATION ORDER No.12.

1. The 60th Divisional Artillery will continue entraining on the 20th & 21st November 1916 in accordance with attached Schedule "A".

2. Units will march to the entraining Station LONGPRE as follows :-

Date		Unit.	Starting Point.	Starting Time.	Route.
20th	(a)	No.2 S.A.A. Section.	BOURDON Cross roads.	5.45 a.m.	HANGEST - CONDE
"	(b)	B/301 Battery RFA	Cross roads S.W. end of BETHEN-COURT.	NOON	FLIXECOURT - CONDE.
21st	(c)	A/301 Battery RFA	(as in (b))	5.15 a.m.	as in (b)
"	(d)	One Battery 303rd. Bde. RFA.	Road junction just W. of BELLOY.	11.40 a.m.	BOURDON - HANGEST - CONDE.

3. A party of 1 Officer and 2 N.C.O's will be sent on to arrive at the Station ½ hour before Units in order to chalk off trucks etc.

Major.
Brigade Major,
60th Divisional Artillery.

18th November 1916.

Copies to :- No. 1 No. 2 S.A.A. Section. 2 & 3 301st. Bde. RFA. 4 303rd. Bde. RFA. 5, War Diary, 6 File.

S E C R E T.   SCHEDULE "A"

Date.	Train No.	Unit.	Offs.	O.R.	Animals	4 Whld.	2 Whld.	Departs LONGPRE.	Train also carries.
20th	22	No.2 S.A.A. Section.	3	255	25	–	–	10.27 am	2/18th Regt & Det. Sigs.
"	23	B/301 Bty. RFA.	5	140	135	1	26	5.27 pm	Det. 2/18th Signals Train.
21st.	24	A/301 Bty. RFA	5	140	135	1	26	10.27 am	Det. Train.
"	25	One Battery 303rd. Bde. RFA	5	140	135	1	26	5.27 pm	ditto.

NOTES.

(a) Guns, limbered wagons, etc. are shown as two 2-wheeled vehicles.

(b) "Halte Repas" will be provided at the following Stations :-

1 hour at MONTEREAU.   9 hours from LONGPRE.
2 "   " MACON.   12 "   "   MONTEREAU.
1 "   " PIERRELATTE.   9   "   "   MACON.

(c) PIERRELATTE to MARSEILLES takes 8 hours.

Major.
Brigade Major.
60th Divisional Artillery.

18th November 1916.

APPENDIX XXII

COPY No. 3

SECRET.   G/S.429.

A.D.C. for G.O.C.   Div. Train.
181 Inf. Bde.   D.S.C.
C.R.A.   A.D.V.S.
"A".   Camp Commandant.
A.D.M.S.   Fourth Army.
Signal Co.   XV Corps.
                           War Diary.

    Units will entrain on the 22nd and 23rd November 1916 in accordance with attached Schedule "A" and Programmes of Entrainment.

    Acknowledge.

H.Q., 60 Div,
20/11/16.
                                      Captain.
                                    General Staff.

SECRET.

COPY No. 3

PROGRAMME OF ENTRAINMENT.

22nd November 1916.

Ref. Map: LENS, Sheet 11. AMIENS, Sheet 17. ABBEVILLE, Sheet 14. 1/100,000.

Troops.	Starting Point	Time of starting.	Route to station.	Entraining Station.	Time due at station.	Time of departure of train.
One Batty., 303 R.F.A. Bde.	Road junction just W. of BELLOY sur SOMME.	4.40.a.m.	BOURDON-HANGEST-CONDE.	LONGPRE.	7.27.a.m.	10.27.a.m.
Det. Div. Train.	(To be arranged by O.C., Div. Train).					
H.Q., 303 R.F.A. Bde.	Road junction just W. of BELLOY sur SOMME.	8.50.a.m.	BOURDON-HANGEST-CONDE.	"	11.17 a.m.	2.17.p.m.
303 R.F.A. Bde. Amm. Col.	"	11.40.a.m.	"	"	2.27.p.m.	5.27.p.m.
One Batty.,303 R.F.A. Bde.						
Det. Div. Train.	(To be arranged by O.C., Div. Train).					

SECRET.

PROGRAMME OF ENTRAINMENT.

COPY No. 3.

Ref. Map: LENS, Sheet 11. AMIENS, Sheet 17. ABBEVILLE, Sheet 14, .. 1/100,000.

23rd November 1916.

Unit.	Starting Point.	Time of starting.	Route to entraining station.	Entraining station.	Time due at station.	Time of departure of train.
H.Q., 181 Inf. Bde.	Cross Roads, BRUCAMPS.	5.20.a.m.	VAUCHELLES les DOMART - LA FOLIE - L'ETOILE - CONDE.	LONGPRE.	7.27.a.m.	10.27.a.m.
2/23 Lond. R.	Cross Roads, ERGNIES.	5. 0.a.m.	AILLY - LONG - LE CATELET.	"	"	"
Y.60 & Z.60 T.M.Battys.	Cross Roads just W. of P. of PONT REMY.	5.30.a.m.	LIERCOURT - FONTAINE.	"	"	"
One Batty. 303 R.F.A. Bde.	Road junction just W. of BELLOY sur SOMME.	8.30.a.m.	BOURDON - HANGEST - CONDE.	"	11.17.a.m.	2.17.p.m.
Det. Div. Train.	(To be arranged by O.C., Div. Train.)			"	"	"
2/21 Lond. R.	Cross Roads, VILLERS-SOUS-AILLY.	12.40.p.m.	LONG - LE CATELET.	"	2.27.p.m.	5.27.p.m.
Det. Mob.Vet.Sec.	Cross Roads, AILLY LE HAUT CLOCHER.	12.30.p.m.	"	"	"	"

SECRET.

COPY No. ......
SCHEDULE "A".

TABLE OF PERSONNEL, ANIMALS and VEHICLES proceeding on the 22nd and 23rd November 1916.

22nd November 1916.

No. of Train.	Type of Train.	Time of departure.	Unit.	Officers.	Other Ranks.	Animals.	Vehicles 4.W.	Vehicles 2.W.
26.	T.C.	10.27.a.m.	One Battery, 303 R.F.A. Bde. Det. Div. Train.	5.	140.	135.	1.	26.
						49.		13.
27.	T.C.	2.17.p.m.	H.Q., 303 R.F.A. Bde. 303 R.F.A.Bde.Amm.Col.	5. 3.	49. 108.	48. 136.	1. 2.	5. 34.
28.	T.C.	5.27.p.m.	One Battery, 303 R.F.A. Bde. Det. Div. Train.	5. 4.	140. 100.	135. 49.	1.	26. 13.

23rd November 1916.

29.	Special *	10.27.a.m.	H.Q., 181 Inf.Bde. 2/23 Lond.R. Y.60 & Z.60 T. Mttys.	8. 39. 2.	40. 958. 46.	21. 24.		
30.	T.C.	2.17.p.m.	One Batty.303 R.F.A.Bde. Det. Div. Train.	5. 4.	140. 100.	135. 49.	1.	26. 13.
31.	Special ∮	5.27.p.m.	2/21 Lond. R. 60 Mob. Vet. Sec.	39.	958. 15.	24. 20.		

Types of Trains. T.C. = Type Combatant, composed of .... 1st Class. Covered Trucks. Flat Trucks.
                                                                   1.   33.   12.
                  T.P. = Type Parc, composed of ....   1.   34.   23.
                  Special * = Composed of ....   1.   47.
                  ∮ = Composed of ....   2.   44.
                                                                   2.   48.   2 Brake Vans.

APPENDIX XXIII

SECRET.   Copy No............

60th DIVISIONAL ARTILLERY.

OPERATION ORDER No. 12.

1. The 60th Divisional Artillery will continue entraining on the .... November 1916 in accordance with attached Schedule "A".

2. Units will march to the entraining Station LONGPRE as follows :-

Date		Unit.	Starting Point.	Starting Time.	Route.
22nd.	(a)	B/303 Bty. RFA.	Road Junction just W. of BELLOY SUR SOMME.	4.40am	BOURDON - HANGEST - CONDE.
	(b)	H.q. 303 Bde.) (303 Bde. Amm.Col)	Do.	8.30am	Do.
	(c)	C/303 Bty. R.F.A.	Do.	11.40am	Do.
23rd.	(d)	Y/60 & Z/60 T.M. Btys.	CROSS ROADS just W. of P in PONT REMY.	5.30am	LIERCOURT - FONTAINE
	(e)	D/303rd. Bty. RFA.	as in (a)	8.30am	as in (a)

3. A party of 1 Officer and 2 N.C.O's will be sent on to arrive at the Station ½ hour before Units in order to chalk off trucks etc.

                        signature
                        Major.
                     Brigade Major.
                60th Divisional Artillery.

21st. November 1916.

Copies to :- No. 1 303rd. Bde. RFA. No. 2 D.O.T.M., No. 3 War Diary. No. 4 File.

S-E-C-R-E-T.   SCHEDULE "A"

Date.	Train No.	Unit.	Offs.	O.R.	Animals	4 Whld.	2 Whld.	Departs LONGPRE.	Train also carries.
22nd.	26	B/303 Bty. RFA.	5	140	135	1	26	10.27am	Det. Div. Train.
	27	303rd. Bde. Amm. Col.	3	108	136	2	34	2.17pm	
		303rd. Bde. H.Q.	5	49	48	1	5	Do.	
	28	C/303 Bty. RFA	5	140	135	1	26	5.27pm	Det. Div. Train.
23rd.	29	Y/60 & Z/60 T.M. Btys.	4	46	-	-	-	10.27am	H.Q. 181st Inf. Bde. 2/23 L.Reg
	30	D/303 Bty. RFA	5	140	135	1	26	2.17pm	Det. Div. Train.

NOTES.

(a) Guns, limbered wagons, etc. are shown as two 2-wheeled vehicles.

(b) "Halte Repas" will be provided at the following Stations :-

   1 hour at MONTEREAU.   9 hours from LONGPRE.
   ½ " " MACON.   12 " " MONTEREAU.
   1 " " PIERRELATTE.   9 " " MACON.

(c) PIERRELATTE to MARSEILLES takes 8 hours.

Major,
Brigade Major.
60th Divisional Artillery.

..........November 1916.

APPENDIX XXIV

SECRET.
COPY NO. 3
G/S. 431

A.D.C. for G.O.C.   Div. Train.
181 Inf. Bde.   D.S.C.
C.R.A.   A.D.V.S.
"A".   Camp Commandant.
A.D.M.S.   Fourth Army.
Signal Co.   XV Corps.
                         War Diary.

    Units will entrain on the 24th November 1916 in accordance with attached Schedule "A" and Programme of Entrainment.

    Acknowledge.

H.Q., 60th Division.
21st November 1916.

C. Bolton.
Captain.
General Staff.

SECRET.

COPY NO. 3

SCHEDULE "A".

TABLE OF PERSONNEL, ANIMALS and VEHICLES proceeding on the 24th November 1916.

No. of Train.	Type of Train.	Time of departure.	Unit.	Officers.	Other Ranks.	Animals.	Vehicles. 4 W.	2 W.
32.	Special	10.27 a.m.	2/22 Lond.R.	39.	958.	24.		
			No. 4 Sec. Div. Sig. Co.	1.	27.	10.		
33.	T.C.	2.17 p.m.	60 San. Sec.	1.	39.	9.		4.
			Div. H.Q.	7.	137.	77.	6.	8.
			Det. 2/6 Fd. Amb.	2.	40.	25.	3.	
			Det. Div. Train.	4.	200.	40.		12.
34.	Special	5.27 p.m.	No. 1 S.A.A. Sec.	3.	255.	25.	1.	1.
			Arm. Col.					
			No. 3 S.A.A. Sec.	3.	255.	25.		
			Arm. Col.	9.	369.	42.		
			Det. 2/6 Fd. Amb.	2.	4.			
			H.Q., Div. R.A.					

Types of Trains. T.C. = Type Combatant, composed of .... 1st Class. Covered Trucks. Flat Trucks.
1. 33. 14.
Special. = Composed of .... 1. 47.

SECRET.   COPY NO. 3.

PROGRAMME OF ENTRAINMENT.

Ref. Map: LENS, Sheet 11. AMIENS, Sheet 17. 24th November 1916.
ABBEVILLE, Sheet 14. 1/100,000.

Unit.	Starting Point.	Time of starting.	Route to entraining station.	Entraining Station.	Time due at station.	Time of departure of train.
2/22 Lond.R.	Crossroads BRUCAMPS.	5.20 a.m.	VAUCHELLES - L's - DOMART LA FOLIE - L'ETOILE - CONDE.	LONGPRE.	7.27 a.m.	10.27 a.m.
H.Q. & Sig. Div. Sig. Co.	"	5.25 a.m.	"	"	"	"
Div. H.Q.	Crossroads AILLY LE HAUT CLOCHER.	9.20 a.m.	LONG - LE CATELET.	"	11.17 a.m.	2.17 p.m.
60 San. S.C.	"	9.20 a.m.	"	"	"	"
Dot. 2/6 Fd. Amb.	LA FOLIE Crossroads	10.15 a.m.	L'ETOILE - CONDE.	"	"	"
Det. Div. Train.	(To be arranged by O.C., Div. Train.)					
No. 1 S.A.A. Col.	Crossroads S.W. of BETHENCOURT.	12 noon	FLIXECOURT - CONDE.	"	2.27 p.m.	5.27 p.m.
Sec. A.M. Col.	Road junction just W. of BOURDON - HANGEST - CONDE.	11.40 a.m.	"	"	"	"
No. 3 S.A.A. Col.	Road junction just W. of BELLOY sur SOMME.	11.40 a.m.	"	"	"	"
Sec. AMM. Col.	"	"	"	"	"	"
Det. 2/6 Fd. Amb.	LA FOLIE Crossroads.	1.0 p.m.	L'ETOILE - CONDE.	"	"	"
H.Q., Div.R.A.	Road junction S. of AILLY LE HAUT CLOCHER.	12.40 p.m.	LONG - LE CATELET.	"	"	"

APPENDIX XXV

SECRET.   Copy No. 3

60th DIVISIONAL ARTILLERY.

OPERATION ORDER No.12.b.

1. The 60th Divisional Artillery will continue entraining on the ....24th.... November 1916 in accordance with attached Schedule "A".

2. Units will march to the entraining Station LONGPRE as follows :-

Date		Unit.	Starting Point.	Starting Time.	Route.
24th	(a)	No. 1 S.A.A. Section.	Cross Roads S.W. of BETHENCOURT.	12 Noon.	FLIXECOURT - CONDE.
	(b)	No. 3 S.A.A. Section.	Road Junction just W. of BELLOY SUR SOMME.	11.40am.	BOURDON - HANGEST - CONDE.

3. A party of 1 Officer and 2 N.C.O's will be sent on to arrive at the Station ½ hour before Units in order to chalk off trucks etc.

4. 3 Motor Lorries for each Section will report at the starting points, 1 hour before starting time.

                                    Major.
                              Brigade Major.
                          60th Divisional Artillery.

....21st. November 1916.

Copies to :-   No. 1   No. 1 S.A.A. Section.
                    2   No. 3 S.A.A. Section.
                    3   War Diary.

S-E C R E T.   SCHEDULE "A"

Date.	Train No.	Unit.	Offs.	O.R.	Ani-mals	4 Whld.	2 Whld.	Departs LONGPRE.	Train also carries.
24th.	34	No. 1 S.A.A. Section.	3	255	25	-	-	5.27 pm	Details 2/6th. Field Ambulance.
		No. 3 S.A.A. Section.	3	255	25	-	-	Do.	

N O T E S.

(a) Guns, limbered wagons, etc. are shown as two 2-wheeled vehicles.

(b) "Halte Repas" will be provided at the following Stations :-

```
1 hour at MONTEREAU.      9 hours from LONGPRE.
½  "   "  MACON.          12   "    "   MONTEREAU.
1  "   "  PIERRELATTE.    9    "    "   MACON.
```

(c) PIERRELATTE to MARSEILLES takes 8 hours.

                                        Major.
                                   Brigade Major.
                                60th Divisional Artillery.

.........November 1916.

60TH DIVISION

ASST. DIR. MED. SERVICES
~~JULY — NOV 1916.~~

1915 AUG — 1915 DEC
1916 JUN — 1916 NOV

www.ingramcontent.com/pod-product-compliance
Lightning Source LLC
Chambersburg PA
CBHW060000240426
43664CB00043B/2746